Call Centre

Call Centre

S. Pankaj

A.P.H. Publishing Corporation
New Delhi - 110002

Published by
Kul Bhushan Nangia
APH Publishing Corporation
5, Ansari Road, Darya Ganj
New Delhi-110 002
☎ 23274050
E-mail: aph@mantraonline.com

2005

ISBN : 81–7648–842–9

Printed in India at
Chaman Enterprises
New Delhi - 110 002

Preface

IT enabled services are emerging as the latest trend in business circles. What started, as a support tool to the mainline industry has today become a separate industry in itself. The cutthroat competition has pushed the organizations to its limit in offering a greater attention to their customers. Call Centres today have emerged as a potent tool with the organizations, which are using them not just to solve and answer the queries of the customers but to sell products, offer them support and even helping them out in general services, etc. Typically there are many formats in which a call Centre works. Most of the times this term is used for voice based Centres but today it covers a wide plethora of formats like email call Centres, technical help desks, interactive chats, etc.

Employing hundreds and thousand of people this industry is at the forefront of technological dynamism and is witnessing a sea change in its operations and management on a daily basis.

This particular book tries to emulate the changes and the happenings of this industry. It offers a comprehensive insight from and industrial and an operational perspective. I am sure this book will provide a better insight to both the experts and the novices of this particular industry.

—Editor

Contents

1

Introduction

You have most likely called a call Centre many times in your life. You may have made an airline reservation, called for directory assistance, ordered a product or called for technical support on a recent purchase. The call Centre is the place where your telephone call is answered.

Depending on how many phone calls are received, call Centres may be very small or extremely large. Some companies need thousands of employees to handle the large volume of calls they receive from customers.

A call Centre is like any other office environment where you will find many people talking on the phone and working with computers. The key difference is that in a call Centre the employees' primary job is to take calls and help customers. When they finish with one customer, they move on to the next customer that is waiting in line.

On a busy day, employees in a call Centre (called customer service representatives or customer service agents) may take more than 100 phone calls. The number of calls that a customer service agent takes depends on the length of each call and their work schedule. On average call times last from three to four minutes, with about one minute of "after call wrap-up" to complete any unfinished work related to the call.

If you work in a call Centre, you will need to be good with people and comfortable talking on the phone, but there is more to it than just the phone call.

Call Centre

A Call Centre is what you interact with when you call a help line, ("my product is not working properly, can you help me"), an order line ("I'd like to order your CD of the month this month"), or when you get a call from one of those annoying sales people right around dinner time.

In each case, these Centres (sometimes referred to as "contact Centres" to reflect the added mediums of email and the web) are usually housed within large, modern office buildings filled with "agents" wearing headsets and sitting in front of computer screens. Those agents are regularly trained on the minutia of the product they are selling or helping with, as well as the procedures used to do their job. The training can range from hands on training using the various software and customer database packages, to "roll playing" drills in techniques for dealing with irate customers. Because of this constant learning and testing atmosphere, the people who work in these Centres are often of greater than average intelligence.

Call Centre definition

A call Centre is a place where customer calls are handled by a customer service organization. Typically, a call Centre has the ability to handle a considerable volume of calls at the same time, aided by computer automation.Calls are screened and then forwarded to the correct customer service representative at the call Centre.

Call Centre definition

A functional area within an organization or an out-sourced, separate facility that exists solely to answer inbounds or place outbound telephone calls. Usually refers to a sophisticated voice operations Centre that provides a full range of high-volume, inbound or outbound call-handling services, including customer support, operator services, directory assistance, multilingual customer support, credit services, card services, inbound and outbound telemarketing, interactive voice response and web-based services

Call Centre definition

A company that answers incoming telephone calls from customers. A call Centre may be an office that makes outgoing telephone calls to customers (telemarketing). Such an office may also responds to letters, faxes, e-mails and similar written correspondence. However the term contact centre (UK) or contact Centre (US) is often applied when such multiple functions are blended in one office.

A call Centre is an umbrella term that refers to reservation Centres, help desks, information lines or customer service Centres, regardless of how they are organized or what types of transactions they handle. Usually refers to a sophisticated voice operations environment that provides a full range of high-volume, inbound or outbound call-handling services, including customer support, operator services, directory assistance, multilingual customer support, credit services, card services, inbound and outbound telemarketing, interactive voice response and web-based services.

The term call Centre can be misleading, as the transactions may be more involved than simple 'calls' and a 'Centre' may not accurately represent the potentially complex, multi-site environment.

A call Centre is a powerful hub of information collection and exchange. There are so many site dedicated to helping make educated decisions about call Centre services for any domestic or global business.

Call Centre services

- Incoming call Centres can be used to answer customer questions, (information hotline, technical support, customer service etc.), to receive customer orders, to redirect customers to pertinent help etc.

- Outgoing call Centres can be used to directly advertise and sell goods or services, to solicit information, (surveys, political poles, customer satisfaction etc.), to campaign or otherwise inform the public.

Advantages of having or using call Centre services

Call Centre services allow a company or organization to contact a large number of people quickly and efficiently. It also provides a greater potential customer market for the sale of goods or services and allows the company to get information from people, or influence public opinion. This allows for:

- Improved customer service to more customers
- More efficient information communication
- Better real-time technical support

Disadvantages

Call Centres can be hard to organize and maintain. Staffing can be a challenge if the call Centre is to function 24 hours a day, 7 days a week. Recruiting and training managers who can effectively educate and motivate the employees can be difficult. Financial management of a call Centre can be tedious and taxing. Call Centre Software is typically needed to allow the employees to contact individuals, and for Management to track employee performance and progress.

Call Centre Options Available

- Establishing and managing call Centre services require strong control over the collection and exchange of information. Seminars, software packages, hardware kits and more things required for companies that wish to begin their own call Centre work.
- Call Centre Outsourcing allows a company to easily solve the problems of organizing and maintaining a call Centre by paying someone else to do those things for them.

- o On shore outsourcing, (using a call Centre within a given country), keeps jobs within that country and has the advantages of drawing from a more uniform language base.
- o Off shore outsourcing, (using a call Centre outside of a given country), often is cheaper and just as effective.

The role of the computer

Technology plays a major role in the call Centre. Most call Centres will have a computer terminal for each customer service agent to use while taking calls from customers. These computers are used to access customer records, product information, ordering status, transaction history and many other types of data. For medical or technical call Centres, these computers will help the customer service agents access medical records or technical data.

For call Centres that accept email from customers, computers are the primary tool for the call Centre agent. A customer service agent will read the email from the customer, access data, conduct research and reply to the customer all from the computer terminal. In state-of-the-art Centres, the call Centre management team has the choice to blend email with phone calls and other customer contact work such as mail, fax and text chat. In this environment, a customer service agent may answer an email one moment and be on the phone for the next customer contact. This is why some call Centres use the term "contact Centre" instead of call Centre because it is more than just phone calls.

The call Centre team

Call Centres are typically organized in groups. Each team has a defined role in the call Centre to support a particular type of customer request. For example, in a call Centre for ordering clothing, one team may support mens' apparel while another team may support teens' or womens' clothing. Each call Centre is organized differently depending on the types of products or services they support.

Call Centre agents have a complete support team to assist them in their work. When difficult questions arise, most call Centres have a help desk for their agents to use, or the call Centre provides support from the supervisors in each area. In some cases it is necessary to escalate the call to experts. If all these options fail, it may be necessary to call the customer back with the information they need.

Other types of teams within the call Centre may include

- The training group (for training new hires and ongoing training of agents).
- The quality monitoring team (for monitoring calls for customer service and quality).
- Human resources (for recruiting and hiring call Centre agents).
- The work force management (for scheduling employees to match the work load).

Covering the globe

Not all call Centres are centrally located in a single building. Large companies may have many call Centres located all around the world. This allows them to handle different time zones and languages. The term for this type of time-zone coverage is "follow the sun". Companies can also route calls to the call Centre that is the least busy thereby better utilizing their resources and shortening the wait time for customers.

This technology also allows companies to hire around the world. For example, you may be calling in the United States and have your call answered by someone in India. In most cases, other than accent differences between regions, you may not be aware that this call was routed to an international location.

Even formal office buildings are not a requirement for call Centres. In some circumstances agents are allowed to work from home or from a branch office. This is called "remote agents" and allows flexibility in both work location and work hours. Home-based agents can work part-time and non-continuous time much easier than agents that must commute to work.

IMPORTANT NOTE RELEVANT TO CALL CENTRE

Variability in the Call Centre

Variability in the call Centre sounds too abstract to be relevant. It is not and we will explain why in a moment. First, what do we mean when we refer to "variability"?

Definition: The range of possible outcomes of a given customer interaction (by phone, email or web).

Variability is often associated with climatic discussions or in manufacturing where variability may result in a less than satisfactory product. Variability and the call Centre is not a common connection but we think it is important to think about.

The intent of this Observations-on-Operations is to raise variability as a consideration when assessing improvements to your call Centre operation. The focus is not to preach uniformity (opposition of variability) so that the call Centre becomes a highly automated "factory". Variability will always exist because people make it so. Customer needs are not always as predicted. Employee responses to customers are not always as expected.

In the world of call Centres (or contact Centres or customer interaction Centres) variability can cause significant seen and unseen impacts to your operation. You are familiar with key variability factors that affect a call Centre such as:

Call volume
Unplanned absences
Average Handling Time (AHT) fluctuations during a period of business change

Call Centres function in the real-time world. A real-time (now) environment is more sensitive to changing variables than a response time (later) environment. Variability is magnified in a real-time context because it can result in longer waits for customers, decreased satisfaction for customers or bottom-line implications (loss of revenue or increased costs).

There are variability factors that may not be as obvious. Here are some potentially less obvious variability factors, prompted with a question, to help you evaluate variability in your call Centre:

1. **Rework**—what percentage of work (order processing, customer enquiry, etc.) is not completed correctly the first time? Variability caused by obscure or ambiguous procedures can create a rework problem requiring additional staff resourcing to solve or affecting customer satisfaction.
2. **First Call Resolution**—what percentage of calls are answered, to the customer's satisfaction, on first call? At a glance, this may seem similar to the rework point above. First call resolution may not have a rework component. A dissatisfied customer may not call back but call the competitor.
3. **Site Variability**—is there a difference in AHT or processing identical call types between your various call Centre sites? One site may be more efficient and have satisfied customers or it could be more efficient with less satisfied customers.

Staff and Variability

Variability is not entirely a call Centre evil. To much uniformity can lead to call Centre agents achieving total boredom because of the repetitious implications of their work. The key point is to provide sufficient variability for staff to ensure that they are engaged fully in the process of satisfying the customer as well as achieving your business objectives.

Technology Performance Gap in Your Call Centre

"We are good at buying the gear but we aren't great at using it". This is a statement that we have heard many times and have said many times ourselves. Buying call Centre technology is normally done through a reasonably extensive process. Often it includes an RFP (Request for Proposal), which may have been proceeded by a RFI (Request for Information).

Technology in the call Centre is complex because it is a multi-platform—multi-vendor undertaking. You often feel like a premarital counsellor making sure there is compatibility before the knot is tied!

We are good at buying the technology but we are not necessarily good at using it. Scenarios unfold that go something like this:

A specific technology was purchased because it met the defined business need. It was driven by a few who had a vision for its capabilities. That was then. Now is now. The "visionaries" behind it have since been

(a) promoted
(b) retired
(c) reassigned
(d) quit (take your pick).

The next generation of leadership is left with a set of call Centre technologies that may not be widely understood. Oh, for the good ol' days when it was clear why the initial investment was made.

What's the solution? One of the best-cost-highest-returns approaches is to get marital counselling of the technology kind. The counselling you need to seek is with your original technology provider (trusting they were not a dotcom that is now a notcom). This seems like a logical step but it isn't out of the norm to be at a loss to know what steps to take. After all, the vast majority of people in call Centres came up through the business ranks not the information technology ranks.

Here is a comparable: Most people use Microsoft Word. Some smart people out there assessed what features people use most frequently. The results are that about 20% of the features are used regularly. The remainder of the features are rarely used. Some users of Word are not even aware of all the features Word provides to make their word-processing lives easier. The same principle applies to our bazillion dollar investment in call Centre technology. We don't even know what the technology might be able to do for us.

Here's a take-away piece that may assist you. Make a list of your top three to five call Centre business issues that you are currently working at resolving in your operation. Which of these are requiring a technology related solution? Next, invite your call Centre technology provider for lunch . Make sure that the sales person brings the techno-know-it-all. Spend lunch casually outlining your issue and probing for solutions that may be hidden in your technology. If it sounds like they have some solid ideas that might solve the problems, consider doing something formal to get their expertise working for you.

The Moral: Give lots of thought to getting more out of your call Centre technology investment before you consider making an investment in more gear and marital counselling. This becomes really critical during a time when we are experiencing some economic slowdowns.

Key Measurements for Call Centre

There is no shortage of call Centre measurements. In fact, it's possible to have a Ph.D. in call Centre measurements but have a failing call Centre. The key is to focus on the few key measurements that ensure your ongoing success.

Measure	*Staff & Operations Mgmt.*	*Customer Interaction*	*Business Process & Systems*
Service Level	A ratio based on how well you are doing at achieving your target (*e.g.* answering 90% of calls within 30 seconds). This should be used as a budgeting driver. Service level is primarily driven by budget allocation.		
Calls Answered by Staff		Measures not just calls received but answered. A reflection	

		of planning and operational efficiency (*i.e.* scheduling). If the calls are not answered, see Abandonment.	
Contacts Answered other than by staff		"Toto, we are not in Kansas anymore". This measures contacts other than traditional phone calls.	
Abandonment rate		Often stated as a ratio against the total number of calls received. High numbers are not necessarily a good thing as far as customers are concerned.	
Calls Complete at First Point of Contact			Measures the percentage of time a customer receives sufficient service so that a follow contact is not required by call Centre staff or the customer. Actually a reflection of business processes and system capability.
Average Handling Time (AHT)	The total time to handle a call or a contact. It is comprised of the Average Talk Time and Average Wrap Time.		
Average Talk Time	The amount of time actually spent talking with the customer.		
Average Wrap Time	The amount of time doing post call or contact work such as notations to the customer database recording the interaction.		
Average Speed of Answer		Measures the average number of seconds	

	required to answer a call. A low number is good but it can also mean that your costs of operation are higher.
Schedule Adherence	The percentage of time a CSR is adhering to their work schedule including coffee and lunch breaks.
Absenteeism	Generally stated as a percentage of days absent either individually or for the entire call Centre. Hint: lower is better…much better.
Turnover	The percentage of staff that leave the call Centre for any reason (to work in the next department or to become a windsurfer in Baja). A low number can be good but if your call Centre has less challenging call types then high turnover can actually be helpful.
Cost Per Call	The actual cost per call. Total operating costs divided into the number of calls. (Simple version)
Cost Per Contact	Similar to Cost per Call but for all other types of non-agent related costs.
Cost Per Minute	Another angle on the Cost Per calculations. This calculation helps to determine the cost per minute of service provided. Where cost per call

		could lead you to reduce AHT to reduce cost per call, cost per minute leads you to reduce your cost per minute of service without necessarily shortening time with the customer. (Whew!)
Customer Loyalty		Oh, fickle customer. A measurement that assesses the churn-rate of customers.
Customer Satisfaction		Very satisfied to "I wouldn't recommend your company to my goldfish" (a.k.a. Dissatisfied). Hint: Very satisfied is another good thing but don't combine the Very, somewhat and just satisfied. Target only the score in the very satisfied category.
Employee Satisfaction	See Customer Satisfaction above and then look out of your office door … yes, the satisfaction of those looking back at you!	
Customer Complaints		Sometimes presented as a percentage against total customer calls.
Training Days (New Staff)	Measures new hire training.	
Training Days (Existing Staff)	Measures the days of training provided to existing staff. In most call Centres this is .003% of training for new hires. Hmmm.	

Dividing Work for Improved Performance

We think we might have a new event for the next Olympics. The name for the event: "Call Centre Tug-o-War". Not a creative name but we think it is a common event in call Centres.

What many don't realize is that call Centres are excellent training ground for the Olympic Call Centre Tug-o-War. On the one team are those who answer the phones. On the other team are those who process the fulfillment work that is generated by the folks talking to customers on the phone. The tug-o-war referees are the call Centre managers and team leaders who work hard to ensure each team is balanced with just enough qualified staff. It's hard to keep the teams balanced and without balanced teams it's not much of a 'war'. Here's why. When the phones get busy, the fulfillment office staff are put on the phone team and now they are out of balance. When the backlog of work in the fulfillment area gets the bosses attention, then those on the phone are sent to getting things back in order. Back and forth staff go between the teams. We have seen where this happens several times in a given day. The process can be very inefficient.

Work in a call Centre generally falls into two broad categories:

Real-time
Fulfillment

Real-time work includes the inbound phone call. When the phone rings it must be answered now—that's real-time! Fulfillment work is that which follows on after the real-time work concludes. Fulfillment activity can include order fulfillment, bill processing, complaint follow-up and service request processing or other similar types of activity.

One key characteristic of fulfillment work is that it can be scheduled, delayed or postponed without significant consequence to the customer and your career! It can occur later—it does not need to happen immediately. On the real-time team, work cannot experience delay. A 27-minute delay in answering the phone is not a best-practices achievement!

Balancing the demands for staff in each area is more an art than a science. The consequences of not working at maintaining the balance can cause either long waits for customers on the phone or lengthy fulfillment delays resulting in customers not getting their shipment or a service rep site visit.

Preparing for the Olympics: Our solutions for the dilemma do not apply equally for all call Centres. We do know that the options work well at achieving the balance when adopted for the specific call Centre.

1. **Scheduling Solution:** Analyze the volume of inbound calls and the fulfillment volume. Look at creating staff schedules that allow you to manage the phone and workload volumes so that the only time the real-time area draws on the fulfillment areas (and *vice versa*) is during special campaigns or unusual events.
2. **Three Team Solutions:** The Real-Time Team who answers the phones, the Fulfillment Team who manages the back office workload and the Swing Team who moves between the other two. This allows staff to be focused on one area for better efficiency. The Swing Team supplement whichever team has the bigger demand. The Swing Team can move between the Real-Time and Fulfillment Teams balancing the workloads. You may even what to stagger the Swing Team start and break times to off set coffee and lunch breaks of the other two teams.
3. **Out the Door Solution:** (sometimes know as Over-the-Wall Solution): Remove the fulfillment work from the call Centre altogether and organize it specifically around fulfillment activity. This is a more extreme approach but it can result in significant operational gains for both the real-time work activity and the fulfillment work activity. You must consider this carefully because you could break business processes that need to be in physically proximity to work well. Some detailed analysis can help determine the right outcome.

From GUI to SUI

Email+Web+SpeechRecognition+ Phone+IVR+ VoiceMail+ Kiosk+Fax.

A History Moment

You do not have to go that far back in computing history to know that the primary interface between computer and human consisted of a black or green screen with text on it. Between 1968 and 1979 Xerox began the development of the first GUI (graphic user interface). A company called Apple pushed the market appeal of GUIs beginning in 1979. Ultimately DOS (being text-based) became Windows and the GUI became commonplace and that is today's history lesson.

From GUI to SUI

What is SUI? It is a Simple User Interface. Not a particularly clever acronym. You could call it a CUI (Customer User Interface) but we digress. The point of this article is that a Simple User Interface is required for each point of contact a customer makes with a call Centre. A SUI is essential to having a good relationship with our customers. This concept isn't new to any of us. When was the last time you trapped your customer in an IVR maze that never ended? We are guilty!

A Call Centre Experience

A recent call to a major call Centre began with a speech recognition interface until we exceeded its depth of capability. It then diverted, unannounced, to a somewhat confusing using-the-buttons-on-the-phone interface otherwise known as IVR. Ultimately we got a call Centre service rep. One call. Three user interfaces—if you count the call Centre rep. as another 'interface'. It was confusing. The reason for the call was solved but it left us pondering the concept of SUI. The changes in interface were abrupt and far from seamless and thus this article was born!

Toto...We Are Not in Kansas Anymore

Another interface era has begun as we all work hard at implementing new access channels (interfaces) into our call Centres. Think of all the new interfaces: Email+Web+ Speech Recognition. Then add to that the existing interfaces: Phone+IVR+VoiceMail+Kiosk+Fax and we see a customer revolt coming! Maybe the customer interface revolt has begun. How many minutes have past since you received your last "I hate your IVR" comment from a customer? As customers move from interface to interface in our multi-channel call Centre world, it forces us call Centre types to develop Simple User Interfaces.

Getting to SUI

Designing a Simple User Interface requires some creative effort but most of all it requires a commitment to testing your interfaces while under development. You will need the help of IT. If they are not willing -- go it alone. Test all of your customer interfaces to ensure that the voice-of-the-customer is heard. Pass the results onto the interface design team. Establish a customer focus group and have them evaluate all of your interfaces. If your channel is in use today, conduct usability surveys with your customers. The real test is if the customer can change call Centre channel interfaces and remain loyal to your company? SUI is part of successful customer relationships.

Marketing Your Call Centre Inside Out

Much of the rest of the organization still doesn't truly understand call Centres or contact Centres. Customer Service Week is a great opportunity to expand the understanding of your call Centre in your company.

Many call Centres are not appreciated for the strategic contribution they make to the company. Although the call Centre has increasing visibility because of e-business, the overall contribution of call Centres is still not widely understood within many companies. This is proven when you hear phrases such as, "aren't they the group that just answer the phones". True, it is the group that "just answer the phones" but call Centres, as we all know, ensure that thousands of customers receive the right service in the right way at the right time!

We think it's time to market your call Centre from the inside out. It's time to focus on marketing your call Centre to the rest of the organization. Market the call Centre's contribution, it's dynamic environment and the people that make the call Centre successful.

What is the value of having an internal marketing plan for your call Centre? We see several reasons to market your call Centre from the inside out:

1. Demonstrate the strategic value of the call Centre to the company executive. Market the competitive advantage and bottom-line value of your call Centre.
2. Showcase the direct contribution CSRs make to the company's profitability, reinforcing the value of the call Centre.
3. Develop new customers for your call Centre. Departments considering new lines of business or providing additional customer service options may overlook the role the call Centre can play.
4. Reduce the "them and us" tensions that can occur between various customer-operating areas.
5. Make it easier to obtain project, technology or operational funding by building credibility with decision makers.
6. Make the boss look good! (We couldn't leave this one out!)

We have considered several internal marketing approaches that help to improve the image of the call Centre within an organization:

1. Call Centre open house

Invite the company to come, see and listen to your call Centre in action. (Hint: don't plan it for your busiest day!) Don't worry about the travel costs—just phone the boss's secretary and get his credit card number!

2. Take the call Centre on the road

Put together a presentation that in 20 minutes says it all in a way that it hasn't been said before. Add a little whiz-bang (like a video clip of the Centre) and market the uniqueness of your customer operation.

3. Produce a regular newsletter (email, paper or fax)

That highlights the people, their talent and contribution. Include customer success stories of your call Centre operation.

4. Create an Introduction to Call Centre course

Team up with your corporate and call Centre training departments to develop an introductory call Centre course. Not only will people learn but it can also be a great way to identify future call Centre staff! (Hint: in the course highlight the global call Centre industry and connect your call Centre to the larger picture.)

5. Create a call Centre intranet segment for the entire organization to surf!

6. Create a one-to-one marketing program

Brainstorm a list of the most influential decision makers in your organization. Put a plan together to invite each person on the list to a unique call Centre learning experience.

Call Centre Incubators

It was only a few years ago when call Centres were considered to be something of a necessary customer service cost. You rarely considered using the call Centre as a means to increase company revenues. You considered the call Centre as a way to handle phone calls. Today this is simply not the case -- or should not be the case.

Call Centres are strategic to the success of any company that wants to be effective in their respective market segment. As the value of call Centres has increased over the last few years, so has the need for those in call Centres to respond quickly to changes in the business. It is an essential element of being strategic.

Call Centres have to be quick to respond to:

Changing competitive demands

New product launches

Variations in customer expectations for sales and support

NOW HERE QUESTION RAISES

How do you make sure your call Centre operation can be as responsive as possible to an ever-changing business model and demands from internal and external pressures?

Answer

Create a call Centre 'incubator' to handle start-ups and changes in your business that requires a quick response. You are thinking, "incubators are for preemies in hospitals and eggs on the farm but not call Centres". Using the metaphor of an incubator can truly help you be quick to make change. Frequently, core operations are eroded while attention is paid to initiating a new process, function or introducing an entirely new line of business. An incubator can isolate disruption to core operations, as it is important to minimize disruption to your core call Centre operations while change is underway.

Here are some of the important elements to think about in creating a call Centre incubator.

1. Separate Structure

Set up the incubator structure outside of day-to-day call Centre operations and where possible, provide the incubator with its own space. Operations folks are great at working to deliver consistent service day-to-day to ensure response time is on target and the quality is just right. These people may not be the best to involve in a start-up because the rules are different—speed to market is better than perfect to market. Good operations people work at perfecting. Good start-up people work at perfecting speed to market.

2. Specific Team

Create a project team headed up by the most entrepreneurial leader you can find who understands your business and your call Centre operation. The rest of the team should consist of every major call Centre discipline necessary to be successful: leaders, supervisors, reps, technical call Centre staff (*e.g.* workforce management), business analysts, trainers and IT folks where necessary. This cross-functional team can be brought together to develop and launch the new process or service. The key measure for this team is teamwork.

3. Stated Objectives

Enable the project team to break the common rules of doing business and to work to deliver the results (*e.g.* email channel incubator). The team must develop the business rules, support, training materials and procedures while they initiate the new service. They typically would be involved in the technology purchasing decision and implementation. The team is accountable for early implementation. By putting reps on the team, the team can move from concept, to design to early experimentation or pilot phases all within the incubator. The team remains involved through to the implementation to core call Centre operations. Make the team accountable for a seamless transfer of the start-up into day-to-day operations. This ensures that at the end of the incubation process you do not end up with an orphan.

4. Think About the Horizon

The incubator period will end. Plan on it and manage to an end date. An end date may mean that everything is completed and it returns to *status quo*. It may mean implementing the results of the incubator call Centre across the entire call Centre. Thinking beyond the focus of the incubator will help the team to deliver beyond the immediate and implement for the long term.

This is not an exhaustive list of suggestions. We could go on at some length. These are just a few ideas that we hope will act as a catalyst for you to think creatively about what an incubator might do for your operation and your company. The concept of an incubator is at work in other industries such as new vehicle design, manufacturing and consumer products. The use of incubators can achieve amazing speed-to-market results and it could well please the boss!

Going K2K in a V2V World

E-business. E-commerce. Put and 'e' in front of anything and you got yourself a whole new industry. Just think. E-fishing. E-lawyers. E-flying. E-smoking. Ya, you get the point. It's been beaten to death but what is coming out of the e-world is a fundamental change for staff in call Centres in meeting the customer's need for excellent service.

Today, most call Centres use V2V customer service representatives. What is a V2V rep?

A voice-to-voice representative—An agent who answers the phone! They use their voice to connect with the customer over the phone. The way they smile when they talk (you can actually hear it in the voice), the tone of voice and the right answer—all are part of the components that really make the event for the customer when calling your call Centre. Call Centre staff learn how to talk on the phone. They do it over and over. Maybe 40 times a day. Maybe 200 times a day. They know how to talk! If they don't, the call mysteri-ously ends up with the supervisor or in the escalation service queue.

Along comes this e-world of ours. With it comes email and with that a whole new expectation—a K2K customer expectation.

What is K2K? As V2V is voice-to-voice customer service, K2K is keyboard-to-keyboard customer service.

As customers who contact our call Centres move to using email, call Centre staff need to learn a whole new way of connecting with the customer. This is a significant challenge for call Centres. Operational questions like "do we use our

V2V agents in a K2K world?" "What do we need to teach a K2K agent that is different from a V2V agent?"

The key point is that not all V2V agents will successfully make the transition to a K2K world. Those who best communicate by voice will not necessarily make a great keyboard agent. Sure you can get the newest whiz-bang email management tool which allows you to standardize a set of answers to FAQs. But you still need K2K agents that are good at putting a smile in email and can write well. This is really true when the customer writes an email in English but it sounds more like Old English when you read it!

It is surprising how poor the quality of email responses are from some companies. Maybe you have experienced it. The K2K agent might as well have sent an email with a single phrase—"duh customer!". "Ya, thank. Sure needed that type of response to make my day". The research gurus, who study the email response times of companies, indicate that most companies time their email responses using a calendar! It might take them one day to reply and more likely five! Compare that to 30 seconds—90% of the time—in the V2V world. Oh, and by the way, how often do you only get a partial answer and you waited one day for that! The result? More calls to the call Centre, which is good for the V2V agents. The K2K agents are helping to ensure the tenure of the V2V agents. The quality of your organization shines brightly through every email response crafted from boilerplate or impromptu responses!

So what is the solution? It is selecting agents that can really do it for you in a K2K world. Chose K2K agents wisely. Lots of people actually express themselves better in written form. Who is a prime candidate in your operation? The staff members who write out their opinion about operations rather than speak out at team meetings? Use typical customer questions received in the V2V world and have the K2K candidate agent write impromptu responses to see how they do.

If you were the customer, would you be satisfied or would you be reaching for the phone to call one of your V2V agents for the rest of the answer? Easy to read. Easy to understand and no "duh customer, my dog is smarter than you" attitudes—important parts to meeting customer expectations in a K2K world. That raise? It's in the E-mail!

Call Centre Properties—Reliability and Reactiveness

Here we are focusing on what we believe about the core properties of a call Centre and how they relate to call Centre operations. The concepts are derived from process modelling used in the design of real-time systems such as aircraft control systems, manufacturing and computer processing. Given that call Centres operate in the real-time environment, these concepts apply equally to call Centre operations.

The core properties of call Centres are:

(a) on-time environment

(b) concurrency

Part 2

(c) reliability

(d) reactiveness

Part 3

(e) dynamic resource allocation

(f) distributed environment.

Reliability

One of the key aspects of buying a car is that you want it to be reliable. After the new car has sat out in the rain all night, you expect that car to start in the morning. Without giving it a thought, you expect the car to be reliable.

Because you call Centre is a communication hub between your products and services and your customers, reliability in the call Centre is a core property for successful call Centre operations. Many events happen concurrently reliability and concurrency go hand in hand. The reliability of the operation is reflected in ensuring that sufficient agents are available to handle the expected call volumes. Reliability is reflected in the 'up-time' of your core systems. The multitude of voice, telephony and data systems you use need to be reliable so that agents can not only connect with the customer but also conduct the transaction with a profitable outcome. When evaluating new systems, make sure that you have done due diligence on the reliability question in your purchasing decisions.

Reliability is reflected in your agent's ability to talk to 30, 50 or 100 customers or more a day! You must ensure that agents are reliably handling customer contact after customer contact. How reliable is your operation? One of the most important factors in developing new business processes within your call Centre is to design the processes to be reliable. To work when they should as they should. To deliver the results to the agents who then can deliver them to the customers.

Learn about your operation: Do a 'reliability audit!' Evaluate the weakness within your operating environment, itemize the unreliable components and work through a plan to improve reliability whether it is your recruiting process, your phone systems, data systems or your agent training program or whatever else your audit reveals. Hint: include the voice-of-the-customer in the audit. Ask customers if they experienced reliability problems in doing business with your call Centre.

Reactiveness

The Marketing Department did it again! Bless their hearts! They 'forgot' to advise the call Centre that the new promotion running in 86 newspapers across the country (which lists a single 800 number on it—yours!) began running this morning. You were expecting a relatively normal call volume day and now you are seeing the queues build. Wait times are beginning to soar to the moon and you still haven't heard from Marketing!

Have a defined plan in place to enable you to respond to the unexpected. To look like a star even when the Marketing department informs you 3 days AFTER the marketing campaign began. It may seem like a contradiction in terms but be proactive about your reactiveness. Develop a plan, a simple plan that will allow you to quickly and easily react to the unexpected. It may mean that you equip back office staff with ACD telephone sets so that they can log into queues and answer calls (even if it takes them twice as long as a regular agent); it could mean that you establish a contract with an outsourcer who can quickly respond to calls that are deflected from your operation to theirs for handling; it could mean that you do nothing more than play a message that advises the customer that 'today is a bad-hair day'; it could mean you get the Manager of Marketing to come down and answer calls (hold it—now that would be a plan!).

Call Centre operations function in the "on-time world", being proactive about your reactiveness will ensure near stardom for you and likely your team getting the bonuses for achieving your sales objectives! After all, the customer doesn't care at all that Marketing didn't tell you—again! Customers want service and they want it now! Build a plan that will allow you to 'grow' your staff to meet the unexpected. To be able to be responsive to anything.

Call Centre Properties: Dynamic Resource Allocation and Distributed Environment

The core properties of call Centres are:

(A) dynamic resource allocation

(B) distributed environment.

Dynamic Resource Allocation

This core principle is the cousin of reactiveness. Reactiveness is the brains (what are we going to do?) whereas dynamic resource allocation is the action (how are we going to do it?). Normally we have two resources available to allocate. People and systems. Agents can be moved between queues in order to respond to the growing wait times or unexpected call volumes. Notice the next time you are in bank and the call for cashiers goes out as the line-up starts to grow! Bank has dynamically reallocated staff from stocking shelves to cashiering. Customers cannot see how we reallocate staff but they definitely are affected by how we do it and the speed in which we do it. Dynamic resource allocation is predicated on teamwork. One of the most effective means of dynamic allocation is teaming up with another department that has staff skilled in many of your call Centre functions.

For example, have staff in a fulfillment Centre trained to a point where they could handle certain types of calls during crunch time. Establish the processes and procedures within your call Centre and between other departments that can ensure the company's success at meeting customer expectations for short wait times.

Systems can also be used to support the concept of dynamic allocation to provide improved call Centre performance. For example, reallocating calls on your 800 lines to other locations or agent groups could be just the trick. Providing different messages to customers estimating an approximate wait time for them, is another form of allocation. The one difference here is that you dynamically allocate the customer's expectations with the normal result of reducing the likelihood of the customer abandoning the call. Dynamically reallocating resources is about developing the ability to alter what people do and how systems support the customer transaction.

Distributed Environment

Many companies have call Centres distributed geographically but networked together. This configuration is called a virtual call Centre. Customers have always been virtual as it relates to call Centres because they are distributed. They can be calling from down the street or from thousands of miles away. When was the last time you looked at a map and compared it to where your customers call you from?

When you look at the environment in this context it provides a renewed sense of just how distributed your business really is. This distributed environment, from a customer perspective, requires you to understand the expectations of customers who are broadly distributed not just geographically but likely cultural as well. The distributed environment of a call Centre may mean that you examine your call Centre for effectiveness in managing the diversity that comes with this distributed environment. For example, what are the wait thresholds for customers by geographic region? Are those factors considered in day to day operations?

Typically, customers from various geographic areas have differing expectations. Being successful at serving customers via your call Centre requires you to have an excellent sense of the distributed environment you manage.

2

TYPE of Call Centre

Telemarketing and outbound call Centres

Not all call Centres receive calls. Many call Centres make calls. These call Centres are called outbound call Centres and include telemarketing companies, debt collection agencies, fund raising organizations and other companies that need proactive contact with customers.

In some cases a call Centre will handle inbound calls from customers during one period of the day and then switch to outbound calling for the remainder of the day. Other call Centres have the ability to blend inbound and outbound at the same time. In other words, if you are not needed for an inbound customer call, then the system can prompt you to place an outbound call. This capability minimizes the time agents sit idle waiting for a call to come in.

Call Centre management and technical positions

In addition to the front-line employees that work with customers, the call Centre offers many other jobs in both management and technical areas. Examples of employment opportunities include:

- Supervisor or team leader
- Training development and delivery
- Workforce scheduling
- Quality monitoring or quality assurance
- Business analyst (reporting and financials)

- Process specialists
- Human resources
- Information technology
- Facility design and maintenance

All of these areas are needed for the call Centre to work effectively and efficiently and offer a strong and diverse career path for customer service representatives working in the call Centre.

Mathematical theory

Queuing theory mathematics can be used to demonstrate that a single large call centre is more effective at answering calls than several smaller centres. The most dramatic improvements come when a large number of offices are centralised. The A call centre (UK) or call Centre (US) is a centralised office, centralised approach aims to rationalise the company's operations and reduce costs, whilst producing a standard, branded, front to the world. The approach naturally lends itself to large companies with a large, distributed customer base. Owing to the size of companies and their customer bases, these offices are often very large, such as converted warehouses. They are often supported by computer technology that manages, measures and monitors the performance and activities of the workers. Examples include utility companies, mail order catalogue firms, and customer support for computer hardware and software.

Call centres have been aided by a range of telecommunications and computer technologies, including automatic call distribution (ACD), interactive voice response (IVR), computer telephony integration (CTI), which allows the actions of the computer to be synchronized with what is happening on the phone. In addition, early customer relationship management (CRM) technologies, such as Siebel and other database systems, were heavily employed in call centres. The latest Internet technologies allow "virtual" call centres to be established across a company's telecommunications network without physically putting all the people in one office.

Call dynamics

Types of calls are often divided into outbound and inbound. Inbound calls are calls that are initiated by the customer to obtain information report a malfunction or ask for help. This is substantially different from outbound calls where the agent initiates the call to a customer mostly with the aim to sell a product or a service to that customer.

The staff of the call Centre is often organized in tiers, with the first tier being largely unskilled workers who are trained to resolve issues using a simple script. If the first tier is unable to resolve an issue the issue is escalated to a more highly skilled second tier. In some cases, there may be third or higher tiers of support.

Call centres have their critics as well. Some critics argue that the work atmosphere in such an environment is dehumanizing. Others point to the low rates of pay and restrictive working practices of some employers. There has been much controversy over such things as restricting the amount of time that an employee can spend in the toilet. Furthermore, call Centres have been the subject of complaints by callers who find the staff of the call Centres often do not have enough skill or authority to resolve problems.

Owing to the highly technological nature of the operations in such offices, the close monitoring of staff activities is easy and widespread. This can be argued to be beneficial, to enable the company to better plan the workload and time of its employees. Some people have argued that such close monitoring breaches human rights to privacy. Yet another argument is that close monitoring and measurement by quantitative metrics can be counterproductive in that it can lead to poor customer service and a poor image of the company.

Many call centres in the UK have been built in areas that are depressed economically. This means that the companies get cheap land and labour, and can often benefit from grants to encourage them to improve employment in a given area. There has also been a trend to move call centres to India, where there is a large pool of cheap English-speaking labour. This phenomenon has led to media reports of poor telephone connections and operators with insufficient local knowledge to do their job. Many American corporations outsource their call Centre operations to Canadian firms due to the low Canadian Dollar and cheap telecommunication rates. SITEL Corporation, which operates call centres in Ottawa, Ontario, Canada and St. Catherines. Ontario, Canada, is one such company.

Around the world there are a number of professional organizations forming to develop and promote call Centre best practice management and operation, to overcome the negative aspects of a call centre.

Telemarketing

Telemarketing is a form of direct marketing where a salesperson uses the telephone to call prospective customers to attempt to sell products or services. The prospective customers are identified and qualified by various means, including past purchase histories, previous requests for information, credit limit, competition entry forms or application forms. Names may also be purchased from another company's customer database, or obtained from a telephone directory or some other public list or forum. The qualification process is intended to find those prospective customers most likely to purchase the product or service being sold or advertised.

Market survey companies often use telemarketing techniques to survey prospective or past customers of a client business to assess market acceptance or satisfaction with a particular product, service, brand or company. Public opinion polls are conducted in a similar manner.

Telemarketing techniques can also be applied to other forms of electronic marketing using e-mail or fax messages.

Telemarketing is often criticized as being a bad or unethical business practice as some companies use/abuse these techniques and technologies to make unsolicited calls or send unsolicited messages to people who do not want to purchase the product or service being offered and are often offended by the high-pressure sales techniques used. Such practices may be subject to regulatory or legislative controls related to privacy in legal jurisdictions. Some countries have professional direct marketing organizations that have codes of ethics that member businesses are supposed to abide by to minimise such offence.

Some jurisdictions have implemented "Do Not Call" listings, either through industry organisations or legislation, in which consumers can indicate that they do not wish to be called by telemarketeers. Legislative versions often provide for heavy penalties for companies calling individuals on these listings. The U.S. Federal Trade Commission has now implemented a national Do Not Call Registry (DNCR) in an attempt to end intrusive telemarketing on a national basis.

To counter unethical telemarketing techniques, some people have developed a range of strategies and tactics for responding to telemarketing calls. Some technical methods rely on the weaknesses of technology that detects a call being answered by a person compared to an answering machine, fax machine or disconnected number. These technologies often simulate the behaviour of machinery that telemarketing technology rejects or otherwise confuses machinery but not human callers. As telemarketeers rarely disclose their own telephone number, using caller ID can allow the targeted subscriber to identify the caller before the call is answered and the subscriber can make a decision to answer or not.

Answer machines and voicemail can also be used to screen calls, as telemarketeers rarely leave messages as the technology generally hangs up first. Other methods rely on upsetting the telemarketer's call script or sales pitch, upsetting the telemarketer, making it uneconomic or undesirable to call a target number, having the target number blacklisted or otherwise having the target number removed from the calling list, or not getting on the calling list in the first place.

HIGHLIGHTS FROM THE STUDY

The figure below shows the current usage levels of different technologies by the study participants (note that participants could indicate more than one technology). CTI jumped from 37% usage in 2001 to 52% usage in 2004. Email and voice response systems retained the top two positions.

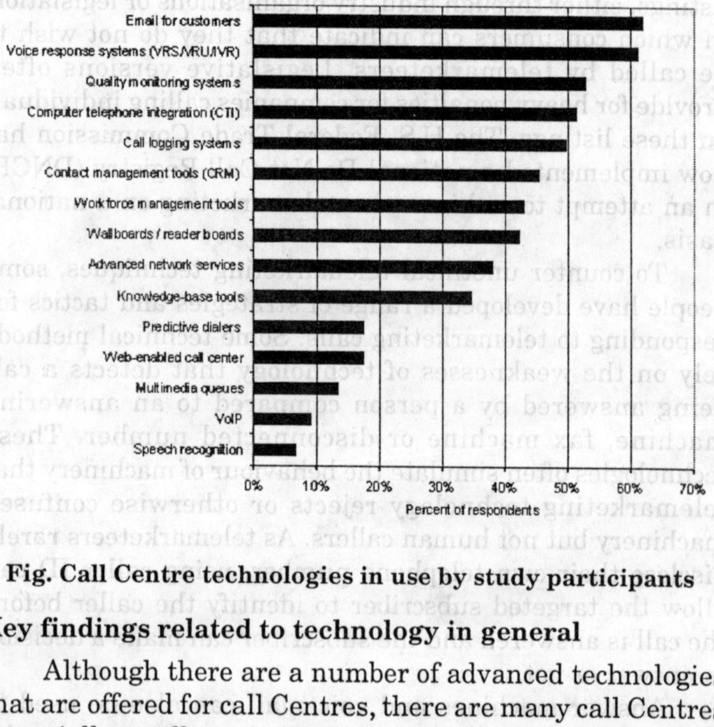

Fig. Call Centre technologies in use by study participants

Key findings related to technology in general

Although there are a number of advanced technologies that are offered for call Centres, there are many call Centres (especially smaller ones) that do not use the most up-to-date technology.

Email and voice response systems, equally considered, have become the most frequently used vehicles for customer contact other than voice calls to agents.

As the different forms of technology have become more readily available and more widely used, implementation and development times have decreased.

Email turnaround times have improved over time, but the reality for email response times is still not matching goals.

The greatest emphasis for future technology projects lies in Web-enabled call Centres and Web-based technology.

Average decrease in talk time

Participants reported decreases in their average talk times due to various technology changes (see the figure below). Contact management systems accounted for the most dramatic decrease in talk times, averaging a reduction of 28 seconds per call. Knowledge-base applications averaged a 26 second decrease per call, quality monitoring systems accounted for an average decrease of 13 seconds per call and CTI accounted for an average decrease of 12 seconds per call.

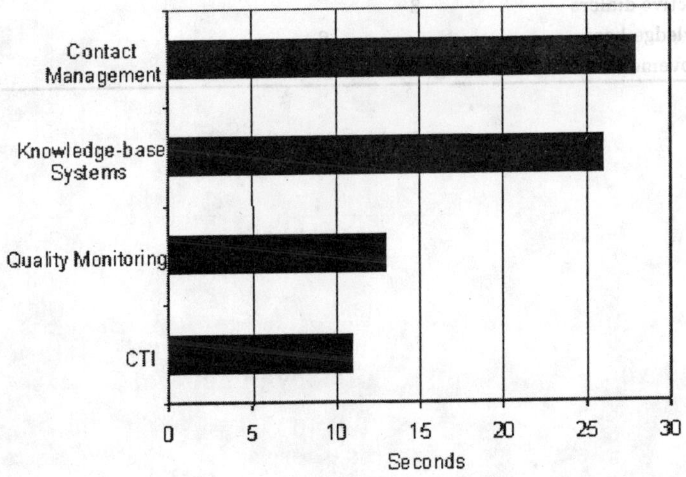

Fig. : Average decrease in talk time from technology implementation

Overall ranking of improvement initiatives

The table below summarizes the technology findings from the studies conducted in 2001 and 2004. The technologies having had the greatest positive impact on call Centre customers and call Centre efficiency are listed and ranked by their impact level. For example, a ranking of "1" in the call Centre efficiency column for voice response systems defines this change as the most cited to positively impact call Centre efficiency in 2004.

Impact full technologies	*Greatest positive impact on customers*		*Greatest positive impact on call Centre efficiency*	
	2004	*2001*	*2004*	*2001*
CTI	1		3	3
Voice response systems	2	4	1	4
Switch and ACD	3	1	2	1
Web-enabled customer contact	4	3	7	5
Workforce management			4	
Quality monitoring	5	5	5	
Desktop software/GUI/CRM	6	2	6	2
New PCs (hardware)	7		8	
Predictive dialers	8			
Knowledge-base		6		
Improvement initiative rankings				

3
Issues in Call Centre Manangement

Call Monitoring

Call monitoring, also known as quality monitoring, is crucial to a call

Centre's success. It gives the organization an idea of how well the Centre is meeting its customer service objectives.

A critical component of any quality-monitoring program is the scorecard and criteria for agent evaluation.

If you are implementing a new call monitoring program, change management will be important for your success as a manager and leader of this new initiative. You should create and implement a change management plan to avoid productivity loss and negative reaction to your new quality monitoring process.

Quality Monitoring Benefits

Introduction

Quality monitoring or call monitoring refers to the process of listening to or observing an agent's phone calls or other multi-media contacts with customers in order to assess and evaluate strengths and weaknesses in performance. There are six basic levels of quality monitoring:

1. Walk-around observation
2. Side-by-side

3. Plug-in/double jack monitoring
4. Silent monitoring
5. Record and review
6. Voice and screen/multi-media monitoring

Companies cite many different benefits from quality monitoring programs. Research results from the 2001 benchmarking study shows that the majority of companies perform quality monitoring with one major goal in mind: to evaluate agent performance and improve service quality. Other reasons for quality monitoring include:

- Assessment and improvement of scripts and processes
- Greater customer satisfaction
- Increased efficiency
- Improved training programs
- Uncovering common customer complaints and concerns
- General troubleshooting

Major Benefits of Quality Monitoring

As a supervisor or manager, there are several key benefits you are trying to address when implementing a quality-monitoring program. The four major benefits of quality monitoring directly impact:

- Efficiency and cost
- Customer satisfaction
- Training improvements
- Quality

CUSTOMER SATISFACTION

Quality monitoring is one of the most effective methods for improving customer satisfaction levels. Many supervisors and managers look for correlation between customer service levels and quality monitoring scores. When performing quality monitoring, you will:

Improve overall employee performance.

Gain valuable customer feedback.

Increase customer satisfaction by addressing common complaints and evaluating customer needs.

Assess agents' listening and comprehension skills.

Evaluate agents' problem-solving abilities.

Gain insight as to how well agents are controlling the pace and flow of the conversation.

Assess agents' customer relationship management skills.

Efficiency and cost

Overall call Centre efficiency is improved with the implementation of a quality monitoring system. In the end, higher levels of efficiency result in lower costs. Quality monitoring allow managers and supervisors to:

- Reduce defective calls that result in callbacks.
- Reduce handle time by improving system navigation skills.
- Troubleshoot problem areas.
- Review scripting for improvement.
- Identify weaknesses in systems operation and navigation.
- Improve employee procedures.

Training improvements

The benefit of quality monitoring that is most often overlooked by supervisors is the improvement of training and new agent orientation programs. Quality monitoring sessions, when recorded and archived, can be especially beneficial during new agent orientation and training. The ability to illustrate with live examples is a major benefit that is often overlooked.

Design improvement programs based on common deficiencies in agents, scripts or policies.

Improve training programs by supplementing them with the "best of" and "worst of" quality monitoring examples.

Implement mentoring, career pathing and in-house training programs using quality monitoring as an aid.

Retain good agents and improve upon existing skills.

Quality

Overall call Centre quality performance is improved with the implementation of quality monitoring systems.

Benchmarking studies indicate a correlation between quality monitoring implementation and overall call Centre performance improvement.

- Helps companies maintain quality standard.
- Increases cost effectiveness through improved efficiencies.
- Accelerates development of agent skills.
- Creates visible accountability for performance.

UNDERSTANDING THE BENEFITS

Quality monitoring is the first step in creating a plan to implement or improve your quality monitoring program. The critical question is:

"Are you realizing these benefits for your call Centre?"

If not, then the first step is—

To evaluate the method being used for quality monitoring. Depending on the method being used, limitations exist for how effective the program can be.

The second step will be to review the quality monitoring process for collecting performance data, analyzing the data and providing feedback to agents and other groups in your call Centre.

Managing the implementation of quality monitoring

Whether you are implementing a brand new monitoring program or simply reorganizing an old one, educating your agents is important because it makes the transition easier for all those involved. Always remember that agents are involved in the process, even though their role may be passive compared to the behind the scenes work you and your team are doing. By including the following five elements in your implementation, you can help ensure agents are educated and aware of the new monitoring process.

1. Clear definitions

The first key element in implementing a successful monitoring program is to provide clear definitions of the monitoring process to your agents. Each element of the process should be concisely defined and explained. This includes identifying:

- New procedures
- New technology
- New tools
- Organizational impacts
- Changes in job roles (*i.e.*, peer monitoring or mentoring)

While many of these items may be explained partially through discussions, handouts or informal conversation, the ideal way to address each of them is to provide agents a visual and verbal description.

For example, you may do this through email, overheads, manuals or newsletters. Whatever method you choose, it is most important to take the time to carefully outline and describe the new circumstances and expectations. Don't gloss over important information or leave out details that impact agents. The goal here is to keep your agents informed and involved—and in the long run, it will make your job easier and improve their perception of the program.

2. Educational and training opportunities

Training and education should be available to all agents, especially when you are implementing a new monitoring program. Training is a critical part of quality monitoring and the overall call Centre improvement cycle.

Training gives agents an opportunity to practice skills, learn new systems, establish goals for themselves and ask questions. Education gives agents the tools to understand why they are doing, what they are doing and how it will benefit them and the call Centre.

Opportunities that should be in place include (but are not limited to):

- Education and training for new systems, tools and procedures.
- New training programs for performance improvement.
- Workshops and team meetings.

Encouraging your agents to take part in these activities is a win-win situation. Your agents gain more ownership over the new process and their goals, and your call Centre sees improvement through better-trained and educated agents.

3. Information about the new process

Provide information that explains how monitoring will affect your agents on a personal level. This gives agents understanding about how their evaluations will affect their job roles and potential for growth, and it keeps them included in the information loop. Some examples of how agents may be affected by monitoring include:

- New expectations for job performance
- Performance tracking
- Training for performance improvement
- Mentoring
- Peer monitoring

Agents are directly affected by and involved in all of the above. The monitoring cycle becomes crystal clear to them when they see the improvement of their own monitoring scores translated into the ability to help others in the call Centre and better serve customers.

4. New performance measures

In order to enforce new performance measures, they must be clearly defined and implemented as goals for the entire call Centre. Your job is to ensure new performance measures and expectations for performance are communicated to agents and instilled as a call Centre requirement. In order to do this, you must:

- Provide clear definitions
- Encourage Q&A sessions so that no uncertainty exists
- Create and maintain a communications channel
- Make these new measures "official"

Leave no stone unturned when implementing new performance measures. Take into account that different agents respond best to different types of communication. You may wish to impart these new measures through a variety of methods (email, posters, meetings, newsletters, workshops). Make sure that all agents are aware of the new measures. Don't unintentionally leave behind members of your own team!

5. Methods for educating agents

Throughout the implementation process, utilize a variety of methods to keep your agents educated about what is taking place. Some people can absorb information simply by hearing it, while others grasp information after seeing it. Your role is to allow both types of learners the opportunity to gain the information the way they need to gain it.

Discussion or Q&A sessions naturally encourage interactivity. This gives everyone the opportunity to speak up and voice an opinion or ask for clarification.

Written communication is equally valuable for two reasons:

1. It puts the new standards in formalized terms and serves as notification that the changes are now requirements.
2. It gives agents a reference and a clear description of what is happening, what is now expected and how it will affect them personally.

According to benchmarking studies, the most effective methods for verbally communicating with and educating your agents are:

- Team (large or small) meetings
- Upper management presentations
- Workshops
- Group demonstrations
- Training events

How to involve your agents in the implementation

Do agents have negative perceptions of quality monitoring? The answer to this question is very important, because it can ultimately decide the success or failure of your quality monitoring program.

What do agents say?

Benchmarking research over recent years indicates that the majority of agents feel quality monitoring is generally okay, and they accept it as a necessary part of the call Centre. Only about 7% of agents view quality monitoring as intrusive and unnecessary and openly oppose it.

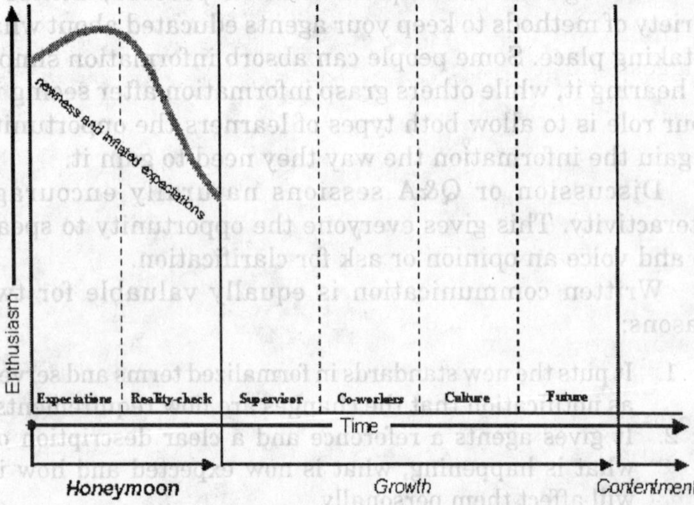

This research indicates that agents' opinions of quality monitoring are generally positive or, at the very least, neutral. Your job is to ensure your quality monitoring program is not only beneficial to the organization, but beneficial to agents as well.

How to combat negative perceptions

Some managers and supervisors find themselves fighting a faceless enemy when implementing quality monitoring because of negative perceptions held by agents. You can overcome these perceptions to create a positive quality-monitoring environment with the help of agent motivation and change management principles.

1. Agent Motivation

Recognition and direct contact and feedback from supervisors are a desired job factors that agents highly value. In addition, agents consider the "positive leadership skills" and the one-on-one relationship with their supervisors to be the most motivating job factor for them on the job, well above incentive programs.

In your communication with agents about the new program, be sure to address these motivating job factors. Stress that the program will allow you to give better feedback to them and help them improve their job performance. Suggested actions include:

- If you are experiencing resistance from certain agents, sit down with them one-one-one to focus on their concerns
- Provide feedback promptly (within 24 hours)
- Implement team discussions and reviews on a weekly or monthly basis
- Maintain regularly scheduled reviews

2. Managing change

Change management will be an important factor in your success when implementing a quality-monitoring program. Be sure to share with employees why the change is taking place, the risk of not changing and what the new program will mean to them personally. Whether you are implementing a brand new monitoring program or simply reorganizing an old one, educating your agents is important because it makes the transition easier for all those involved. Always remember that agents are involved in the process, even though their role may be passive compared to behind the scenes work you and your team are doing.

There are several actions you can take to minimize resistance to the new program. Among the most successful are:

- Implement a quality monitoring process that uses the full Quality Monitoring Lifecycle Involve the agents in the implementation or improvement of the monitoring process

- When hiring new agents, introduce the program as part of the work process for improving and not as punitive mechanism or simply an evaluation tool

The most critical times for you to focus your efforts are:

- When implementing a new quality monitoring program
- When hiring new agents
- When agent perception is already poor
- Methods for quality monitoring
- Benefits of quality monitoring
- Perception and legality
- The complete Quality Monitoring Lifecycle
- Survey criteria
- Scorecard content—with a sample based on best practices research
- Implementation and improvement guidelines

Quality Monitoring Lifecycle?

The goal of this tutorial series is to present the Quality Monitoring Lifecycle and to explain the role this program has in the call Centre. Quality monitoring is an essential part of call Centre operations, but many times the real benefits of call monitoring are not realized—the monitoring takes place for the sake of monitoring. The first tutorial in this series presents the Quality Monitoring Lifecycle. Modules 2, 3 and 4 examine each of the steps—monitor, feedback and coaching—in detail. The module examines how to make the most of a quality monitoring program and the key lessons and improvements your program can produce.

The Quality Monitoring Lifecycle

The Quality Monitoring Lifecycle shown in the figure below is a critical model for designing or improving your quality monitoring program.

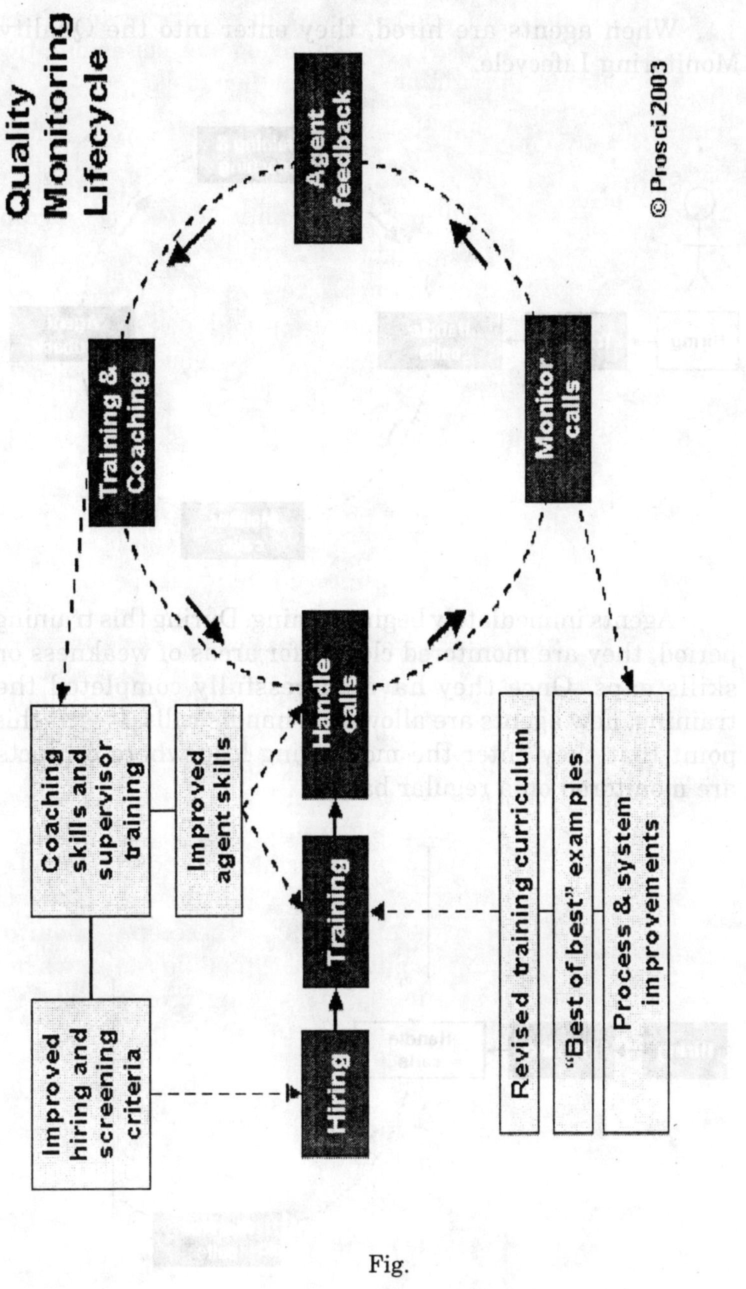
Quality Monitoring Lifecycle
Agent feedback
Training & Coaching
Monitor calls
Handle calls
Coaching skills and supervisor training
Improved agent skills
Training
Improved hiring and screening criteria
Hiring
Revised training curriculum
"Best of best" examples
Process & system improvements
© Prosci 2003

Fig.

When agents are hired, they enter into the Quality Monitoring Lifecycle.

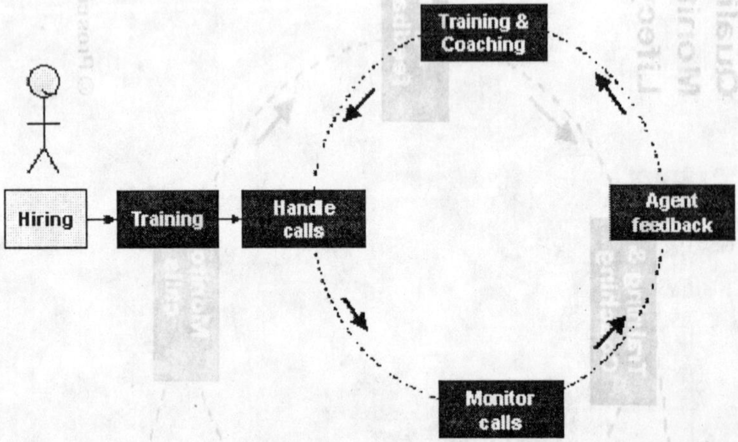

Agents immediately begin training. During this training period, they are monitored closely for areas of weakness or skills gaps. Once they have successfully completed the training, new agents are allowed to handle calls. It is at this point that they enter the monitoring loop where contacts are monitored on a regular basis.

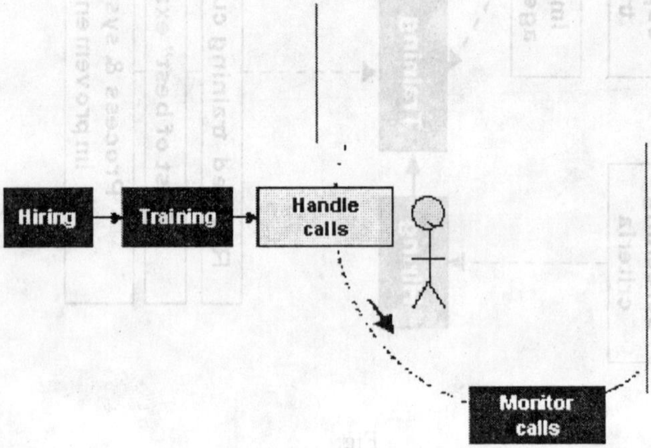

Monitoring often immediately brings to light various issues and information that result in changes to the current process or alterations in training methods.

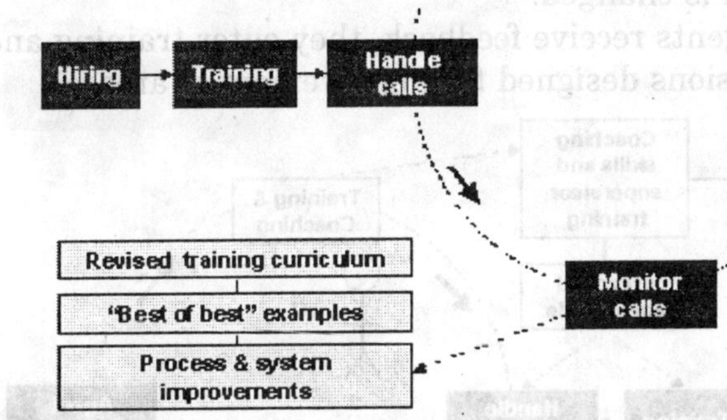

Issues that relate to process and system improvements, revised training curriculum and coaching are often easy to spot once quality monitoring commences. These and related issues may be raised throughout the monitoring cycle and usually impact training and work processes.

Feedback is the next step in the lifecycle. Agents are given evaluations based on their monitored contacts.

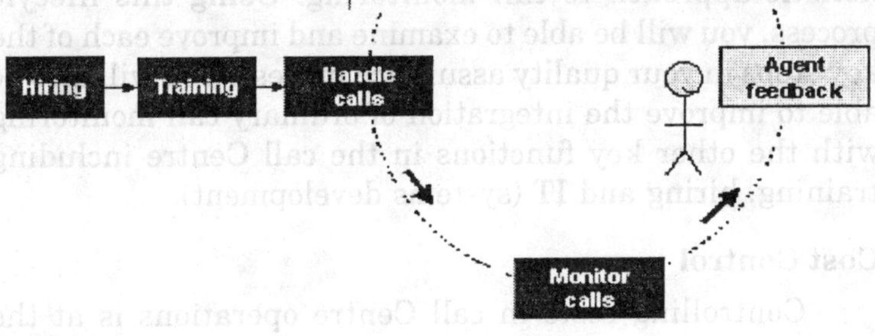

Feedback goes to two major destinations: to the agent and to the system.

Agent feedback is an evaluation that directs the agent toward training or coaching sessions in order to improve performance. The system benefits because group or process issues come to the forefront. Often system changes are implemented, training or hiring is altered, or the monitoring process itself is changed.

Once agents receive feedback, they enter training and coaching sessions designed for improvement of areas.

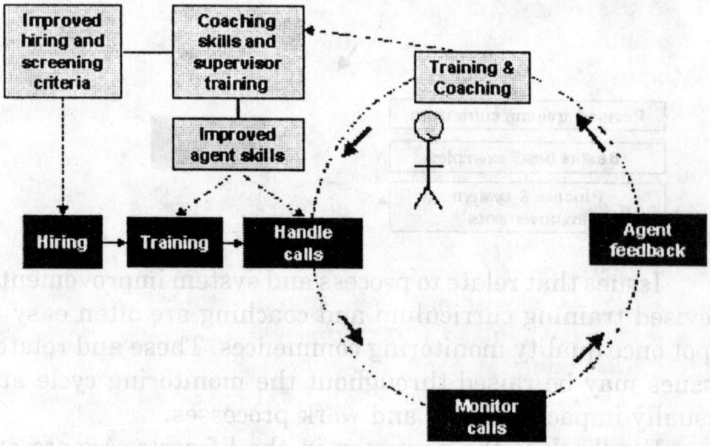

These training and coaching sessions are created to address common areas of weakness and group issues. They also provide a way for agents to interact with superiors in a non-threatening environment.

The quality monitoring lifecycle introduced in this is a holistic approach to call monitoring. Using this lifecyle process, you will be able to examine and improve each of the key steps in your quality assurance process. You will also be able to improve the integration of ordinary call monitoring with the other key functions in the call Centre including training, hiring and IT (systems development).

Cost Control

Controlling costs in call Centre operations is at the

forefront of business initiatives across the globe. Call Centre managers are facing constant pressure to do more with less. Improve service, cut costs.

Moreover, peak calling periods and seasonal variations also require call Centre managers to find ways to handle these peaks without "blowing the budget" by hiring more staff.

The first resource is a comprehensive ways to reduce handle time
Lower resource costs
And reduce contact volume.

Controlling the Cost of Call Centre Operations provides a systematic approach to reducing your call Centre costs. With this, you will critically examine multiple channels for reducing expense. The outcome is a set of identified and prioritized cost saving initiatives that are most suited for your contact Centre :

- need to reduce the cost of your call Centre operations
- are under pressure to deliver the same level of service with fewer resources
- are faced with increasing costs in your call Centre
- need to manage peak calling periods or seasons without 'breaking the bank'

Lowering handle time (*e.g.*, talk time plus after-call work time for a phone call)
Reducing resource costs for handling contacts (fully loaded cost per unit time).
Decreasing total volume of contacts (volume of inbound contacts for all media).

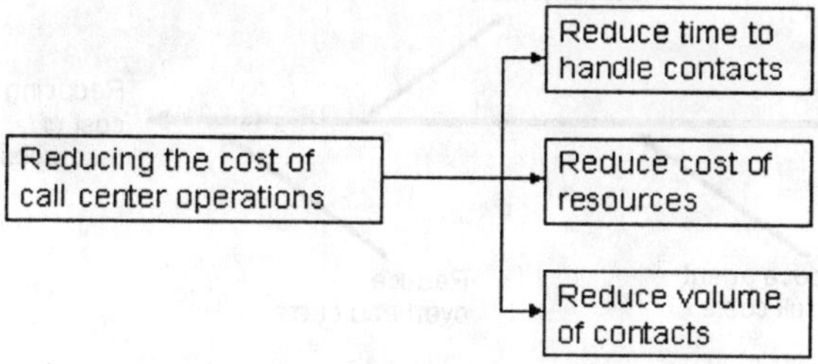

Reducing any one of these three variables will reduce the cost of operating a contact Centre. This framework is critical to a systematic analysis of your contact Centre costs. In the following summary, we will build on this framework to begin the process of analyzing the potential areas for cost reduction.

Reducing the handle time

Reducing the contact handle time can be accomplished by improving one of the following three areas:

- Improve agent capability
- Improve systems support
- Improve or redesign contact processes

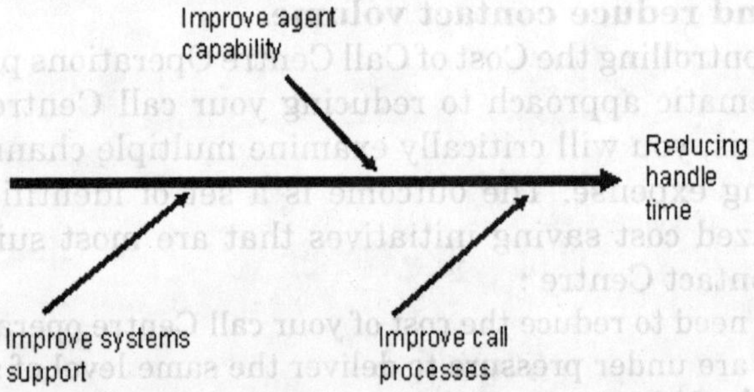

Reducing the cost of resources

Reducing the cost of resources (including the cost of people, equipment or facilities necessary to handle customer contacts) can be achieved by one of the following methods:

- Drive volume to lower cost channels
- Reduce agent payroll costs
- Reduce overhead costs

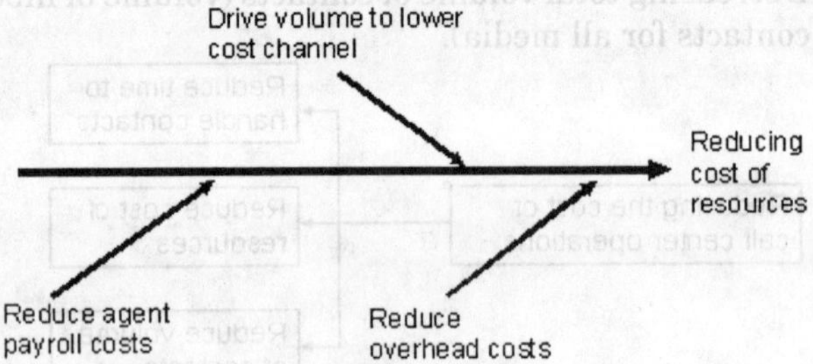

Reducing the volume of contacts

Reducing the volume of contacts can be achieved by one of the following methods :

- Eliminate reason to contact
- Minimize misdirected calls
- Reduce repeat calls

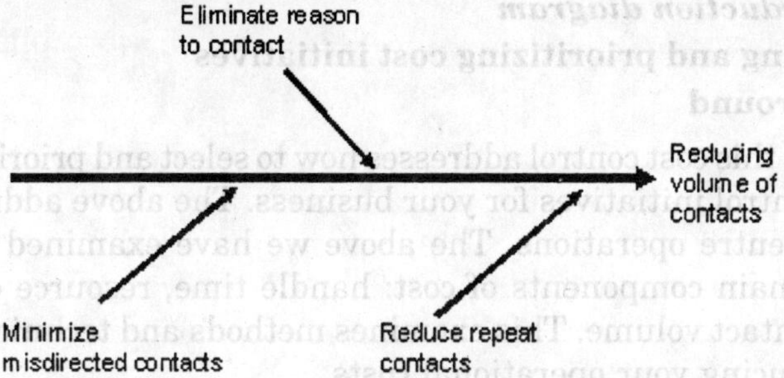

Note that redistributing volume to alternate media (*i.e.*, moving phone calls to IVR or web self-service) does not appear on this diagram. That type of cost reduction initiative is addressed in the category of "Reducing the Cost of Resources" under the area "Drive volume to lower cost channel".

Putting the framework together

By taking each component and putting them together, you can create a master framework for identifying cost

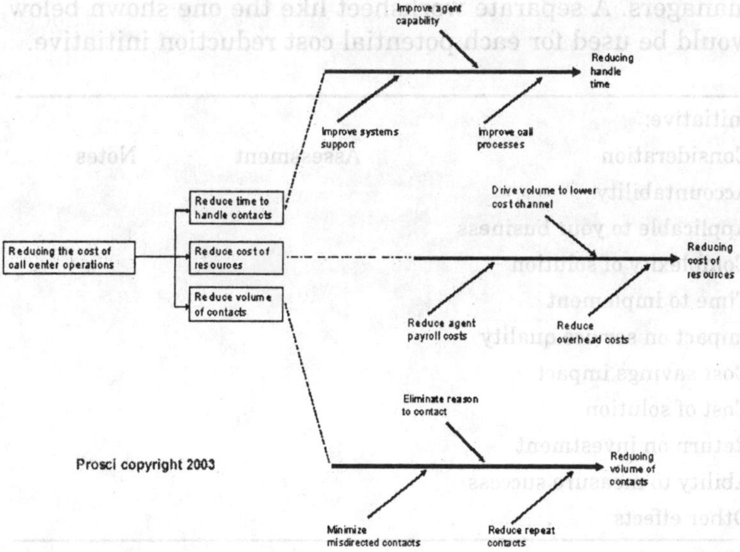

reduction initiatives for your call Centre as shown in the cost reduction diagram.

Cost reduction diagram

Selecting and prioritizing cost initiatives

Background

In this cost control addresses how to select and prioritize cost control initiatives for your business. The above address calls Centre operations. The above we have examined the three main components of cost: handle time, resource cost and contact volume. This examines methods and techniques for reducing your operational costs.

Initiative selection considerations

The table below can be used to capture the key considerations for a particular cost initiative. This helps call Centre leaders, managers and consultants think about all of the implications (both positive and negative) of a particular initiative. In other words, reducing the cost of call Centre operations does not come without a price in many cases, and understanding the tradeoffs is important for call Centre managers. A separate worksheet like the one shown below would be used for each potential cost reduction initiative.

Initiative:

Consideration	Assessment	Notes
Accountability		
Applicable to your business		
Complexity of solution		
Time to implement		
Impact on service quality		
Cost savings impact		
Cost of solution		
Return on investment		
Ability to measure success		
Other effects		

• **Accountability**

Does the contact Centre have the sole authority for this improvement idea or are other organizations involved? For example, offering self-service on the web would require working with the department that manages the website, if it is not the call Centre. What other groups or organizations need to be involved?

• **Applicable to your business**

Is this initiative applicable to your business strategy, business model, contact Centre strategy, contact Centre model, etc.? For example, efforts to reduce handle time with universal agents may not be applicable to a contact Centre that delivers very specialized and highly specific technical support.

- Complexity of solution: How complex is the solution? How many different groups and systems are impacted? Will implementation be easy or difficult? How much change wills the solution introduce into the organization?
- Time to implement: How long will the solution take to implement (week, month, quarter, year, etc.)?
- Impact on service quality: Will the initiative hurt service quality? Will the initiative improve service quality? How will the change impact customers?
- Cost savings impact: What are the bottom-line cost savings from this change?
- Cost of solution: What are the initial costs and ongoing costs to implement this solution?
- Return on investment: What is the ROI? Does it meet the financial threshold for new investments?
- Ability to measure success: Can we measure the impact of this change?
- Other effects: What other benefits will be derived from this change?

Go/no-go criteria

Once you have documented the implications of each initiative, you will need to narrow your long list of potential projects down to a short list. In most cases you can narrow the field by setting threshold criteria.

Example criteria could be:

- ROI—initiatives must have a ROI of more than 15%
- Time—initiatives must have a payback period less than 12 months
- Cost—initiatives must be less than $500K in the implementation cost in the first year
- Strategy—initiatives must be directly aligned with a given business or call Centre strategy
- Customer—initiatives must result in positive impact on customer relationships

These examples and others that may be unique to your situation can be used as a "GO" or "NO GO" decision that will result in a shorter list of initiatives to consider.

Prioritizing and moving forward

Given a final short list of initiatives, you can rank these initiatives with a simple scoring process. Begin by creating a spreadsheet like the table below. Your potential projects will be listed in the first column, with your selection criteria in the first row. For each project, rank on a scale of 1 to 5 each criteria (1 being the worst score, 5 being the best). Note that each criteria item also has a separate weighting factor (1 is lowest, 3 is highest). In some cases it is useful to use a non-linear weighting approach. For example, 1, 3 or 10. This non-linear weighting scale allows some criteria to play a dominating role in the final scoring.

In the spreadsheet model you have created, you can add up the total score for each potential project and the result is a ranking of the best projects for your call Centre.

Example :

	Time to implement	*Cost to implement*	*Total cost*	*Return on investment*	*Customer impact savings*	*Total (sum of score* weighting factor)*
Criteria weight	1	2	3	3	2	
New email system	2	3	1	5	2	31
Update IVR	1	1	2	1	1	14
Use part-time agents	2	1	1	4	2	23
New desktop software	3	4	5	5	5	51

In this example, the "new desktop software" project ranks the highest, and the updated IVR ranks the lowest. You can use this technique for just a few projects or for ranking 50 projects.

The most important aspects of this type of process are:

· get agreement on the criteria early in the process

· decide for each criteria what results in a score of 1, 2, 3, 4 or 5 and be consistent across all projects

· agree in advance what the relative weighting of criteria will be

Call Centre Measurement

Call Centres are often measured by their performance on key indicators. These indicators tell how the call Centre is doing in terms of efficiency, cost, service quality and performance. Some key indicators that many call Centres track include:

Abandon Rate
Availability and Agent Utilization
Average Speed of Answer (ASA)
Cost per contact by media
Contact Volume
Customer Satisfaction
Handle Time

One Call Resolution Rate
Quality Monitoring
Schedule Adherence
Service Level
Span of Control
Turnover Rate

Three Steps For Creating Effective Call Centre Measures and Reports

Step 1: Define your goals

Rather than trying to organize and process the reams of data that piles up in databases, on desks and in filing cabinets, be selective. Focus on what is really important to your needs. Consider all the sources and types of data generated and decide which ones directly impact the business needs and goals of your organization. Do you want to provide better customer service? Improve processes and work flows? Increase revenue and decrease costs?

Keep the list manageable. Focus on three to five really important measurements that will truly reflect the success of your Centre. The list will be different for every call Centre. If yours is a revenue-generating Centre, for example, you may want to monitor abandon rate, service level and sales volume. A help desk or technical support line might be more concerned with "done in one" resolution and customer satisfaction. Use phone sats as well as other sources of data to provide a holistic view of the call Centre's objectives.

The following table provides some examples of measurements to consider in three very different categories:

ACD	Processes and Operations	Systems and Contacts
Calls Answered	Calls Completed on First Contact	Cost per Minute
Average Speed of Answer	Turnaround Time	Cost per Call/ Contact
Average Talk Time	Customer Satisfaction	System Utilization
Average Wrap-up Time	Save Rate	System Availability
Abandoned Calls or Rate	Up sell/Cross-sell Revenue	Network Busies
Service Level	Schedule Adherence	Hit Rate (ANI, etc.)

No golden rules

It is important to decide which measures matter to YOUR call Centre, to YOUR business goals and to YOUR customers. There are no magic industry standards to strive for. If you run a customer contact Centre that provides car insurance quotes to potential customers, you don't want to keep them waiting too long—they could spend that time looking through the yellow pages for your competition's phone number. However, if you're giving away free samples of a new product, your callers may accept a slightly longer hold time. What matters is setting logical, realistic targets that are specific to your environment.

Beware of conflicting objectives

The goals you set for your call Centre should be a means to an end: mainly the high level business and operational needs of the organization. Although the big picture is key here, don't forget to examine the individual goals in detail. Think each measure through—what is involved, what the end result will be and the resources and skills necessary to accomplish them—to be sure they do not conflict with one another.

For example, if decreasing costs is a primary business goal, you may meet this need by targeting a shorter average handling time. However, if customer satisfaction is also a primary goal, a conflict may arise. These two measures may drive different behaviors. Reps who are tasked with handling a high volume of calls may not take the extra time to develop a warm and fuzzy rapport with callers or may "accidentally" hang up on customers in the quest for an acceptable AHT.

To avoid the pitfalls of conflicting objectives, don't focus on measurements as the only objectives. Make the high level business and operational needs the primary objectives and use measurements as a guide to get you there. People do what they are incented to do, and you must give them clear, obtainable targets to work towards.

Principles for Effective Measures

There are five main principles to effective measures:

1. Simplicity: Measures should be easy to communicate and comprehend. Your associates and supervisors need to really understand what the measures are and what they mean.
2. Drive the right behavior: Measures are a means to an end. Make sure reps don't confuse measurements and objectives, and that the measure don't drive them to do the wrong thing.
3. Measurable: The data needs to be available and correct to accurately calculate the measure.
4. Accountability associated with control: avoid holding someone accountable for a measure for which they cannot control the outcome.
5. Support high level business goals: Remember the big picture. Your measures should "roll-up" to support the entire organization.

Action step

Prepare a list of the business goals for your call Centre. For each business goal, write down the measures in the call Centre which have the most impact on that business goal. Identify any potential conflicting measures, and select those that you believe will most influence the success of your call Centre and drive behavior toward the overall business goals. Assess each measure against the principles listed above.

Step 2: Create methods for measurement.

Once you've identified which measures are most important to the business goals and mission of your organization, the next step is to decide how you will measure. This is more complicated than it sounds. You can't rely on industry standards, as there are no industry standards. Just peek at a glossary, pick up an industry rag, or visit a vendor web site—everyone defines and calculates differently.

Take turnover as an example. Most call Centres have

some idea of their turnover, and how it compares with their "industry standard". But exactly how are these numbers calculated? Do you count positive (promotions) and negative (resignations) aspects? What about folks who don't make it through training—do you count them too? Are your answers the same as everyone else's? Probably not. You need to determine how you will define your measurements to best serve your needs.

What is everyone else doing?

Every call Centre is different, with unique goals and targets based on different experiences and expectations. Because of this fact, you can't go out and find a statistical survey and expect to find all the answers. But it is useful to be aware of what other call Centres are doing—what works, what doesn't work, what they've learned and would do differently. Several benchmarking studies are available that will help you understand what other call Centres are measuring, and how they are performing. Pay attention to the lessons that relate to your own business goals, and forget the rest. There is no need to be a slave to someone else's 80/20-service level if those numbers aren't based in the reality of your call Centre. If your callers are happy with 80/30 or 80/40, stay with it. Don't strive to achieve a goal that doesn't matter—it only costs money.

Bad data in, bad data out

The key to good measurement is consistency. Review business policies and procedures that guide contact handling, processes and the associated measurements to make sure everyone is working the same way. Common call handling procedures are important.

Consider the use of the not ready state. Rep A completes a call and immediately makes himself available to accept a call. Rep B however, completes a call and then sits in the not ready state the queue builds up a little, and then makes herself available to accept a call. This procedural difference results in very different availability statistics for the individuals and skews the group averages. To maintain consistent measurements, reps must be trained on the correct processes and procedures, be given obtainable targets to aim for, and be given periodic performance reviews. Without proper and consistent use of tools and procedural guidelines, the associated measurements are meaningless.

How you measure is just as important as what you measure. Remember to calculate in a standard fashion, and strive for consistency in all processes and procedures to create measurements that are useful to your call Centre.

Action step

For each measure you have selected, clearly define how the data will be collected. Assess the accuracy of the source. Ensure that procedures are in place in the call Centre to ensure that the measure accurately reflects the actual performance and that you will not be mislead by the results of the data. If the data is coming from a system (*e.g.*, ACD, IVR, CIS, etc.), then you will need to meet with the technology support group in your Centre to fully understand the data from this system. Ask a lot of questions and make sure the data is representing the measure you need.

Step 3: Putting measurements to work

Measurements themselves are not a goal, but rather an indication of how your business is functioning. With careful analysis of the measurements that reflect the business goals of your organization, you can learn a great deal about how your call Centre is doing. Don't measure for the sake of measuring, but rather create a plan to review and use the information that is generated.

Action steps

Chart the data

Once the data starts pouring in, it can be a bit overwhelming. But don't let the reams of data and endless columns of figures get you down. Put the data into a format that is easy to understand and use. Taking the time to chart out the important information in a readable and workable form is worth the effort. Bar graphs, pie charts and comparison matrices are all much easier to work from than the standard system-generated report. And you won't be doing this just for yourself—remember other folks will review the data too. These charts will eventually show a wider audience the progress that your call Centre has made over time!

Set targets and benchmarks

It is important to develop measures that are accurate and correct for your environment. Moreover you will need benchmarks and targets. Each of your charts and graphs should reflect the long-term target for your call Centre, and if you have good benchmark data, show how well you are performing against these benchmarks. You will also need to revisit your benchmarks and targets periodically to ensure that they meet the business goals of the call Centre.

You also need to communicate that targets and objectives are dependent on the business conditions and time period. Let's say that you're the manager of a call Centre for a local utility. And based on your business objectives and customer expectations, you've targeted an average speed of answer of 40 seconds. Now, should that be the target for every hour of every day? Will you accept worse performance during an outage? How about striving for a shorter talk time to handle that increased volume? Different situations sometimes demand different measurements and processes. The list below highlights some other factors that may influence performance targets:

- Time of day, day of week
- Season
- Marketing events
- Special focus in the call Centre
- Customer/product
- Media/contact type

Create situational targets and processes when necessary and be sure everyone knows what is expected.

Communicate your results

Measurements are used by different people for different things, so it is important to clearly communicate the goals and measurements to your entire team. The following table shows some of the users of call Centre measurement data, and how they might use it in real-time and historically.

	Immediate Use	*Long Term Use*
Management	Analyze activity Assess performance	Business planning Product/ service changes Technology changes Marketing changes Set new goals and targets
Supervisors	Analyze activity Assess performance Refine training Daily management	Justify staffing Resource allocation Refine training Process, call flow and work flow changes
Reps	Decisions for activity Personal assessment	Personal growth decisions Career planning

Since measurements and their associated goals have such a widespread impact, it is important not to keep them to yourself. Everyone in the Centre needs to know what is expected of them, and how their efforts contribute to the overall success of the call Centre. Management and supervisors may benefit from status meetings and summary reports. Providing reps with the necessary feedback can be as simple as posting messages on a reader or bulletin board, or as complex as elaborate reward programs. The key is to convey the message that everyone has a responsibility for the high-level business objectives that are reflected in the measurements.

Staff in other departments needs to know what's going on in the Centre, so don't forget to tell them, too. Is the marketing plan working effectively and generating calls? Are calls coming in on the new product release? Is the volume dropping off now that the problem's been solved? People in marketing, product management/development and other areas will understand the call Centre better and work more closely with it when they are informed.

Act on areas for improvement

Sometimes the measurements do not meet the set targets. This is the time to review your environment, processes and procedures, and develop plans to better meet your goals. For example, let's say a call Centre manager is tracking total transaction time and the numbers are well over the target. Process analysis might be a logical first step to create more efficient work patterns. Once the best processes have been identified, a technology assessment could be in order. The automation of the new processes makes the goal for total transaction time more realistic. A plan based on measurement analysis can help you do it to better, smarter and faster.

1. Set Targets	2. Collect Measurements	3. Show Results	4. Create ActionPlans

There may even be times when the targets just can't be met—they were unrealistic to start, staffing is low, or other hurdles exist. It is important to assess and refine measures, rather than continuously operate in an environment where targets can't be met.

Conclusion

The next time someone asks you, "So how's your call Centre doing?" you can give them an earful. Explain exactly what your key measurements are, how they are calculated and how they are tied directly to your organization's business goals. Tell them who uses the measurements and how and what actions are taken if the targets aren't met. Most importantly, show your progress over time. These are the characteristics of good call Centre management.

4

Strategy

With the introduction of multi-media and VoIP into the call Centre, the playing field for the next generation call Centre will be changing dramatically. Vendors are here today and gone tomorrow. Concepts like CRM are still struggling to demonstrate a return on investment. Call Centre consolidations and cost-cutting dominates the scene for some companies during this time of economic downturn.

Strategic planning for new call Centres and call Centre consolidations is now a requirement for providing the lowest cost, highest quality service. Whether you are starting a new call Centre or reengineering your current environment, a sound blueprint and future vision is an important foundation.

Where to start is typically the question. Several general guidelines will support your planning process.

External focus

External focus is certainly a requirement for good strategic planning. This includes your customers as well as other companies. This is an excellent overview of the changing operations and technology in the call Centre space.

Strategy Roadmap

Organizing the strategic planning process is also critical to success. What should you consider? How should you organize your strategic plan? What process, technology, HR and facility components should be considered?

Change management

If you are implementing a new call Centre or redesigning your existing Centre change management will be important for your success as a manager and leader of this new initiative.

Technology enablers

Technology continues to shift the foundation of customer contact with new media and access channels, higher bandwidth, changing protocols and rapidly changing vendor positioning.

Call Centre Strategy
The Mission Statement and Contact Strategy
Background
Call Centre Mission Statement

Every contact Centre should have a mission statement. The mission consists of a few lines or a brief paragraph that describes the Centre and what it does. At a high level, some of the questions it answers include:

- What is our main function or purpose?
- How do we fit in with the overall business mission?
- What are our defining characteristics?
- How do we want to be recognized by our customers?
- What are our priorities?
- What is our market segment/industry focus?

At the planning stage of a contact Centre, a mission statement is a useful tool. It succinctly identifies the end result of your efforts, and it functions as a "sanity check" to ensure that all work and planning support the mission. After the Centre is in place, it provides employees at all levels with a quick reminder of what you are all about. The three main benefits to your organization and to employees are:

1. Helps define and align strategies
2. Focuses discussions
3. Aids in decision-making

Well-crafted mission statements share some common features:

- Short and snappy
- Easy to understand
- Meaningful
- Lasting

Everyone in the contact Centre should know the mission statement and understand how their role supports it.

Develop a customer contact strategy

A customer contact strategy defines the desired customer experience and how the contact Centre fits within the organization's overall process of serving customers. The strategy document acknowledges the "today" state and identifies the future state (usually 2 to 3 years out) that everyone in the organization is working towards. A customer contact strategic plan is useful to:

1. Define the overall role of the contact Centre.
2. Align corporate strategies (*e.g.*, technology, self-service, marketing, organization).
3. Provide a blueprint for change and create your vision for the future.

Your research with customers and benchmarking of competitors and non-competitors will contribute to this customer contact strategy development.

Topic list for a customer contact strategy

Some topics that should be addressed in your strategic plan are:

1. Overall contact Centre mission.
2. Relationship and role of the contact Centre with the overall organization.
3. High-level objectives and benchmarks for performance.
4. Products and services available.

5. Target customers.
6. Access methods and media (current and future).
7. Technology directions.
8. Self-service options.
9. Organizational structure.
10. Operations and processes.
11. Priorities and values.

The customer contact strategy is a high-level description of the call Centre that can be read by anyone in the organization to learn about the who you are, what you will be doing and how to relate to the operation as a whole.

The process

The steps in creating a strategic plan require gathering data and then developing the strategy.

1. Gather data and ideas from your research

- Document customer requirements (from your research on customer needs and expectations)
- Review best practices and look at the competition (from your benchmarking)
- Interview key stakeholders
- Brainstorm viewpoints internal and external to the organization

2. Conduct strategy design session

- Vision "x" years out
- Phased plan
- Follow up with business case or other actions as needed

3. Document and communicate the strategy using the topic list presented earlier in tutorial

Your contact Centre mission statement and strategy document are key components for planning a new call Centre or for introducing significant improvements into your existing Centre. These tools will help you communicate with your stakeholders (senior management), your peers (including other departments) and your call Centre employees.

Guidelines for creating a contact Centre strategy

A customer contact strategy defines the desired customer experience and how the contact Centre fits within the organization's overall process of serving customers. If you do not have a customer contact strategy, now is a good time to prepare one for your Centre. This tutorial will help you get started.

If you already have a contact strategy, it should be updated annually. Use this tutorial to compare your strategy framework and contents.

Topics that should be addressed in strategic plan are:

1. Overall contact Centre mission
2. Relationship and role of the contact Centre with the overall organization
3. High-level objectives and key performance indicators
4. Products and services available
5. Target customers
6. Access methods and media
7. Technology
8. Self-service options
9. Organizational structure
10. Operations and processes
11. Priorities and values

The customer contact strategy is a high-level description of the call Centre that can be read by anyone in the organization to learn about who you are, what you will be doing and how to relate to the operation as a whole.

Four viewpoints that must be considered

Four key viewpoints must be considered in any strategic plan: the customer, customer service representatives, the call Centre managers and the organization. By responding to the questions and concerns on the following worksheet, you will begin to understand each viewpoint and be on your way to defining a customer contact strategy.

1. The Customer's View
   How can I contact the Centre?
   When can I contact the Centre?
   Can I talk with a person?
   What alternate contact media/channels are available?
   Will I get stuck waiting long?
   Can I do it in a single contact?
   Do I get good customer service?
   How does this compare to the other companies I work with (your competition)?

2. The Customer Service Representative's View
   What tools do I need to help customers?
   What skills do I need to help customers?
   What opportunities and career paths are available to me?
   What do I have to do to succeed?

3. The Call Centre Manager's View
   How many contacts are handled?
   Is there skilled staff available?
   What metrics are in place?
   How do we meet performance targets?
   How do we drive CSR behavior?
   Do the tools exist to support CSRs?

4. The Organization's View
   What are our priorities?
   Are all customers treated the same?
   How do we drive more revenue or profitability?
   How do we reduce contact handling costs?
   What does the competition offer?
   Do we want to be best in class?
   Do we have the technology we need?
   How can we drive customer behavior?
   What do we need to provide to other organizations?
   What do we need from other organizations or departments?

Learning about your competition

As with most aspects of business, when developing a strategy you want to keep an eye on the competition. A good working knowledge of how they treat their customers will give some insight into what your customers expect of you.

But who is your competition? You can start by naming the top players in your vertical market, but that's only part of the answer. Your customers have relationships with a variety of businesses and will very likely compare their experience with your contact Centre to every other customer service experience they have ever had. So how do you figure out what the competition is doing? Benchmarking. Benchmarking gives you and your team a snapshot of a variety of contact Centres and helps you to gauge how your Centre measures up. It allows you to set up your Centre based on what works for others.

There are two ways to get benchmarking information:

(1) Your team can gather its own data
(2) You can purchase the data.

We recommend both approaches. You can purchase benchmarking reports to learn not only about performance measures, but also best practices in call Centre management and the use of technology. You should also gather your own data.

Gathering your own data

Gathering data on your own can be an effective way to understand your competition. The steps involved are:

1. Ask your team to create a list of the competitors and non-competitors you are interested in benchmarking against.
2. Brainstorm the elements of customer contact you want details about (see worksheet below).
3. Assign a resource or resources to do the benchmarking.
4. Prepare for calls to the competition:
   (a) Create a worksheet to capture notes.
   (b) Research telephone numbers.
   (c) Open accounts or place orders.

5. Place calls and populate the worksheets.
6. Summarize findings.

It is a good idea to call each organization on your list more than once, varying the times (peak and off peak perhaps) and reasons for calling (sales, service, general inquiry) to get a better sample.

Documenting customer requirements (learning about your customers)

You cannot develop a strategy to meet the needs of your customers if you don't know who they are. This may sound obvious, but a surprising number of contact Centres do not have a good handle on their customers. Understanding exactly who your actual and target audiences are, their relationship with your organization, their likes, dislikes and expectations, will allow you to plan a contact Centre that successfully addresses those specific needs.

Gathering basic demographic information is a good first step: age, sex, marital status, geographical location/time zone, income range, access to internet, current usage of your products/services and warranty status. This information can be found hiding in a number of places (*e.g.*, corporate databases, forms/applications, customer surveys). It might take a bit of digging to find, but it is well worth the effort. You do not want to staff your Centre for extended business hours only to find your average customer is retired and could call weekdays between 9 and 5. Understanding demographics will help you make the right decisions.

Customer relationships

Now that you know some general characteristics about your customers, the next step is to identify their relationship with your organization.

Knowing the products or services that you provide to the customer can give you clues about the following:

- reason for calling/contact type
- complexity/call length
- up sell/cross sell opportunities

- level of customer service required

A financial institution, for example, may find that 75% of their customers have only one checking account. For planning purposes then, you may assume that the average call will be regarding a single product (a checking account) and that customers will not have a great need to transfer funds between accounts. However, the up sell/cross sell opportunities are significant.

Customer relationships provide valuable information that will help you define the functions and characteristics of your Centre. How do you find out about your customers likes and dislikes or what they expect from your organization? Ask them! Focus groups and customer surveys are two methods for getting the scoop directly from the source.

The process for creating your strategic plan

The steps in creating a strategic plan require gathering data and then developing the strategy.

1. Gather data and ideas
   - Review best practices and learn about your competition (from your benchmarking work as described above)
   - Document customer requirements (from your research on customer needs and expectations)
   - Interview key stakeholders—Brainstorm viewpoints
2. Conduct strategy design session—Vision "X" years out and develop a phased plan; follow up with business case or other actions as needed
3. Document and communicate the strategy using the topic list presented above.

5

Technology

A new age of technology

When call Centres first began, it was not unusual to walk into a call Centre and hear ringing phones. When a customer called, the telephone system would ring the telephone of any agent that was not busy with another call. If more than one call was coming in at the same time, many phones could be ringing.

In today's modern call Centres, when a customer calls they wait in line in what is called a "queue". A telephone queue is a holding place for calls until an agent becomes free to take a new call. Since most agents in call Centres today wear headsets, you will not hear ringing phones. The waiting call is transferred to the agent that has been idle the longest, and all the agent hears is a tone that alerts them a call is coming through.

Within the call Centre area, usually on an electronic display board, you can see how many calls are waiting on hold and how long the longest caller has waited. This information helps the agents and managers know when to take special steps to speed up the process or to add more agents to handle calls in queue.

Also commonplace today in call Centres is automated attendant technology (Press 1 for sales, Press 2 for...). This technology allows customers to tell the telephone system the type of call they are placing. Recall from the earlier discussion on teams that the call Centre is organized in groups supporting different areas. The automated attendant ensures that the customer is routed or directed to the right group to meet their needs. In some companies, they have taken the automated attendant one step further. Instead of only routing calls, the automated system can help the customer directly. For example, banks have long used these automated systems to provide account information or to initiate transactions such as balance transfers. In state-of-the-art call Centres, you will find speech recognition technology that allows the customer to speak their request and avoid pressing buttons on their telephone.

Technology improvement initiatives

Top 10 technology changes made over the past two years

Changes with the greatest positive impact on customer service

Changes with greatest impact on call Centre efficiency

Average decrease in talk time

Overall ranking of improvement initiatives

Future plans

Short-term changes planned

Long-term technology changes

Business drivers for change

Future technology changes with the greatest impact on customer satisfaction

Future technology with the greatest impact on call Centre efficiencies

Desired technology capabilities

Technology improvement initiatives

Table 1—Summary of changes and associated impact

Largest technology changes in last two years (in rank order)	*Greatest impact on customer service*	*Greatest impact on call Centre efficiency*
1. Switch and ACD replacements or upgrades	1	1
2. Web-enabled call Centre	2	4
3. Desktop and contact management applications	2	2
4. Voice response applications	4	4
5. Customer relationship management	5	4
6. Computer-telephone integration	-	3
7. Email and multimedia management	3	5
8. Quality monitoring	4	-
9. Knowledge-based applications	5	-

* Items with the same number indicate an equal frequency of listings by participants. The ranking of "1" indicates highest impact.

World-class call Centres

Participants outlined the primary characteristics of a world-class call Centre. The number one standard for a world-class call Centre is multimedia functionality. This multimedia environment for a world-class call Centre includes:

- the ability for universal queues for all media types
- web-enabled call Centre with online interactive support
- complete customer self-service applications through the Internet and voice response systems
- integrated reporting across media
- comprehensive customer relationship management for all contact channel

DIFFERENT TECHNOLOGY

1. ACD

In telecommunication, an automatic call distributor (ACD) is a device that distributes incoming calls to a specific group of terminals.

If the number of active calls is less than the number of terminals, the next call will be routed to the terminal that has been in the idle state the longest. If all terminals are busy, the incoming calls are held in a first-in-first-out queue until a terminal becomes available.

2. CRM

The stated purpose of customer relationship management (CRM) is to enable a company to better serve its customers through the introduction of reliable service automated processes, personal information gathering and processing, and self-service. It attempts to integrate and automate the various customer serving processes within a company.

It typically involves three general areas of business.

Customer service system

The customer service part automates some service requests, complaints, product returns and information requests.

A marketing information system

The marketing information part provides information about the business environment, including competitors, industry trends and macroenviromental variables.

A sales force management system

The sales force management part automates some of the company's sales and sales force management functions. It keeps track of customer preferences, buying habits and demographics and also sales staff performance.

Integrated CRM software is often also known as "front office solutions". This is because they deal directly with the customer.

Many call Centres use CRM software to store all of their customer's details on. When a customer calls, the system can be used to retrieve and store information relevant to the customer. By serving the customer quickly and efficiently, and also keeping all information on a customer in one place, a company aims to make cost savings and also encourage new customers.

CRM solutions can also be used to allow customers to perform their own service via a variety of communication channels. For example, you might be able to check your bank balance via your WAP phone without ever having to talk to a person, saving money for the company and saving your time.

CRM ACHIEVEMENTS

Improving customer service

- CRMs are claimed to improve customer service. Proponents say they can improve customer service by facilitating communication in several ways:
  - Provide product information, product use information, and technical assistance on web sites that are accessible 24 / 7
  - Help to identify potential problems quickly, before they occur
  - Provide a user-friendly mechanism for registering customer complaints (complaints that are not registered with the company cannot be resolved, and are a major source of customer dissatisfaction)
  - Provide a fast mechanism for handing problems and complaints (complaints that are resolved quickly can increase customer satisfaction)
  - Provide a fast mechanism for correcting service deficiencies (correct the problem before other customers experience the same dissatisfaction)
  - Identify how each individual customer defines quality, and then design a service strategy for each customer based on these individual requirements and expectations
    use internet cookies to track customer interests and personalize product offerings accordingly
    use the internet to engage in collaborative customization or real-time customization
  - Provide a fast mechanism for managing and scheduling followup sales calls to assess post-purchase cognitive dissonance, repurchase probabilities, repurchase times and repurchase frequencies

- Provide a fast mechanism for managing and scheduling maintenance, repair and on-going support (improve efficiency and effectiveness)
- Provide a mechanism to track all points of contact between a customer and the company, and do it in an integrated way so that all sources and types of contact are included, and all users of the system see the same view of the customer (reduces confusion)
- The CRM can be integrated into other cross-functional systems and thereby provide accounting and production information to customers when they want it

Improving customer relationships

- CRMs are also claimed to be able to improve customer relationships. Proponents say this can be done by:
  - CRM technology can track customer interests, needs, and buying habits as they progress through their life cycles and tailor the marketing effort accordingly. This way customers get exactly what they want as they change.
  - The technology can track customer product use as the product progresses through its life cycle and tailor the service strategy accordingly. This way customers get what they need as the product ages.
  - In industrial markets, the technology can be used to micro-segment the buying centre and help co-ordinate the conflicting and changing purchase criteria of its members
  - When any of the technology driven improvements in customer service (mentioned above) contribute to long-term customer satisfaction, they can ensure repeat purchases, improve customer relationships, increase customer loyalty, decrease customer turnover, decrease marketing costs, increase sales revenue and thereby increase profit margins

Technical functionality

- A CRM solution is characterized by the following functionality:
  - Scalability—the ability to be used on a large scale

and to be reliably expanded to whatever scale is necessary.
multiple communication channels—the ability to interface with users via many different devices (phone, WAP, internet, etc)

- Workflow—the ability to automatically route work through the system to different people based on a set of rules.
- Database—the centralised storage (in a data warehouse) of all information relevant to customer interaction
- Customer privacy considerations, *e.g.* data encryption and the destruction of records to ensure that they are not stolen or abused.

3. CTI

Computer telephony integration, also referred to as CTI, is technology that allows interactions on a telephone and a computer to be integrated or coordinated.

The following functions can be implemented using CTI:
Calling Line Information Display (Caller's Number, Number Called, IVR Options).
Screen Population on answer, with or without using calling line data.
On Screen Dialling. (Fast dial, predictive dialling).
On Screen Phone Control. (Ringing, Answer, Hang-up, Hold, Conference etc.).

THERE ARE TWO FORM OF CTI
First Party Call Control

First Party Call Control is the easiest to implement. This requires a connection between the computer and the telephone. Effectively the computer has a telephone built into it. Only the computer associated with the phone can control it. The computer can control all the functions of the phone, normally at the computer user's direction.

Third Party Call Control

Third Party Call Control is more difficult to implement

and often requires a dedicated Telephony Server to interface between the Telephone Network and the Computer Network. Information about a phone call can be displayed on the corresponding computer workstation's screen while instructions to control the phone can be sent from the computer to the telephone network. Any computer in the network has the potential to control any phone in the telephone system. The phone does not need to be built into the computer, and may only need to have a microphone and headset in the circuit, without even a keypad, to connect to the telephone network.

4. Databases

Database systems can allow management to better control their campaigns. Contacts can be selected by any available value, so as to maximize efficiency in targeting and delivery. By selecting a database system and call Centre software that is compatible with advanced databases such as Microsoft's SQL Server and Oracle, efficiency can be improved even more and information formatting problems can be avoided.

5. IVR

In telephony, interactive voice response, or IVR, is a computerized system that allows a person, typically a telephone caller, to select an option from a voice menu and otherwise interface with a computer system. Generally the system plays pre-recorded voice prompts to which the person presses a number on a telephone keypad to select the option chosen, or speaks simple answers such as "yes", "no" or numbers in answer to the voice prompts.

The latest systems use natural language speech recognition to interpret the questions that the person wants answered.

IVR systems are found operating voicemail systems and telephone banking services and are often the first point of contact when calling many larger businesses. These systems are generally used at the front end of call Centres to identify what service the caller wants and to extract numeric information such as account numbers as well as provide answers to simple questions such as account balances or allow pre-recorded information to be heard.

IVR systems are often criticised as being unhelpful and difficult to use due to poor design and lack of appreciation of the callers' needs. A properly designed IVR system should connect callers to their desired service promptly and with a minimum of fuss.

6. Predictive dialers

Predictive Dialer Software: A predictive dialer processes potential contacts and identifies disconnected numbers, busy signals, unanswered calls and detects answering machines. Such calls can be avoided, scheduled for later contact, or pre-recorded messages can be left, allowing live agents to only deal with established connections that are directed to them.

7. Text-to-speech

TTS—A general term to describe the act of using technology to convert digitally stored text into audible human speech (such that it mimics the human voice). Also a term that denotes methods, functions and technologies used to do the same (that is, convert text into spoken language).

7. World-class call Centres—the next generation Background

In 1999 we presented the core principles around world-class call Centres from our research with 102 call Centres. This update of the orginal article incorporates the results from the 2001 call Centre study. Overall the core principles have proven to be lasting concepts for creating a contact Centre that delivers excellent customer service at the lowest possible cost (with only one addition to the list with this update). On the other hand, the top-10 process and technology areas reflect shifting priorities from 1999 and show the increased focus on multi-media contact handling as a core competency for the call Centre.

The one addition to the core list of principles is based on market growth and revenue generation opportunities. This principle addresses the changing role of the call Centre from a pure "cost Centre" for the organization to an integral part of the company's growth strategy in the marketplace. Call Centres are migrating to "profit Centres" for revenue generation or transitioning to a more visible role in creating customer goodwill and building a wealth of customer data for use by product development, marketing and sales.

Here is the list of principles for the next generation of world-class call Centres.

The principles driving world-class call Centre design

Principle 1—Give customers choice

Customers expect to choose how they interact with you. Your service must be by their standards and by the media of their choice. Telephone service cannot be the only media for customer service.

Principle 2—Provide access anytime anywhere

Access to services will be every hour of every day, from whereever the customer chooses.

Principle 3—Enable customers to help themselves

Customers will have access to information and can choose self-service or agent-assisted service. Many customers will prefer to find information or initiate transactions on their own.

Principle 4—Personalize every customer interaction

Every transaction should personalize the service so that each customer is treated like the only customer. This level of customization may be based on the type of customer, their past transaction history, or other critical flags that are set by the business.

Principle 5—Know your customers

Employees and systems will know the customer and build on that knowledge with every customer contact.

Principle 6—Enable employees to deliver great service

Employees are the cornerstone to great service and must be enabled with the right tools, processes and information so that they are empowered to help the customer every time.

Principle 7—Demand to be the best and measure your performance toward this goal

The only standard is excellence, and the only way to achieve excellence is to measure your success with every transaction and improve over time with both continuous process improvement and discontinuous (dramatic) process improvement through business process reengineering.

Principle 8—Treat every customer contact as an opportunity for market growth or revenue generation

Every transaction, whether sales oriented or not, results in a direct impact on the future growth of the organization. More and more the contact Centre is the "face of the business" to the customer, and the impression and opportunities developed through that contact have a direct impact on market share, market growth and revenue generation opportunities. Upsell, cross-sell and customer segmentation strategies will result in overall growth for the business.

Top-10 outlook for processes and technology

Each of the opportunities listed below have process elements and enabling technologies. They bring to life the concepts for excellent customer service, low cost operation and market growth listed above. Since 1999, the emphasis has shifted and the list below represents that shift in focus and priority.

Opportunity 1—Integrated multi-media queues

Integrate voice and electronic transactions into a single

workflow with integrated queues that allow work blending and load balancing of multiple media types.

Opportunity 2—Web-enabled contact Centres

Create Internet sites for customer service that provide comprehensive information access and the ability to initiate transactions. Tightly link the contact information and processes from the Internet with processes, contact management systems and databases in the call Centre to ensure timely and synchronized data access.

Opportunity 3—Email and text chat

Develop email and text chat as a reliable transaction channel in addition to inbound and outbound voice calls. Teach customers how to use this tool effectively and ensure that your email processes are responsive to your customer's expectations.

Opportunity 4—Customer relationship management

Develop customer relationship management systems that can integrate email, fax, phone, and Internet transaction information into a comprehensive history of customer contact that flag opportunities for new products and services.

Opportunity 5—Voice Response Systems and Speech Recognition

Tightly integrate ACD and voice response systems to allow seamless transfers back and forth between VRU and agent-assisted service. Simplify voice response interactions to make them fast and easy to use. Use automated speech recognition and voice recognition to reduce transaction times and enable greater functionality of voice response systems including faster transaction speed and security.

Opportunity 6—Desktop applications

Provide employees with the capability to access internal and external (Internet) data rapidly, to see what the customer sees, and to execute transactions with a fully integrated desktop such that all employees are fully empowered to deliver excellent customer service every time.

Opportunity 7—Computer Telephone Integration

Use computer telephone integration (CTI) to provide personalized routing and work-object handling and to produce reports on both electronic and voice transactions.

Opportunity 8—Quality monitoring

Implement quality monitoring tools and processes to enable a continuous improvement cycle for call Centre associates and ongoing improvement to hiring and training programs.

Opportunity 9—Integrated Reporting

Enable full multi-media reporting capabilities to provide integrated reports across all media types.

Opportunity 10—Virtual Centres and Management Tools

Create virtual Centres that allow employees to choose work locations including remote offices and to provide the organization with follow-the-sun capability for international customer service. Develop new resource management tools for effectively managing resources that are geographically dispersed.

Summary

Achieving world-class performance for the next generation of contact Centres will require call Centre managers to fundamentally rethink the value of the call Centre to the customer and to the business. Managers will need to drive strategic planning and design decisions from a set of guiding principles that are customer focused and that leverage new technology. Incremental improvements will not be adequate to keep pace with growing customer demands for service that is anytime and anywhere. The need to redesign or reengineer the basic business processes around customer service will be an imperative for call Centre managers who are planning ahead for the next generation.

NEW ACHIEVEMENT

Focusing on a Few Things—Consistently

One of the most significant reasons call Centres under perform boils down to one word—distractions—a loss of focus.

Getting Too Comfortable

You can reach a point where you find your call Centre operation performing well week over week. You get comfortable with the success of that performance. The pressure of managing the real-time environment eases and you can sit back and actually enjoy the success. The boss is happy. Staff is not dealing with Mr. Screaming Customer who is reacting to long wait times and it is all looking pretty fine.

Inevitably, your attention turns to projects or other activities that often get pushed to the side of the desk when the call Centre is in a state of service level chaos. And then it happens. Usually it is subtle, maybe it even goes unnoticed but service levels start to slide. Your AHT (average handling time) raises. Your operation misses its service level goals by 24 seconds one week. Big deal right?

Real-Time Reality

One day you realize that service levels have fallen like that stock you invested last year! "What?" "How did this happen?" The phone rings, it is the boss. Not a good day! Customers are complaining about long waits. Sales are off. Revenue per call is falling. The boss is calling to talk about it. "How?" "What happened?" "Why?" Frequently it has to do with a loss of focus. Distractions. Important distractions but distractions nonetheless.

So what is the solution? Successful call Centre operations occur when you maintain a consistent focus on just a few things. Consistently doing a few things right consistently. Keeping that focus for staff and supervisors takes creative efforts in communication and management.

Practical Suggestion

Here is an exercise that may be helpful. Think about the few activities that, if done consistently each week, ensure stable call Centre performance for your operation. Keep the list short—3 - 5 activities. Think this through carefully. It is not one-size fits all. Every call Centre is different. Even for companies with multiple Centres, this list is likely different for each operation. Write out the list. Are you sure these are the few things that if done consistently right each week results in your success? Double check. Ask others. Test the list next week. Are you right? When you think you have it, teach the list!

Take a few minutes and figure out how to teach the importance of those items to everyone in your call Centre operation. Are you an agent? Teach your team leaders. Are you a team lead? Teach the boss. Make them look good. Determine the best way to get your team to 'own' that list. Consider having one person responsible for ensuring that one activity on the list is fulfilled each day or week or month. Rotate the activity responsibilities to others to keep complacency from affecting outcomes.

One last comment—remember to focus on just those few things. No matter what distractions come your way, do not ever forget to take care of these basic items. It is like gas for your car, ignore the gas gauge and you can only go so far and we have all been there before!

Quality—The Competitive Advantage for Indian Call Centres An Initiative by NASSCOM and STQC Ministry of Communication and Information Technology, Government of India

Ministry of Communication and Information Technology (MCIT) and NASSCOM have joined hands to step up the quality movement in the nascent Indian call Centre industry. A workshop on quality initiatives in call Centres was organised at New Delhi to discuss various quality-related issues and evolve a strategy for India to emerge as a sustainable destination for the call Centre and back-office industry.

Ministry of Communication & Information Technology emphasized the need for Quality of Service in IT Enabled Sector.

Call Centre business offers enormous employment opportunities and revenue growth. However, inadequate quality of service and mushrooming growth can adversely effect India's image and potential opportunities.

Call Centre organizations can follow to improve upon their processes and operational methodology. He said, 'adequate training infrastructure is the need of the hour along with quality and standardization, and Nasscom through its Call Centre Forum has already initiated steps towards the same'.

Currently there are no standards that cover the entire spectrum for ITES, especially in the context of overseas outsourcing. There are of course existing ISO standards and some standards that are specific to Call Centres but this particular initiative of MCIT with Nasscom for quality improvement in call Centre operations will play a significant role in bringing standardization in the Call Centre industry.

They highlighted the initiatives that STQC has already taken in terms of standardization by evolving draft guidelines for call Centres based on world wide accepted ISO 9001 standard. Moreover, a core team of STQC engineers is in the process of framing certification scheme, compliance to which shall ensure adequate level of quality in operations of call Centres.

They have planned to formulize schemes for certification of personnel at agent as well as manager level so that skilled manpower is available to the industry in this area. Depending upon the response of the industry these certification schemes could be extended to other IT enabled services like Geographical Information

MIT has set up STQC Directorate to provide standardization, testing and certification support to Indian electronics industry for improving their product quality and increasing their competitiveness in the global market. The STQC functions through 22 laboratories throughout the country, providing services to Industries in testing and calibration, product development assistance, system reliability prediction and assessment, education and on the job training in Quality and Reliability, with a manpower strength of 600 engineers/scientists.

Virtual Call Centre

The virtual call Centre allows organizations to manage and use agents in multiple locations as a single entity, provides every agent with all functions and features and enables seamless call routing and transferring across the organization. Everyone is talking about virtual call Centres, but until virtualization is technologically feasible and economically affordable, few organizations will enjoy its many benefits. With its all-IP platform, Virtual by Design, enabling the rapid and cost-effective deployment of a virtual call Centre with far less complexity and cost than in other contact Centre environments.

The evolution to IP communication has gained tremendous momentum in the past two years. It is not just an IP variation on the traditional PBX design. It was designed from the ground up as a "switchless" system, taking full advantage of the switching function that is inherent in an IP network for all communication channels.

Unity

All major functions—ACD, IVR, CTI, administration and reporting, recording, and predictive dialing—reside on the same platform. And all contact channels—telephone, email, voice mail and web chat/voice/video/collaboration-were implemented from the ground up on that one unified platform. Thus, no separate middleware platform is needed to mediate between ACD, IVR and Agents. All information about a call simply moves with the call automatically. A single Agent GUI serves all contact channels.

All queues and routing rules are universal, and all channels are tracked and managed through one database and one set of reports. Administrative changes are implemented once and propagated immediately through the entire virtual call Centre. Unity reduces the cost of integration, speeds implementation, streamlines operations, and reduces the cost of management and maintenance. Perhaps more important, it enhances the quality of customer care.

Integratability

Because of its unity, much of the integration required in legacy call Centres is unnecessary. IVR, ACD and Agent are automatically synchronized and always have the same complete call-related information available.

Integration to external systems such as CRM is also greatly simplified because of this unity. External systems only need to exchange information and synchronize with one point in the system, usually the Agent application, while legacy CTI integrations require a separate CTI server to coordinate the actions of ACD, IVR and Agent with the external application.

Leading CRM applications, further simplifies the process. The result is that integration is completed more quickly and much less expensively than in the legacy environment, typically in hours or days, rather than weeks and months. This is not a slogan or an exaggerated claim, but a fact based on field experience.

Land-line based phone systems and fixed telephony PSTN

The network that connects most phones together is known as the PSTN (public switched telephone network).

Fixed phone lines are usually copper wirelines, which form a circuit between the subscriber and a subscriber-line interface. The SLI is nondescript street furniture, usually a box on the ground, or a silver can on a telephone pole. The SLI provides dial tone, and converts voice and dialed numbers to digital signals, which are sent on a few wires to the exchange. SLIs were invented so that central offices could be smaller, thus less expensive, while giving better service. Some recent installations may use optical fiber to connect an SLI to the exchange. Some old installations may connect subscribers directly to an exchange without using SLIs.

An analog phone's twisted pair is self-contained, self-testing and designed to fail safely. It typically modulates incoming and outgoing conversations on the same pair of wires and biases the lines at 48 volts DC to power the telephone. The power is provided from multiply redundant power systems at the exchange—most phones will continue to work in a power-failure. Further, the dial tone is presented only when the SLI's and exchange's computer believe the network is up.

An analog line uses frequencies of 0-3.5 kHz, with frequencies higher than this filtered at the SLI before it is converted to digital samples. The analog speech signals are carried over the digital backbone network as a stream of digitally encoded samples at a sample rate of 8 kHz (8,000 numeric samples representing sound-pressure per second). The frequencies on the copper above 4 kHz can be utilized for DSL connections.

A line is a single voice communications circuit between the subscriber and the central switching office. A trunk is a single circuit between an SLI or central offices and may be analog or digital and is transmitted via copper, microwave, or fiber optics. A trunk group is a grouping of identical trunk circuits between two specific central offices.

Automatic telephone systems generally use numeric addresses, more commonly known as telephone numbers. The addressing system often distinguishes local, long-distance and international calls. Local calls are initiated by dialling the local number. A long-distance number is indicated by a long-distance prefix (ITU-T recommends "0") followed by area code and a number local to that area. International phone calls require an international prefix (the ITU-T recommends "00") followed by area code and local number. US and Canadian phone systems use "1" as the long distance prefix and "011" for international prefix.

Larger companies and organizations often employ a PABX (Private Automatic Branch Exchange). This is a telephone switch that defines its own local phone number range, which is commonly embedded in a public local phone number range. Some of the largest companies now even have their own internal telephone networks across the country, or even throughout the world, with limited gateways into the PSTN.

Most PSTN systems use analog communication between individual phones and the local switch. If digital communication is used for an individual phone, the system used is usually ISDN (Integrated Services Digital Network).

Between switches in the PSTN, most signalling is now digital using

VOIP

IP Telephony also called Internet telephony is the technology that makes it possible to have a telephone conversation where the signal is carried over the Internet or a dedicated network in Internet Protocol (IP) packets, instead of over dedicated voice transmission lines. This allows the elimination of circuit switching and the associated waste of bandwidth. Instead, packet switching is used, where IP packets with voice data are sent over the network only when data needs to be sent, *i.e.* when a caller is talking.

Its advantages over traditional telephony include:

lower costs per call, especially for long-distance calls

lower infrastructure costs: once IP infrastructure is installed, no or little additional telephony infrastructure is needed.

Note that voice over IP traffic does not necessarily have to travel over the public Internet: it may also be deployed on private IP networks.

The protocols used to carry the signal over the IP network are commonly referred to as Voice over IP, or VoIP protocols. VoIP protocols include H.323, which also provides videoconferencing and data capability and is the most widely deployed VoIP protocol in enterprise and carrier markets, MGCP (Media Gateway Control Protocol), SGCP (Simple Gateway Control Protocol), and SIP (Session Initiation Protocol), a protocol to initiate VoIP connections.

Corporate and Telco use of VoIP

Although few office environments and even fewer homes use a pure VoIP infrastructure, telecommunications providers routinely use IP telephony, often over a dedicated IP network, to connect between their switching stations, where they convert the dedicated voice signal to IP packets and back. The result is a data-abstracted digital network that the provider can easily upgrade and use for multiple purposes.

Corporate customer support Centres that provide support over telephone often use IP telephony exclusively to take advantage of the data abstraction that comes with it.

The benefit of using this technology is the need for only one class of circuit connection and better use of the available bandwidth. IP telephony is commonly used to route traffic that may be originated from and terminated at conventional PSTN telephones.

VoIP is now widely deployed by carriers, especially for international telephone calls. Most commonly, users are completely unaware that their telephone call is being routed over IP infrastructure for most of its distance, instead of entirely over the circuit switched PSTN.

VoIP is also used by large companies to eliminate call charges between their offices, by using their data network to carry inter-office calls. They may also use VoIP to reduce the costs of calls outside the company, by carrying them to the nearest point on their network before handing them off to the PSTN.

There are companies, which offer a gateway to the PSTN from any VoIP phone. You can simply dial a conventional telephone number and the telephone call will be routed over your Internet connection to the company that operates the gateway, and they will bill you, not the local phone company.

Electronic Numbering (ENUM) makes it possible to dial

traditional E.164 phone numbers, but be connected entirely over the Internet if the other party uses Enum, so you do not incur any expenses other than the Internet connection fees.

VoIP implementation challenges

Because IP does not by default provide any mechanism to ensure that data packets are delivered in sequential order, or provide any Quality of Service guarantees, implementations of VoIP face problems dealing with latency and possible data integrity problems.

One of the central challenges for VoIP implementers is restructuring streams of received IP packets, which can come in any order and have packets missing, to ensure that the ensuing audio stream maintains a proper time consistency. Another important challenge is keeping packet latency down to acceptable levels, so that users do not experience significant lag time between when they speak and the signal is decoded on the other end of the connection.

Solutions to these problems

Certain hardware solutions can distinguish VoIP packets and provide priority queuing for this class of service.

Alternatively packets can be buffered but this can lead to an overall delay similar to that encountered on satellite circuits.

The network operator can also ensure that there is enough bandwidth end-to-end to guarantee low-latency low-loss traffic: this is easy to do in private networks, but much harder to do in the public Internet.

Jitter (delay variance) problems are mainly generated in low band access (less than 256 Kbps) because of serialization of big (1500 bytes) data packets. Over this access, a mechanisms of fragmentation of these big packets are needed (interleaving small voice packets) to reduce the delay. Over access less than 256 Kbps it is almost impossible to ensure quality voice without a fragmentation mechanism

VoIP protocols

In the overwhelming majority of implementations, the RTP protocol is used to transmit VoIP traffic ("media").

For signaling, there are several alternative protocols:

SIP, the IETF Session Initiation Protocol, a newcomer gaining popularity

H.323, an older protocol still used by many legacy applications

Skinny Client Control Protocol, proprietary protocol from Cisco

MeGaCo (a.k.a. H.248) and MGCP, both Media Gateway control protocols

MiNET, proprietary protocol from Mitel

IAX, the Inter-Asterisk exchange protocol used by the Asterisk open source PBX server and associated client software.

Mass-market telephony over broadband Internet access

A new development has been the introduction of mass-market VoIP services over broadband Internet access services, in which subscribers make and receive calls as they would over the PSTN. This requires an analog telephone adapter (ATA) to connect a telephone to the broadband Internet connection. Companies in the US, such as Vonage, Voice Pulse and Packet, use IP to offer unlimited calling to the US, and sometimes to Canada or to selected countries in Europe or Asia, for a flat monthly fee. One advantage of this is the ability to make and receive calls as you would at home, anywhere in the world, at no extra cost. As calls go via IP, this does not incur charges as call diversion does via the PSTN, and the called party does not have to pay for the call.

For example, somebody may call you on a number with a US area code, but you could be in London, and if you were to call another number with that area code, it would be treated as a local call, regardless of where you are in the world. However, the broadband phone is likely to complement, rather than replace a PSTN line, as it still needs a power supply, while calling the US emergency services number 911, may not automatically be routed to the nearest local emergency dispatch Centre, or be of any use for subscribers outside the US.

Another challenge for these services is the proper handling of outgoing calls from Fax machines, TiVO boxes, satellite television receivers, alarm systems, conventional modems or Fax modems and other similar devices that depend on access to a voice-grade telephone line for some or all of their functionality. At present, these types of calls sometimes go through without a hitch, but in other cases they won't go through at all. And in some cases, this equipment can be made to work over a VoIP connection if the sending speed can be changed to a lower bits per second rate. If VoIP and cellular substitution becomes very popular, some ancillary equipment makers may be forced to redesign equipment, because it can no longer be assumed that a conventional voice-grade telephone line will be available in nearly every home in the United States and Canada.

There is also a free service called Free World Dialup (FWD), that permits users to make free telephone calls to other FWD users, and that has only limited connections to and from the public switched telephone network.

Internet Protocol (IP)

TCP/IP

Transmission Control Protocol / Internet Protocol—The two main protocols which, taken together, comprise the network protocol used on the Internet. The protocol is also used for most data networks in operation today. Internet Protocol, or "IP" is a low-level, unreliable, packet protocol. Transmission Control Protocol ("TCP") sits (logically) on top of IP and uses the unreliable services provided by IP to provide reliable connection oriented network communication services.

The Internet Protocol (IP) is a data-oriented protocol used by source and destination hosts for communicating data across a packet-switched Internet work.

Data in an IP internet work are sent in blocks referred to as packets or datagrams (the terms are basically synonymous in IP). In particular, in IP no setup is needed before a host tries to send packets to a host it has previously not communicated with.

The Internet Protocol provides an unreliable datagram service (also called best effort); *i.e.* it makes almost no guarantees about the packet. The packet may arrive damaged, it may be out of order (compared to other packets sent between the same hosts), it may be duplicated, or it may be dropped entirely. If the application needs reliability, the Transport layer adds this.

Packet switches, or Internet work routers, are used to forward IP datagrams across interconnected layer 2 networks. The lack of any delivery guarantees means that the design of packet switches is made much simpler. (Note that if the network does drop, reorder or otherwise damage a lot of packets, the performance seen by the user will be poor, so most network elements do try hard to not do these things—hence the best effort term. However, an occasional error will produce no noticeable effect.)

IP is the common element found in today's public Internet. It is described in IETF RFC 791, which was first published in September 1981. This document describes the current and most popular network layer protocol in use today. This version of the protocol is assigned as version 4. IPv6 is the proposed successor to IPv4; the Internet is slowly running out of addresses, and IPv6 has 128-bit source and destination addresses, providing more addresses than IPv4's 32 bits. Versions 0 through 3 were either reserved or unused. Version 5 was used for an experimental stream protocol. Other version numbers have been assigned, usually for experimental protocols, but have not been widely used.

IPv4 Header Format

{| align="Centre" border="1" cellpadding="3" cellspacing ="1"

|- align="Centre"

! colspan="1" | +
! colspan="4" | 0 - 3
! colspan="4" | 4 - 7
! colspan="8" | 8 - 15
! colspan="3" | 16 - 18
! colspan="13" | 19 - 31
|- align="Centre"
! colspan="1" | 0
| colspan="4" | Version
| colspan="4" | Header length
| colspan="8" | Type of Service
(now DiffServ and ECN)
| colspan="16" | Total Length
|- align="Centre"
! colspan="1" | 32
| colspan="16" | Identification
| colspan="3" | Flags
| colspan="13" | Fragment Offset
|- align="Centre"
! colspan="1" | 64
| colspan="8" | Time to Live
| colspan="8" | Protocol
| colspan="16" | Header Checksum
|- align="Centre"
! colspan="1" | 96
| colspan="32" | Source Address
|- align="Centre"
! colspan="1" | 128
| colspan="32" | Destination Address
|- align="Centre"
! colspan="1" | 160
| colspan="32" | Options
|- align="Centre"
! colspan="1" | 192
| colspan="32" |
Data
|}

The first header field in an IPv4 datagram is the 4-bit version field.

The second field is a 4-bit Internet Header Length (IHL) telling the number of 32-bit words in the IPv4 header. Since an IPv4 header may contain a variable number of options, this field essentially specifies the offset to the data portion of an IPv4 datagram. A minimum IPv4 header is 20 bytes long, so the minimum value in decimal in the IHL field would be 5.

In RFC 791, the following 8 bits were allocated to a Type of Service (ToS) field—now DiffServ and ECN. The original intention was for a sending host to specify a preference for how the datagram would be handled as it made its way through an internet work. For instance, one host could set its IPv4 datagrams' ToS field value to prefer low delay, while another might prefer high reliability. In practice, the ToS field has not been widely implemented. However, a great deal of experimental, research and deployment work has focused on how to make use of these eight bits. These bits have been redefined and most recently through DiffServ working group in the IETF and the Explicit Congestion Notification code points.

The next 16-bit IPv4 field defines the entire datagram size, including header and data, in 8-bit bytes. The minimum-length datagram is 20 bytes and the maximum is 65535. The maximum size datagram, which any host is required to be able to handle, is 576 bytes, but most modern hosts handle much larger packets. Sometimes subnetworks impose further restrictions on the size, in which case datagrams must be fragmented. Fragmentation is handled in either the host or packet switch in IPv4 and in the host only in IPv6.

The next 16-bit field is an identification field. This field is primarily used for uniquely identifying fragments of an original IP datagram. Some experimental work has suggested using the ID field for other purposes, such as for adding packet-tracing information to datagrams in order to help trace back datagrams with spoofed source addresses.

A 3-bit field follows and is used to control or identify

fragments.

The fragment offset field is 13-bits long, and allows a receiver determine the place of a particular fragment in the original IP datagram.

An 8-bit time to live (TTL) field helps prevent datagrams from persisting (*e.g.* going in circles) on an internet work. Historically the TTL field limited a datagram's lifetime in seconds, but has come to be a hop count field. Each packet switch (or router) that a datagram crosses decrements the TTL field by one. When the TTL field hits zero, the packet is no longer forwarded by a packet switch and is discarded.

An 8-bit Protocol field follows. This field defines the next protocol used in the data portion of the IP datagram. The Internet Assigned Numbers Authority maintains a list of Protocol numbers. Common protocols and their decimal values include ICMP (1), TCP (6) and UDP (17).

The following field is a 16-bit checksum field for the IPv4 datagram header. Some values in a IPv4 datagram header may change at each packet switch hop, so the checksum must be adjusted on its way through an internet work.

The checksum is followed by a 32-bit source address and 32-bit destination address respectively. (Note: IPv6 source and destination addresses are 128 bits each.)

Additional header fields (called options) may follow the destination address field, but these are not often used. Option fields may be followed by a pad field which ensures that the user data are aligned on a 32-bit word boundary. (In IPv6, options move out of the standard header and are specified by a Next Protocol field, similar in function to IPv4's Protocol field).

IPv4 Addressing and Routing

Perhaps the most complex aspects of IP are addressing and routing. Addressing refers to how end hosts are assigned IP addresses and how subnetworks of IP host addresses are divided and grouped together. IP routing is performed by all hosts, but most famously by internetwork routers, which typically use either interior gateway protocols (IGPs) or external gateway protocols (EGPs) to help make IP datagram forwarding decisions across IP connected networks.

Routing

Forms the backbone of the Internet. Without it no Internet would exist. Routing provides the means of forwarding logically addressed packets from their local sub network toward their ultimate destination. In large networks packets may pass through many intermediary destinations before reaching their destination. Routing occurs at layer 3 of the OSI seven-layer model.

Hubs and switches move data on the local network, while the router has an awareness of the neighboring routers.

Knowing where to send packets requires knowledge of the structure of the network. In small networks, routing can be very simple, and is often configured by hand. In large networks the topology of the network can become complex, and may change constantly, making the problem of constructing the routing tables very complex.

As routers can only recalculate the best routes very slowly relative to the rate of arrival of packets, routers keep a routing table that maintains a record of only the best possible routes to certain network destinations and the routing metrics associated with those routes.

Routing protocols facilitate the exchange of routing information between networks, allowing routers to build routing tables dynamically. Traditional IP routing stays simple because it uses next-hop routing where the router only needs to consider where it sends the packet, and does not need to consider the subsequent path of the packet on the remaining hops.

Although this dynamic routing can become very complex, it makes the Internet very flexible, and has allowed it to grow in size by more than eight orders of magnitude over the last thirty(?) years since adopting IP in 1983.

Routing algorithms use two basic technologies:

- Telling the world who your neighbors are: link-state routing protocols such as OSPF
- Telling your neighbors what the world looks like: distance-vector routing protocols such as RIP

A routing metric consists of any value used by routing algorithms to determine whether one route is superior to another. Metrics can cover such information as bandwidth, delay, hop count, path cost, load, MTU, reliability and communication cost. The routing table stores only the best possible routes, while link-state or topological databases may store all other information.

Depending on the relationship of the router relative to other autonomous systems, various classes of routing protocols exist:

Ad hoc network routing protocols appear in networks with no or little infrastructure. For a list of a couple of the proposed protocols

- Interior Gateway Protocols (IGPs) exchange routing information within a single autonomous system. Common examples include:
- IGRP/EIGRP (Interior Gateway Routing Protocol/ Enhanced IGRP)
- OSPF (Open Shortest Path First)
  RIP (Routing Information Protocol)
- IS-IS (Intermediate System to Intermediate System)
- Exterior Gateway Protocols (EGPs) route between separate autonomous systems. EGPs include:
- EGP (the original Exterior Gateway Protocol used to connect to the former Internet backbone network—now obsolete)
- BGP (Border Gateway Protocol: at version BGPv4 as of 2002)

INTERNET PROTOCOL SUITE

The Internet protocol suite is the set of protocols that implement the protocol stack on which the Internet runs.

It is sometimes called the TCP/IP protocol suite, after the two most important protocols in it: the Transmission Control Protocol (TCP) and the Internet Protocol (IP), which were also the first two defined.

The internet protocol suite can be described by analogy with the OSI model, which describes the layers of a protocol stack, not all of which correspond well with internet practice.

In a protocol stack, each layer solves a set of problems involving the transmission of data and provides a well-defined service to the higher layers.

Higher layers are logically closer to the user and deal with more abstract data, relying on lower layers to translate data into forms that can eventually be physically manipulated.

The internet model was produced as the solution to a practical engineering problem.

The OSI model, on the other hand, was a more theoretical approach and was also produced at an earlier stage in the evolution of networks.

Therefore, the OSI model is easier to understand, but the TCP/IP model is the one in actual use.

It is helpful to have an understanding of the OSI model before learning TCP/IP, as the same principles apply, but are easier to understand in the OSI model.

Layers in the TCP/IP stack

There is some discussion about how to map the TCP/IP model onto the OSI model. Since the TCP/IP and OSI protocol suites do not match precisely, there is no one correct answer.

In addition, the OSI model is not really rich enough at the lower layers to capture the true layering; there needs to be an extra layer (the Internetworking layer) between the Transport and Network layers. Protocols specific to a particular network type, but which are run on top of the basic hardware framing, ought to be at the Network layer. Examples of such protocols are ARP and the Spanning Tree Protocol (used to keep redundant bridges idle until they are needed). However, they are local protocols and operate beneath the internet work functionality; to place both groups (not to mention also protocols which run on top of the internet work protocol, such as ICMP) all at the same layer can be confusing.

The following diagram attempts to show where various TCP/IP and other protocols would reside in the original OSI model:

7	Application	*e.g.* HTTP, SMTP, SNMP, FTP, Telnet, SSH, NFS, RTSP
6	Presentation	*e.g.* XDR, ASN.1, SMB, AFP
5	Session	*e.g.* ISO 8327 / CCITT X.225, RPC, NetBIOS, ASP
4	Transport	*e.g.* TCP, UDP, RTP, SCTP, SPX, ATP
3	Network	*e.g.* IP, ICMP, IGMP, X.25, CLNP, ARP, RARP, OSPF, RIP, IPX, DDP
2	Data Link	*e.g.* Ethernet, Token ring, PPP, HDLC, Frame relay, ISDN, ATM
1	Physical	*e.g.* electricity, radio, laser

Commonly, the top three layers of the OSI model (Application, Presentation and Session) are considered as a single Application Layer in the TCP/IP suite. Because the TCP/IP suite has no unified session layer on which higher layers are built, these functions are typically carried out (or ignored) by individual applications. A simplified TCP/IP interpretation of the stack is shown below:

Application"layer 7"	*e.g.* HTTP, FTP, DNS(routing protocols like RIP, which for obscure reasons run over UDP, may also be considered part of the network layer)
4 Transport	*e.g.* TCP, UDP, RTP, SCTP(routing protocols like OSPF, which run over IP, may also be considered part of the Network layer)
3 Network	For TCP/IP this is the Internet Protocol (IP)(required protocols like ICMP and IGMP run over IP, but may still be considered part of the network layer; ARP does not run over IP)
2 Data Link	*e.g.* Ethernet, Token ring, etc.
1 Physical	*e.g.* physical media, and encoding techniques, T1, E1

The Physical layer

The Physical layer describes the physical characteristics of the communication, such as conventions about the nature of the medium used for communication (such as wires, fiber optic links or radio links), and all related details such as connectors, channel codes and modulation, signal strengths, wavelength, low-level synchronization and timing and maximum distances.

The Data-Link layer

The Data link layer specifies how packets are transported over the physical layer, including the framing (*i.e.* the special bit patterns which mark the start and end of packets). Ethernet, for example, includes fields in the packet header which specify which machine or machines on the network a packet is destined for. Examples of Data-link layer protocols are Ethernet, Wireless Ethernet, SLIP, Token Ring and ATM.

PPP is a little more complex, as it was originally specified as a separate protocol, which ran on top of another data link layer, HDLC/SDLC.

This layer is sometimes further subdivided into Logical Link Control and Media Access Control.

The Network layer

As originally defined, the Network layer solved the problem of getting packets across a single network. Examples of such protocols are X.25, and the ARPANET's Initial Connection Protocol.

With the advent of the concept of internetworking, additional functionality was added to this layer, namely getting data from the source network to the destination network.

This generally involves routing the packet across a network of networks, known as an internet.

In the Internet protocol suite, IP performs the basic

task of getting packets of data from source to destination, and also supports other protocols, such as ICMP (used to transmit diagnostic information about IP transmission) and IGMP (used to manage multicast data).

ICMP and IGMP are layered on top of IP but perform network layer functions, illustrating an incompatibility between the internet and OSI models.

The Network Layer Internet Protocol (IP) can carry data for a number of different higher level protocols. These protocols are each identified by a unique IP Protocol Number. ICMP and IGMP are protocols 1 and 2, respectively.

The Transport layer

The protocols at the Transport layer can solve problems like reliability ("did the data reach the destination?") and ensure that data arrives in the correct order. In the TCP/IP protocol suite, transport protocols also determine which application any given data is intended for.

The dynamic routing protocols which technically fit at this layer in the TCP/IP Protocol Suite (since they run over IP) are generally considered to be part of the Network layer; an example is OSPF (IP protocol number 89).

TCP (IP protocol number 6) is a "reliable", connection-oriented transport mechanism providing a reliable byte stream, which makes sure data arrives undamaged and in order, is re-transmitted if lost and eliminates duplicate copies. TCP tries to continuously measure how loaded the network is and throttles its sending rate in order to avoid overloading the network. Furthermore, TCP will attempt to deliver all data correctly in the specified sequence. These are its main differences from UDP and can become disadvantages in real-time streaming or routing applications with high layer 3 loss rates.

UDP (IP protocol number 17) is a connectionless datagram protocol. It is a "best effort" or "unreliable" protocol —not because it is particularly unreliable, but because it does not verify that packets have reached their destination and gives no guarantee that they will arrive in order.

If an Application requires these guarantees, it must provide them itself, or use TCP.

UDP is typically used for applications such as streaming media (audio and video, etc.) where the time TCP requires for retransmission and re-ordering might not be available, or for simple query/response applications like DNS lookups, where the overhead of setting up a reliable connection is disproportionately large.

Both TCP and UDP are used to carry a number of higher-level applications. Their TCP or UDP Port Number distinguishes the applications at any given network address. By convention certain well-known ports are associated with specific applications.

RTP is a datagram protocol that is designed for real-time data such as streaming audio and video.

Although RTP uses the UDP packet format as a basis, it provides a function that is at the same protocol layer.

The Application layer

The Application layer is where most common network programs reside.

These programs and their corresponding protocols include :

HTTP (The World Wide Web)
FTP (File transport)
SMTP (Email)
SSH (Secure remote login)
DNS (Name ↔ IP Address lookups) and many others.
Applications most commonly run on TCP or UDP, and are often associated with a well-known port number. Some examples are:
HTTP on TCP port 80 or 8080.
SSH on TCP port 22,
DNS lookups on UDP (or sometimes TCP) port 53,
RIP routing updates on UDP port 520.

6

Future Call Centre

Having never heard of the Call Centre industry fifteen years ago, an individual told me there was incredible opportunity in this business. After thinking about WHY they were telling me this... when they had nothing to gain... it was clear, there must be opportunity in the call Centre business!

This is even more true today. As a person with over 15 years of Call Centre experience, I can truly say ... "there is incredible opportunity in this business".

Traditional Call Centres

The image of row after row of telemarketers calling consumers, desperately trying to persuade them to purchase a product or service is the common perception of most call Centres. Unfortunately, too many call Centres today still operate in this environment. Using even modern predictive dialers still does not relieve the cost and stress of trying to promote a product or service. Although many telemarketeers use different introductions or gimmicky approaches and techniques, consumers are getting wary and tired of this type of selling. And after a long shift, the enthusiasm and morale of an outbound telemarketeer wanes significantly. The quality of the message delivered to the last prospect of the shift is generally not the same as was delivered to the first prospect of the day. Plus a call Centre can only contact as many prospects as can be handled by the number of agents in the Centre. Even predictive dialers only eliminate busy signals, no answer and answering machine calls. However, since well over 90% of cold calls are made to uninterested parties, telemarketeers spend most of the day handling "No Interest" calls.

Advanced Call Centre Solutions

Imagine having a call Centre with ALL of your telemarketeers talking ONLY with interested prospects. With technology from Database Systems Corp. this type of advanced call Centre is now a reality. By letting your phone system do more work and qualification of your called prospects, your call Centre agents can spend more productive time selling and promoting rather than just trying to keep a prospect on the line. Prospects can now be called and introduced with a consistent, professional message. Your call introduction will be a clear, concise message that YOU want to present.

Fewer agents can now process far more calls in this new call Centre. You can hire call Centre agents that can work from your Centre or from home. Recruiting telemarketeers into this environment is much easier. Call Centres can become as much as 10 times more productive using this smart and professional marketing approach. Calling campaigns that take days or weeks to perform can now be accomplished in just hours!

Features of Advanced Call Centres

The advanced call Centre will be far more productive and cost effective. By letting technology unburden routine tasks, your Centre will be capable of assuming any type of call campaign at a lower cost. The following features of this call Centre of the future are available NOW from Database Systems Corp.

Call campaigns with voice messaging—Let our phone system qualify prospects or introduce your product or company BEFORE transferring to your agents. Messages can be left on answering machines as well. No more dropped calls, plus your message can properly identify your organization and products conforming to proposed FTC regulations.

- *Call Centre agents working from home*—Now your call Centre agents can work from home, from remote offices or at your call Centre. Using the Web, our technology can connect calls with your agents, no matter where they are.
- *Professional inbound call processing*—Inbound calls can be professionally answered using our intelligent IVR and call routing features. Information can be easily given to callers without ever having to speak with an agent. Of course, we can still intelligently route calls to different agent groups and do outside call transfers.
- *Flexible dialing programs*—Our PACER phone system can perform just about any type of dialing, from simple auto dial, progressive dialing, predictive dialing and of course our message dialing—whatever your calling campaign requires.
- *Fully automated contact management*—Our award winning CRM software system, Telemation, is our flagship product. Installed in all different types of call Centres, Telemation can manage your call Centre information and provide it in a timely manner to your agents.
- *Telephony links to corporate applications*—To further increase the productivity of your call Centre, calls can be launched from the PACER dialer and connected to your agents using our computer telephony software. Existing PC, Linux, or Web applications can be fully integrated into our call Centre products using this CTI software.
- *Online administration and reporting*—Products from Database Systems Corp. include a comprehensive online reporting system plus the ability to customize reports and graphs to your specific needs through our phone software.

Reports

The Call Centre Reporter, enables you to run more than a dozen detailed reports on your call Centre activity. Based on Microsoft Excel, it presents·information-packed graphs in colorful, easy-to-read format, for any time period you want, automatically updated with the latest data. Keep track of your callers' wait times, how many calls are being abandoned, how long calls are taking once connected, and more. Discover who your busiest and most effective agents are. Quantify what times of day have your heaviest volumes, and whether you need to add more trunks to the system. Let your business grow with help from the Call Centre Reporter.

Special reports to track advertising campaign success

Planning a marketing blitz? Keep track of results to the second with TeleVantage's specialized reports. Have agents mark campaign-related calls with an account code, then use the Call Volume By Account Code Report to track them. Or, place an ad with a phone number that TeleVantage recognizes as the contact "Campaign", then use the Call Volume By Identified Caller Report to track all calls from "Campaign". And if your agents are placing outbound calls, use the Call Trends Report to track just those.

Compare multiple queues

The Queue Comparison Report gives you an easy way to find out where your business' energies are being drawn and react quickly to trends. It measures the performance of one queue against another in terms of total calls, average wait time, and the breakdown between calls handled, abandoned and sent to voice mail. Compare sales queues for different product lines, or your sales queue with your customer support queue. Nothing beats having the numbers in front of you.

Report on your regular phone traffic too

Most reports that can be run to track an agent can also be run to track non-agent users. For example, the User Activity Report shows how much time a user is spending in each personal status. Many queue-level reports can also be run against workgroups, such as the Average Wait Time and

Call Volume by Time of Day Report. And the valuable Trunk Performance Report lets you measure the traffic on your phone system as a whole, giving you insight into the growth patterns of your overall business.

Reports

Activity History by Agent—Shows an agent's activity history by displaying a row for every change in agent state, and how long the agent spent in each state, for all the queues to which the agent belongs.

Activity History by Queue—Shows a history of all of the agent activity in a queue by displaying a row for every change in agent state, and how long each agent in the queue spent in each state. Shows data for all agent activity in the queue.

Agent Performance Trends—number of calls and average talk time for a specific agent.

Agent Performance Trends by Queue—zeroes in on an agent's performance for a specific queue.

Average Wait Time and Call Volume by Time of Day—average wait time and inbound call volume displayed by hour

Call Centre Queue Information—Shows all vital information for every Call Centre Queue and a breakdown of information on each Agent in those queues.

Call Log—By date range, shows an agent's or queue's call log entries.

Call Trends—total outbound calls by agents in a queue. For example, measure the performance of a sales calling campaign.

Call Volume by Account Code—total calls and total talk time for calls using each account code. Track any type of call for which agents have entered an account code, for example a recurring support problem or calls relating to an ad campaign.

Call Volume by Identified Caller—by TeleVantage contact, shows total calls a user, queue, or workgroup received and average talk duration. For example, if you created 5 contacts, each to track a different promotional advertisement code, this report would show how many people called for each promotion.

Cumulative Calls and Average Talk Time by Agent—by agent, shows total calls made and received and average talk time for any queue or workgroup.

Custom Data—total calls and average talk time associated with calls from a user, queue, or all system calls, that are identified by a specific custom data variable. For example, an auto attendant could be configured to set the "Product" custom variable to "Apples" or "Oranges" based on the menu choice selected. This report would show how many callers selected Apples versus Oranges, and the average length of those calls.

Inbound Call Outcome Trends—total calls handled by one agent, multiple agents, abandoned, sent to voice mail and the total number of calls for any queue.

Inbound Call Volume Trends—total calls a queue received, average wait time and longest wait time.

Queue Comparison—compares all queues on total number of calls, average wait time, and total calls handled, abandoned, and sent to voice mail. For example, you can see how well your sales queue performs compared to your technical support queue.

Service Level—by wait time, shows the percentage of calls answered, abandoned, or sent to voice mail during a time range for a queue.

Trunk Performance—by hour, shows the average number of inbound and outbound calls handled by the trunks you specify and the percentage of these trunks in use. Tells you if you need to add or remove trunks from your TeleVantage system, and can also help you predict future trunk performance.

User Activity—pie charts showing the percentage of an agent's time spent in active versus other statuses. Shows the kinds of calls that make up the active calls.

Wait by Outcome—how long callers waited before their calls were handled, abandoned, or sent to voice mail.

7

Legal Implications for The Call Centre Industry

The Laws of Call Centres
Idle Time is NOT Slack Time

Idle time—what a juicy target! Finance departments see the idle time numbers in our forecasts or history, representing, say, 20 seconds or so per call where no work is being done! Think of the savings! If the Centre takes 100,000 calls per week, then this 20-second idle time represents 29,000 hours of productivity just waiting to be nabbed! It's one-half million dollars to be saved!

But there is a problem with that "Idle Time Savings" cell in their big financial spreadsheet. Idle time behaves according to one of the Laws of Call Centres.

A Law of Call Centres: Given a Centre's size, handle time, call volume, service goal and staffing level, idle time is fixed, and is an output, not an input.

Corollary: If you give employees something to do with those free "idle time" hours you'll reduce the service offered to your customers.

The graph above represents the ironclad relationship between occupancy (the inverse of idle percentage) and service level for a particular call Centre. If I change occupancy by pulling "idle hours" out of the Centre, then service level will necessarily decrease.

In 1994, Congress passed the Telemarketing and Consumer Fraud and Abuse Prevention Act to combat telephone fraud. It serves to provide law enforcement agencies with powerful new tools and gives consumers new protections and guidance on how to differentiate between fraudulent and legitimate telemarketing. Under the Act, the Federal Trade Commission (FTC) adopted the Telemarketing Sales Rule, which went into effect December 31, 1995 and requires telemarketeers to formalize their existing policies and, where necessary, create new ones to bring their operations into compliance.

Businesses not covered by the Rule

The following four types of businesses, even though they may use interstate telephone calls to sell goods or services, are not subject to the FTC's jurisdiction and, therefore, are not covered by the Rule:

- Banks, Federal Credit Unions and Federal Savings and Loans
- Common carriers, such as long distance telephone companies and airlines
- Non-Profit Organizations
- Insurance companies—to the extent that this business is regulated by state law

However, individuals or companies that contract with one of these four types of entities are covered and must comply with the Rule. For example, if you provide services to, or on behalf of, a bank or airline, or if you are profiting from services provided to a nonprofit organization, you are covered by the Rule. This does not apply to individuals and companies selling investments, who are subject to the jurisdiction of the Securities and Exchange Commission or the Commodity Futures Trading Commission.

Calls not covered by the Rule

Some types of calls are not covered by the Rule, regardless of whether the business or individual receiving the call is covered:

- Consumer calls in response to a catalog advertisement, as long as the catalog is issued at least once a year and contains a written description/illustration of the goods or services offered for sale and the business address of the seller. If, during the call, the telemarketeer offers goods or services not included in the catalog or not prompted by the consumer, the sales transaction is covered by the Rule. Catalog merchandise sales are covered by the FTC's Mail and Telephone Order Merchandise Rule.
- 900 number pay-per-call telephone calls, which must comply with the FTC's 900-Number Rule.
- Calls related to the sale of franchises or business opportunities that are covered by the FTC's Franchise Rule.
- Unsolicited calls from consumers, such as hotel, airline and car rental reservations, take-out food orders, technical support, or calls to retailers that have not been prompted by an advertisement or solicitation.
- Follow-up calls after a face-to-face sales presentation. For sales made at the consumer's home or away from the seller's place of business, the FTC's Cooling Off Rule applies.
- Business-to-business calls that do not involve retail sales of non durable office or cleaning supplies, such as paper, toner and cleaning solvents.
- Consumers' calls made in response to general media advertising, such as television commercials, infomercials, home shopping programs, magazine and newspaper ads, and yellow pages or similar directory listings.
- Calls responding to direct mail advertising, if the solicitation material clearly, conspicuously and truthfully discloses cost and quantity, material restrictions, limitations or conditions, and any "no refund" policy. Calls responding to direct mail advertising related to credit repair, recovery services, advance-fee loans, investment opportunities or prize promotions are not exempt.

Proper Identification

All outbound telemarketing calls must promptly disclose, in a clear and conspicuous manner, the identity of the seller, that the purpose of the call is to sell goods/services, the nature of the goods/services being offered, and in the case of a prize promotion, that no purchase or payment is necessary to participate or win.

Calls initiated strictly to welcome new customers or to ascertain customer satisfaction do not require these four oral disclosures. Calls made by for-profit companies on behalf of non-profit entities need only disclose the name of the nonprofit organization on whose behalf they are calling, the nature of the offered goods/services and the request for a donation.

Calling Hour Restrictions

The Rule expressly forbids calls to private residences before 8:00 a.m. or after 9:00 p.m. (local time at the consumer's location). Any exceptions to this must be with the expressed consent of the called party.

Required Information to Consumers

The Rule requires telemarketeers—whether making outbound calls to consumers or receiving inbound calls from consumers - to provide the following information so that the consumer can make an informed purchase decision from that particular seller before paying for the goods/services that are the subject of the sales offer:

- **Cost and quantity**—The Rule requires disclosure of the total cost to purchase, receive or use the offered goods/services and the total quantity of goods/services the consumer must pay for and receive. An exception to the Rule is if the telemarketeer is offering a "negative option plan", such as record or book clubs that require the consumer to purchase a specific number of items over a specified time period, or a "continuity plan", where the consumer can purchase some or all of a collection over the course of the plan. Since neither the seller nor the consumer knows the quantity of products that will ultimately be purchased or the total cost, only the costs and quantity of goods/services that are part of the initial offer must be disclosed, along with the total quantity of additional goods/services the consumer must purchase over the duration of the plan and the range of costs to purchase each individual additional good/service.

- **Material restrictions, limitations or conditions to purchase, receive or use the offered goods/services**—This includes such things as method of payment, deposit or advance reservation requirements, any restrictions, limitations, conditions or additional expenses that may be incurred to redeem the offer.
- **"No refund" policy**—Refund, cancellation, exchange or repurchase policies must be disclosed only if they are part of the sales presentation. On the other hand, if "all sales are final", the consumer must be informed of this fact before paying for the offered goods/services.
- **Prize promotions**—A prize is anything offered and given to a person by chance. For purposes of the Rule, chance exists if a person is guaranteed to receive an item and, at the time of the offer, the specific item the person will receive is not identified. (You can tell them they will receive one of several prizes, but not which prize.) The telemarketeer must, however, promptly disclose, in a clear and conspicuous manner, the odds of winning the prize(s) and/or the factors used in calculating the odds—that no purchase is necessary to participate in the promotion or win a prize, the no-purchase/no-payment entry information, and any costs or conditions to receive or redeem any prize.

Authorization for Payment

The Rule requires a consumer's "express verifiable authorization" for use of bank account information to obtain payment through "phone checks" or "demand drafts". This can be done by advance written authorization (a fax or voided signed check will do) by a tape recording of the consumer giving authorization, or by a written confirmation of the transaction sent to the consumer before the draft is submitted for payment.

The taped authorization and written confirmation must include the date and amount of the draft(s), the name on the account from which the funds will be paid, the number of draft payments authorized, if more than one, a telephone number answered during normal business hours that the consumer can call with questions and the date of the consumer's authorization.

Many states require advance consent of the recorded party; the taped confirmation must show that the consumer understands and acknowledges each term of the transaction and authorizes it. Written confirmations must include a refund policy in the event that the consumer disputes the authorization.

Prohibitions Under the Rule

Claims which are false or misleading are strictly prohibited. All offers must be stated clearly and honestly so that the parties know exactly what they have committed to, how much it will cost and what they will be getting in return.

Misrepresenting any material aspect of the product, service, prize promotion or investment opportunity—or of the refund, repurchase or cancellation policy—is also prohibited. The Rule prohibits the telemarketeer from misrepresenting their affiliation with, or endorsement by, any charitable, governmental, police, civic or similar third-party organization.

The Rule prohibits knowingly assisting and/or facilitating telemarketing practices that violate the Rule—or deliberately remaining ignorant of Rule violations. For example, third parties that provide names of consumers with poor credit records to credit repair services will not be protected from liability. (Credit repair services cannot request or receive payment until the time frame within which the promised service has expired and evidence of the promised improvement in the consumer's credit record has been achieved.)

Credit card "laundering"—obtaining access to the credit card system through another's merchant account without the authorization of the financial institution—not only violates the Rule, it is a criminal offense under federal law as well as under the law of some states.

Finally, the Rule prohibits the use of threats, intimidation or profane or obscene language to pressure a consumer into accepting a sales offer. Repeated calls to an individual who has declined to accept an offer are considered acts of intimidation and is an abusive practice.

"Do not call" Policies

Sellers may not call, or cause a telemarketeer to call, a consumer who has requested to receive no more calls from, or on behalf of, the particular goods/services being offered. The Rule further requires sellers to maintain "Do not call" lists of those consumers who do not wish to be contacted by phone, to develop a written policy implementing this "Do not call" list-keeping requirement, and to train its telemarketing personnel in these procedures.

Enforcement and Penalties

Calling a consumer who has requested not to be called is a Rule violation and could result in civil penalties of up to $10,000 per violation, nationwide injunctions prohibiting certain conduct or redress to injured consumers. If a written "Do not call" policy is in place and the call was the result of error, there may be no Rule violation, but the complaint could be subject to an enforcement investigation into the effectiveness of the "Do not call" policy, how it is implemented and if all personnel are properly trained in its procedures.

Ultimately, the seller is responsible for keeping a current "Do not call" list, whether it is through a telemarketing service it hires or through its own efforts. However, if the investigation reveals that the telemarketeer ignored the seller's written "Do not call" procedures, then the telemarketeer would be liable for the Rule violation. The Rule further states that, without an agreement to do otherwise, the seller must maintain advertising and promotional materials, information about prize recipients, sales records, employee records and all verifiable authorizations for demand drafts for a period of two years from the date that the record is produced.

The FTC, the states and private citizens may bring civil lawsuits in federal district courts to enforce the Rule. Actions by the states may be brought by the attorney general or any officer authorized to bring actions on behalf of its residents. Private persons may bring action if they have suffered $50,000 or more in actual damages. In both cases, written notice must be provided to the FTC prior to filing a complaint or immediately upon instituting the action.

ETHICAL MARKETING GUIDELINES

Overview: The ATA promotes and supports courteous, ethical and relevant telephone communication between consumers and businesses. We promote adherence and compliance with all state and federal laws pertaining to telephone and marketing communications to our membership. We also strongly promote training and processes for our member employees to ensure that telephone marketing is professional and consumer friendly.

The ATA develops, promotes and supports ethical marketing guidelines created by best practices developed within the industry that support professional, accurate and courteous communication.

The ATA encourages its members and member clients to use on-going quality and feedback programs that allow consumers to provide feedback to the business and industry relating to personal teleservice experiences.

General: ATA requires (1) that members adhere to state and federal laws, (2) adopt professional communication standards and practices that minimize potential annoyance associated with telephone marketing offers; (3) develop marketing processes and targeting to ensure the call has relevance; (4) develop and use procedures to control the timing and frequency of communication.

Target Marketing & Frequency

ATA supports a targeted marketing approach, recognizing that untargeted calling is not in the best interest of consumers, businesses or the telemarketing industry. Calls should always be targeted to people or companies likely to have a use for the particular product or service being offered. With the exception of legitimate market research requiring random sampling, the ATA does not condone random or sequential dialing without regard to the potential usefulness of the product or service offered to the call recipient.

ATA recognizes that consumer interest may change over time and therefore an offer that was not relevant may become so in the future. Consumers receive multiple targeted offers throughout a year and the ATA supports a time span between marketing promotions from the prior contact (excepting follow-up service, customer satisfaction and new account introduction calls).

Attempted Contact Frequency

For any given marketing, political or charitable calling program, consumer contact should be limited to avoid excessive contacts. The ATA supports limiting the number of maximum attempts to reach an individual regardless of who answers the phone. Placing a limit on attempting to reach a specific individual will minimize the frustration experienced by any other individual answering the phone who is not the targeted recipient of the call. This limit is supported for those calls that are answered by an individual and not by an electronic device.

In addition to the contact limit, if the individual answering the phone requests that the telemarketeer not call again or requests a specific time for a call back, such a request should be honored whether or not the individual is the targeted recipient of the call.

Consumer Requests and Feedback

Consumer requests should be explicitly honored by industry. For example;

- Customers declining an offer should not be called again during that marketing campaign or for the recommended 'rest period' between marketing campaigns. Members are encouraged to educate their telephone representatives to recognize early refusals and only continue if the customer needs additional information to understand the offer.
- Requests to be placed on company/client specific do not call lists should be handled expeditiously, and such requests should be recognized and honored and not requiring the consumer to use specific language to distinguish a do not call request from a refusal request.
- The request to be placed on company/client do not call requests should be consumer friendly and not require the consumer to place additional calls.

In accordance with the TCPA, consumers should be provided with a method to contact marketeers to ask questions or provide feedback. ATA strongly recommends that every contact be provided a toll free number to call that is answered during business hours by an industry professional who can respond to the consumer's needs. Members are encouraged to use timely and efficient multi marketing media that makes it convenient and easy for customers to ask questions, follow-up on orders and provide other feedback to the respective business

"Do Not Call" Compliance

ATA strongly advocates and promotes the value of company/client specific do not call lists. Federal law mandates that companies maintain internal, company/client specific do not call lists to honor requests from consumers to not receive future solicitation calls. All such requests from consumers should be honored. Companies must adhere to this mandate whether using internal or contracted telephone representatives. Policies and procedures must exist to ensure that all Do Not Call requests are honored. Training should be frequently conducted with all representatives regarding how to correctly respond to the consumer and handle any such requests.

ATA requires all members comply with federal and state laws, including those relating to state and federal do not call lists. Marketeers should adhere to the various frequency guidelines relating to downloading the updated state/federal lists of those consumers who have requested not to receive solicitation calls for those marketing programs and industries that are bound by such laws.

Business Relation & Prospect Inquiry Definition

ATA supports the business relationship exemption present in federal and most state do not call laws. The definition of business relationship should be legislated to ensure a standard interpretation. ATA supports a business relationship definition to be defined for customers with current and recent relationships with marketeers, as well as a definition for prospective customers who inquire about a company's product or service.

Call Flow Adherence

Outbound solicitation communication should be brief and engaging to allow consumers to state interest and engage in conversation if they choose. ATA supports laws that require marketeers to engage consumers by restricting the initial solicitation pitch to include an introduction, purpose of call and gaining of the consumer's interest to proceed. Delivering efficient communication is beneficial to both consumers and business and allows interested consumers to assess their interest in the offer being presented.

Consumers who express no interest in the offer or call should be respected. Marketeers should not continue the call once they have offered a response to a consumer's objection unless the customer asks additional questions or clearly states interest in the offer. Continuing dialogue with a consumer who expresses no interest is not in the best interest of consumers, businesses or the telemarketing industry.

Call Abandon Rules

Federal law requires that those calls abandoned/not answered by a live operator have a recorded message delivered to the consumer stating the marketeer's name, reason for calling and phone number that is answered during business hours. ATA supports this law and practice. The message allows consumers to receive information regarding who has attempted to reach them and services that may be of value. Requiring this message eliminates 'phantom' calls. In addition, the ATA requires its members to comply with all federal legislation, which requires that no more than 3% of all callers attempted on a given day for a campaign would receive an automated voice recording due to the unavailability of a live representative.

Calling Hour Restrictions

The ATA requires members to adhere to the federally mandated calling hours for marketing offers and promotes member companies to use those same calling hours for non-marketing calls. All ATA members must honor any state laws further restricting calling hours or days.

What the ATA and these Ethical Guidelines are all about

The American Teleservices Association (ATA), a not-for-profit trade association founded in 1983 to represent and serve the telemarketing profession for all industries that use the telephone as a means to communicate with customers and prospective customers. It is committed to meeting the needs of its members, as well as protecting the rights of consumers and businesses who have telephone contact with its members.

Through professional programs and activities, the ATA attempts to educate its members, the public and public officials concerning the ethical behavior for both inbound and outbound telemarketing. We have also developed these Ethical Marketing Guidelines to help any business, consumer or legal entity objectively measure telemarketing program integrity and professional performance.

·The ATA supports the Federal Trade Commission (FTC) Telemarketing Sales Rule and the Federal Communications Commission (FCC) Telephone Consumer Protection Act.

- The ATA strongly encourages its members to review all federal, state and local laws for compliance before initiating any telephone solicitation campaign.
- The ATA advocates the highest standards of professionalism and ethical behavior for all telemarketing operations. These guidelines, when conscientiously adhered to and practiced call-by-call; help assure the long-term satisfaction of ATA members, their employees and customers while preserving the future of the call Centre industry.

This Ethical Guidelines are an educational tool developed under the premise that professional, reputable programs have specific goals, achieved through closely supervised high-quality performance, with the public interest—business and consumer—in mind. It is anticipated that these Ethical Marketing Guidelines will be an evolving set of principles that should grow over time as changes in the industry and changes in the various laws governing the industry come about.

As direct marketeers ("sellers") move forward with telephone solicitations, several do not call compliance issues must be considered pursuant to the FTC's Telemarketing Sales Rule (the "TSR") and the FCC's rules under the Telephone Consumer Protection Act (the "TCPA Rules"). Generally, in order to ensure compliance, it is imperative that sellers: (a) develop, implement, and follow a written Do Not Call Policy; (b) train personnel and third party telemarketeers ("telemarketeers") in procedures established as part of the Do Not Call Policy; (c) scrub calling lists against the Registry, as well as any remaining state lists; (d) understand the parameters of the existing business relationship exemption for themselves and their affiliates; (e) ensure compliance with company-specific internal do not call obligations; (f) keep accurate, detailed records of compliance; and (g) appoint a specific person to be a "Chief Telemarketing Officer".

Develop a Written Do Not Call Policy

Both the TSR and TCPA Rules offer a "safe harbor" pursuant to which sellers and telemarketeers will not be liable for calling a number on the Registry, if: a call is the result of an error and the seller or telemarketeer can demonstrate that its routine business practices include: (a) establishment and implementation of a written policy for compliance procedures; (b) training in the compliance procedures for its personnel and any other entities assisting in compliance; (c) mainta-nence of a company-specific list of telephone numbers that must not be called; (d) a process to prevent calling numbers on the Registry; and (e) the monitoring and enforcement of its written compliance policy on an on-going basis.

Creating a written Do Not Call Policy is the first step to establish compliance and without it, sellers and telemarketeers will never be able to meet the remaining prongs of the safe harbor. The written policy must explain the seller's or telemarketeer's procedures for complying with the Registry. The policy should, at a minimum, address the following:

- Subscribing to and paying for the use of the Registry.
- Downloading telephone numbers on a timely and quarterly basis from the FTC's website at https://telemarketing.donotcall.gov/.
- Procedures for accepting and recording company-specific do not call requests and maintaining a company-specific do not call list ("Company Specific List").
- Time frame for responding to requests to be placed on the Company Specific List.

- Scrubbing calling lists against the Registry and the Company Specific List.
- A procedure for dealing with a person who claims his or her number is on the Registry or the Company Specific List.
- Procedures for dealing with an inadvertent call to a person whose number is on the Registry or the Company Specific List.
- Training personnel and, in the case of sellers, third party telemarketeers, to comply with the requirements of the Registry and the Company Specific List.
- Use of the Registry list and the Company Specific List is prohibited for any purpose other than to honor such do not call requests.
- Ensuring that compliance with the Registry and the Company Specific List is monitored.

Once the written Do Not Call Policy has been completed, it can be used as a road map for working out the specific technical details of how to comply. The written Do Not Call Policy should be used as general guide for all internal and external operations that are implicated in telemarketing activities.

Train Personnel and Vendors

Sellers and telemarketeers must periodically train their own personnel, and, in the case of sellers, any telemarketing vendors acting on their behalf, with respect to the practices and procedures that are necessary to comply with the policy and ideally, the laws that impact telemarketing activities.

Scrub Calling Lists

While the Do Not Call safe harbor is helpful, it cannot be relied upon as a substitute for scrubbing calling lists against the numbers on the Registry and on any Company Specific List.

Don't Forget About State Specific Lists

There are two important issues to be aware of with

respect to state-specific lists. First, the states have been given approximately eighteen months to download any existing state do not call registries into the Registry. Even though most states have folded their state specific lists into the Registry, there are a few holdout states, including Alaska, Georgia, Idaho, Indiana, Louisiana, Missouri, Texas, Wisconsin and Wyoming. Therefore, marketeers must still scrub against these state lists in addition to the Registry. In November 2003, the State of Texas demonstrated its strong enforcement posture with respect to its state do not call list when the Texas Attorney General brought lawsuits against fifteen telemarketeers that allegedly violated the "Texas No-Call" law.

Second, even in those states which have merged their lists into the Registry, state regulators retain their ability to enforce do not call violations made to state residents under state specific statutes. This leaves open the possibility of both state and federal regulatory action, as well as private causes of action, for violation of both state and federal do not call provisions.

Be Wary of Affiliates' Existing Business Relationships

Sellers can take advantage of an exemption to the do not call provisions of both the TSR and TCPA Rules, if there is an "existing business relationship" ("EBR") between the seller and the person being called. An EBR exists where a purchase or transaction has occurred within eighteen months, or where an inquiry or application regarding offered products or services has been made within three months, immediately preceding the solicitation and the relationship has not been terminated by either party.

Whether an affiliate or company otherwise related to the company with which the EBR exists can also take advantage of the EBR is a much more complicated issue. The test here is the reasonable expectation of the consumer. The FTC has indicated that "[a]n established business relationship is between a seller and a customer; it is not necessarily between one of the seller's subsidiaries or affiliates and that customer.

The test for whether a subsidiary or affiliate can claim an established business relationship with a sister company's customer is: would the customer expect to receive a call from such an entity or would the customer believe such a call is inconsistent with having placed his or her number on the National Do Not Call Registry".

In considering whether or not a consumer would reasonably expect to be called by an affiliate, one must ask are the affiliate's goods or services similar to the seller's and is the affiliate's name identical or similar to the seller's? The greater the similarity between (1) the nature and type of goods sold by the seller and any subsidiary or affiliate, and (2) the identity between the seller and any subsidiary or affiliate, the more likely it is that the call would fall within the EBR exemption.

Both the FCC and the FTC make specific use of the words "affiliate" and "subsidiary" under their respective rules, and these terms generally have established meaning under corporate law. An "affiliate" is generally understood to mean a company, incorporated or not, in which a certain percentage or greater interest is owned, directly or indirectly, by another company. A "subsidiary", is generally understood to mean a company that is owned by another company and such other company has the ability to control the subsidiary. Entities such as franchisees or independent car dealerships, both of which are independently owned entities, would not typically be considered "affiliates" or "subsidiaries" of a marketeer under these definitions. Accordingly, a strict interpretation of the EBR exemption would suggest that these and similar types of entities could not take advantage of the EBR exemption with their franchisor or motor vehicle manufacturer, respectively, despite the fact that the goods and services offered and the names of the entities are likely to be virtually identical.

Don't Forget About Company Specific Do Not Call Obligations

One of the most important factors to remember in

complying with the do not call provisions of the TSR and TCPA Rules is the need to maintain a Company Specific List. As a practical matter, scrubbing a calling list against the Registry is not enough, since a consumer's request to be placed on a company specific do not call list trumps any exemptions under the Registry between the seller and the consumer. Once a calling list has been scrubbed against the Registry, it must also be scrubbed against any Company Specific List.

Keep Records

Even if a written Do Not Call Policy has been developed, and all of the other procedures and practices necessary to meet the Do Not Call safe harbor have been implemented and followed, such efforts will be wasted if compliance cannot be proven. In general, the TSR requires records to be kept for a period of twenty-four months, and under the TCPA Rules, the retention period, for records of those consumers who have requested not to be called, is five years. Therefore, a document retention policy relating to telemarketing records must be implemented and followed. Detailed and accurate records may be the only defense against claims of a Do Not Call violation.

Put Someone in Charge

All of the foregoing is meaningless if someone is not appointed to oversee and ensure compliance with the TSR, TCPA Rules and state telemarketing laws. A responsible person must be appointed to monitor and ensure compliance with the Do Not Call Policy and applicable laws—a "Chief Telemarketing Officer". This person must be familiar with the company's telemarketing practices and related laws and act as a central point of contact for coordination and compliance questions. Without designating such a person, adherence to regulations and policies may lapse and the risk of regulatory action is likely to rise.

Conclusion

Telemarketing can still be an effective part of any sales and marketing strategy. However, in the new era of the Do Not Call Registry and increased regulatory and private actions, it is essential that both sellers and telemarketeers know how to comply with the law, and ultimately, understand how to reduce their legal risks. With enforcement actions likely to increase in the months to come, taking the steps outlined above will help achieve that goal.

Chapter 265 of the Acts of 2002

AN ACT REGULATING TELEMARKETING SOLICITATION

Be it enacted by the Senate and House of Representatives in General Court assembled, and by the authority of the same, as follows:

SECTION 1. Inserting after chapter 159B the following chapter hereby amends the General Laws:

CHAPTER 159C
TELEMARKETING SOLICITATION

Section 1. As used in this chapter, the following words shall, unless the context clearly requires otherwise, have the following meanings:—

- "Caller identification service or device", a telephone service or device which permits a consumer to see the telephone number of incoming calls.
- "Consumer", an individual who is a resident of the commonwealth and a prospective recipient of consumer goods or services.
- "Consumer goods or services", an article or service that is purchased, leased, exchanged or received primarily for personal, family or household purposes including, but not limited to, stocks, bonds, mutual funds, annuities and other financial products.
- "Doing business in the commonwealth", conducting telephonic sales calls: (i) from a location in the commonwealth or (ii) from a location outside of the commonwealth to consumers in the commonwealth.

"Existing customer", a residential telephone subscriber with whom the person or entity making a telephonic sales call has maintained an account or had a business relationship within the previous 24 months.

"Marketing or sales solicitation", the initiation of a telephone call or message to encourage the purchase or rental of, or investment in, property, goods or services, that is transmitted to a consumer, but not including a telephone call or message: (i) to a consumer with that consumer's prior express written or verbal invitation or permission; (ii) by a tax-exempt nonprofit organization; (iii) by an individual or organization for a noncommercial purpose, such as a poll or survey; or (iv) to a consumer in response to a visit made by such consumer to an establishment selling, leasing or exchanging consumer goods or services at a fixed location.

"Office", the office of consumer affairs and business regulation.

"Telephonic sales call", a call made by a telephone solicitor to a consumer for the purpose of: (i) engaging in a marketing or sales solicitation; (ii) soliciting an extension of credit for consumer goods or services; or (iii) obtaining information that will or may be used for marketing or sales solicitation or exchange of or extension of credit for consumer goods or services.

"Telephone solicitor", an individual, association, corporation, partnership, limited partnership, limited liability company or other business entity, or a subsidiary or affiliate thereof, doing business in the commonwealth who makes or causes to be made a telephonic sales call.

"Unsolicited telephonic sales call", a telephonic sales call other than a call made: (i) in response to an express written or verbal request of the consumer called; (ii) primarily in connection with an existing debt or contract, payment or performance of which has not been completed at the time of the call; (iii) to an existing customer unless such customer has stated to the telephone solicitor that such customer no longer wishes to receive the telephonic sales calls of such telephone solicitor; or (iv) in which the sale of goods and services is not completed, and payment or authorization of payment is not required, until after a face-to-face sales presentation by the telephone solicitor or a meeting between the telephone solicitor and customer.

Section 2. The office shall establish and maintain a no sales solicitation calls listing of consumers who do not wish to receive unsolicited telephonic sales calls. The office may contract with a private vendor to establish and maintain such listing, provided that: (i) the private vendor has maintained national no sales solicitation calls listings for more than 2 years; and (ii) the contract requires the vendor to provide the no sales solicitation calls listing in a printed hard copy format and in any other format offered at a cost that does not exceed the production cost of the format offered. The office shall provide notice to consumers of the establishment of a no sales solicitation calls listing. A consumer who wishes to be included on the listing shall notify the office by calling toll-free number provided by the office, or in such other manner and at such times as the office may prescribe, which may include electronic notification. A consumer on such listing shall be deleted from such listing upon the consumer's written request or in such other manner and at such times as the division may prescribe, which may include electronic notification. The office shall update such listing not less than quarterly and shall make such listing available to telephone solicitors and other persons for a fee as the office shall prescribe.

Section 3. A telephone solicitor shall not make or cause to be made an unsolicited telephonic sales call to a consumer: (i) if the consumer's name and telephone number appear on the then current quarterly no sales solicitation calls listing made available by the office under section 2; (ii) to be received between the hours of 8:00 p.m. and 8:00 a.m., local time, at the consumer's location; (iii) in the form of electronically transmitted facsimiles; or (iv) by use of a recorded message device.

Section 4. No telephone solicitor shall intentionally cause to be installed or shall intentionally use a blocking device or service to circumvent a consumer's use of a call identification service or device.

Section 5. (a) A person who obtains the name, residential address or telephone number of a consumer from published telephone directories or from any other source and republishes or compiles such information, electronically or otherwise, and sells or offers to sell such publication or compilation to telephone solicitors for marketing or sales solicitation purposes shall, in accordance with this chapter, exclude from any such publication or compilation and from any database used exclusively for marketing or sales solicitation purposes, the name, address and telephone number of a consumer whose name and telephone number appears in the then current quarterly no sales solicitation calls listing made available by the office under section 2.

(b) This section shall not apply to: (i) a telephone company, subject to the authority of the department of telecommunications and energy, for the sole purpose of compiling, publishing or distributing telephone directories or causing the compilation, publication or distribution of telephone directories or providing directory assistance; and (ii) a person, for the sole purpose of compiling, publishing or distributing telephone directories for such telephone company pursuant to an agreement or other arrangement with such telephone company.

Section 5A. (a) A telephone solicitor shall disclose all of the following information within the first minute of a telephonic sales call and before requesting, accepting or arranging for payment by a consumer: (i) that the purpose of the telephone call is to make a sale or solicit funds; (ii) the correct name of the telemarketing company that employs the individual telemarketeer who is making the call; (iii) the correct name of the ultimate seller whose goods or services are being offered by means of the telemarketing call; and (iv) a complete and accurate description of the goods or services being offered including, but not limited to, the retail market value of the goods or services.

(b) The telemarketeer shall provide all of the following

information before requesting, accepting or arranging for payment by a consumer: (i) the cost to the consumer of the goods or services that are the subject of the telemarketing sales call including, but not limited to, any applicable tax, shipping and handling fees; (ii) any restrictions, limitations or conditions attached to purchasing the goods or services; (iii) the complete terms of any applicable refund, return, cancellation, exchange or repurchase policies; (iv) any material aspect of an investment opportunity being offered including, but not limited to, the price of the land or other investment, the location of the investment and the fact that an investor may lose some or all of their original investment.

Section 6. The office shall promulgate regulations to carry out this chapter which shall: (i) require each local exchange company to inform consumers of the opportunity to provide notification to the office or its contractor that such consumer objects to receiving unsolicited telephonic sales calls; (ii) specify the methods by which each such consumer shall give notice to the office or its contractor of the consumer's objection to receiving such sales calls or revocation of such notice; provided, however, that there shall be no cost to the consumer for joining the listing; (iii) specify the length of time for which a notice of objection shall be effective and the effect of a change of telephone number on such notice; (iv) specify the methods by which such objections and revocations shall be collected and added to the no sales solicitations calls listing; (v) specify the methods by which a person or entity desiring to make telephonic sales calls may obtain access to the no sales solicitation calls listing as required to avoid calling the telephone numbers of consumer included in such listing; and (vi) specify such other matters relating to the listing that the office deems desirable.

Section 7. If the Federal Communications Commission establishes a single national database of telephone numbers of consumers who do not wish to receive unsolicited telephonic sales calls pursuant to 47 U.S.C. section 227(c)(3), the office shall include that part of such single national database that relates to the commonwealth in the listing established pursuant to this chapter.

Section 8. (a) The attorney general may initiate proceedings relating to a knowing violation or threatened knowing violation of this chapter. Such proceedings may include, without limitation, an injunction, a civil penalty of not more than $5,000 for each knowing violation, but not less than $1,500 for a knowing violation involving a consumer who is 65 years of age or older and additional relief in a court of competent jurisdiction. The attorney general may also issue investigative demands and subpoenas, administer oaths and conduct hearings in the course of investigating a violation of this chapter.

(b) A person who has received more than 1 unsolicited telephonic sales call within a 12-month period by or on behalf of the same person or entity in violation of this chapter may: (i) bring an action to enjoin the violation; (2) bring an action to recover for actual monetary loss from such knowing violation or to receive not more than $5,000 in damages for such knowing violation, whichever is greater; or (iii) bring both such actions.

(c) In a civil proceeding resulting from a transaction involving a violation of this chapter, the prevailing party, after judgment in the trial court and exhaustion of all appeals, if any, shall be awarded reasonable attorney's fees and costs from the nonprevailing party.

Section 9. It shall be a defense in any action or proceeding brought pursuant to this chapter that the defendant has established and implemented, with due care, reasonable practices and procedures to effectively prevent unsolicited telephonic sales calls in violation of this chapter.

Section 10. No action or proceeding shall be brought pursuant to this chapter: (i) more than 3 years after the person bringing the action knew or should have known of the occurrence of the alleged violation; or (ii) more than 3 years after the termination of a proceeding or action arising out of the same violation by the commonwealth, whichever is later.

Section 11. Information contained in the no sales

solicitation listing established pursuant to this chapter shall be used only for the purposes of compliance with this chapter or in a proceeding or action under section 8. Such information shall not be subject to public inspection or disclosure.

Section 12. A court of the commonwealth may exercise personal jurisdiction over a nonresident or his executor or administrator as to an action or proceeding authorized by this chapter.

Section 13. The remedies, duties, prohibitions and penalties provided in this chapter shall not be exclusive and shall be in addition to all other causes of action, remedies and penalties provided by law, including any applicable remedies pursuant to chapter 93A.

Section 14. The office shall establish an advisory group comprised of government entities, local telecommunications companies, businesses, senior citizens and other community advocates to compile and promote a list of educational literature to help consumers understand their options with regard to telephonic sales calls. The office shall work with local telecommunications companies to disseminate to their residential subscribers information about the availability of and instructions on how to request educational literature from the office. The office shall include on its internet website information that informs consumers of their rights to be placed on the no sales solicitation calls listing and the various methods, including notice to the office, of placing their names on the no sales solicitation calls listing.

SECTION 2. This act shall take effect on January 1, 2003.

Approved August 10, 2002.

Laws Governing Call Centres

In 1994, Congress passed the Telemarketing and Consumer Fraud and Abuse Prevention Act to combat telephone fraud. It serves to provide law enforcement agencies with powerful new tools and gives consumers new protections and guidance on how to differentiate between fraudulent and legitimate telemarketing. Under the Act, the

Federal Trade Commission (FTC) adopted the Telemarketing Sales Rule, which went into effect December 31, 1995 and requires telemarketeers to formalize their existing policies and, where necessary, create new ones to bring their operations into compliance.

Businesses not covered by the Rule

The following four types of businesses, even though they may use interstate telephone calls to sell goods or services, are not subject to the FTC's jurisdiction and, therefore, are not covered by the Rule:

- Banks, Federal Credit Unions and Federal Savings and Loans
- Common carriers, such as long distance telephone companies and airlines
- Non-Profit Organizations
- Insurance companies—to the extent that this business is regulated by state law

However, individuals or companies that contract with one of these four types of entities are covered and must comply with the Rule. For example, if you provide services to, or on behalf of, a bank or airline, or if you are profiting from services provided to a nonprofit organization, you are covered by the Rule.

This does not apply to individuals and companies selling investments, who are subject to the jurisdiction of the Securities and Exchange Commission or the Commodity Futures Trading Commission.

Calls not covered by the Rule

Some types of calls are not covered by the Rule, regardless of whether the business or individual receiving the call is covered:

- Consumer calls in response to a catalog advertisement, as long as the catalog is issued at least once a year and contains a written description/illustration of the goods or services offered for sale and the business address of the seller. If, during the call, the telemarketeer offers goods or services not included in the catalog or not prompted by the consumer, the sales transaction is covered by the Rule. Catalog merchandise sales are covered by the FTC's Mail and Telephone Order Merchandise Rule.

- 900 number pay-per-call telephone calls, which must comply with the FTC's 900-Number Rule.
- Calls related to the sale of franchises or business opportunities that are covered by the FTC's Franchise Rule.
- Unsolicited calls from consumers, such as hotel, airline and car rental reservations, take-out food orders, technical support, or calls to retailers that have not been prompted by an advertisement or solicitation.
- Follow-up calls after a face-to-face sales presentation. For sales made at the consumer's home or away from the seller's place of business, the FTC's Cooling Off Rule applies.
- Business-to-business calls that do not involve retail sales of non durable office or cleaning supplies, such as paper, toner and cleaning solvents.
- Consumers' calls made in response to general media advertising, such as television commercials, infomercials, home shopping programs, magazine and newspaper ads, and yellow pages or similar directory listings.
- Calls responding to direct mail advertising, if the solicitation material clearly, conspicuously and truthfully discloses cost and quantity, material restrictions, limitations or conditions, and any "no refund" policy. Calls responding to direct mail advertising related to credit repair, recovery services, advance-fee loans, investment opportunities or prize promotions are not exempt.

Proper Identification

All outbound telemarketing calls must promptly disclose, in a clear and conspicuous manner, the identity of the seller, that the purpose of the call is to sell goods/services, the nature of the goods/services being offered, and in the case of a prize promotion, that no purchase or payment is necessary to participate or win.

Calls initiated strictly to welcome new customers or to ascertain customer satisfaction do not require these four oral disclosures. Calls made by for-profit companies on behalf of non-profit entities need only disclose the name of the nonprofit organization on whose behalf they are calling, the nature of the offered goods/services and the request for a donation.

Calling Hour Restrictions

The Rule expressly forbids calls to private residences before 8:00 a.m. or after 9:00 p.m. (local time at the consumer's location). Any exceptions to this must be with the expressed consent of the called party.

Required Information to Consumers

The Rule requires telemarketeers—whether making outbound calls to consumers or receiving inbound calls from consumers—to provide the following information so that the consumer can make an informed purchase decision from that particular seller before paying for the goods/services that are the subject of the sales offer:

- **Cost and quantity**—The Rule requires disclosure of the total cost to purchase, receive or use the offered goods/services and the total quantity of goods/services the consumer must pay for and receive. An exception to the Rule is if the telemarketeer is offering a "negative option plan", such as record or book clubs that require the consumer to purchase a specific number of items over a specified time period, or a "continuity plan", where the consumer can purchase some or all of a collection over the course of the plan. Since neither the seller nor the consumer knows the quantity of products that will ultimately be purchased or the total cost, only the costs and quantity of goods/services that are part of the initial offer must be disclosed, along with the total quantity of additional goods/services the consumer must purchase over the duration of the plan and the range of costs to purchase each individual additional good/service.

- **Material restrictions, limitations or conditions to purchase, receive or use the offered goods/services**—This includes such things as method of payment, deposit or advance reservation requirements, any restrictions, limitations, conditions or additional expenses that may be incurred to redeem the offer.
- **"No refund" policy**—Refund, cancellation, exchange or repurchase policies must be disclosed only if they are part of the sales presentation. On the other hand, if "all sales are final", the consumer must be informed of this fact before paying for the offered goods/services.
- **Prize promotions**—A prize is anything offered and given to a person by chance. For purposes of the Rule, chance exists if a person is guaranteed to receive an item and, at the time of the offer, the specific item the person will receive is not identified. (You can tell them they will receive one of several prizes, but not which prize.) The telemarketeer must, however, promptly disclose, in a clear and conspicuous manner, the odds of winning the prize(s) and/or the factors used in calculating the odds—that no purchase is necessary to participate in the promotion or win a prize, the no-purchase/no-payment entry information, and any costs or conditions to receive or redeem any prize.

Authorization for Payment

The Rule requires a consumer's "express verifiable authorization" for use of bank account information to obtain payment through "phone checks" or "demand drafts". This can be done by advance written authorization (a fax or voided signed check will do) by a tape recording of the consumer giving authorization, or by a written confirmation of the transaction sent to the consumer before the draft is submitted for payment.

The taped authorization and written confirmation must include the date and amount of the draft(s), the name on the account from which the funds will be paid, the number of draft payments authorized, if more than one, a telephone number answered during normal business hours that the consumer can call with questions, and the date of the consumer's authorization.

Many states require advance consent of the recorded party; the taped confirmation must show that the consumer understands and acknowledges each term of the transaction and authorizes it. Written confirmations must include a refund policy in the event that the consumer disputes the authorization.

Prohibitions Under the Rule

Claims which are false or misleading are strictly prohibited. All offers must be stated clearly and honestly so that the parties know exactly what they have committed to, how much it will cost and what they will be getting in return.

Misrepresenting any material aspect of the product, service, prize promotion or investment opportunity—or of the refund, repurchase or cancellation policy—is also prohibited. The Rule prohibits the telemarketeer from misrepresenting their affiliation with, or endorsement by, any charitable, governmental, police, civic or similar third-party organization.

The Rule prohibits knowingly assisting and/or facilitating telemarketing practices that violate the Rule—or deliberately remaining ignorant of Rule violations. For example, third parties that provide names of consumers with poor credit records to credit repair services will not be protected from liability. (Credit repair services cannot request or receive payment until the time frame within which the promised service has expired and evidence of the promised improvement in the consumer's credit record has been achieved.)

Credit card "laundering"—obtaining access to the credit card system through another's merchant account without the authorization of the financial institution—not only violates the Rule, it is a criminal offense under federal law as well as under the law of some states.

Finally, the Rule prohibits the use of threats, intimidation or profane or obscene language to pressure a consumer into accepting a sales offer. Repeated calls to an individual who has declined to accept an offer are considered acts of intimidation and is an abusive practice.

"Do not call" Policies

Sellers may not call, or cause a telemarketeer to call, a consumer who has requested to receive no more calls from, or on behalf of, the particular goods/services being offered. The Rule further requires sellers to maintain "Do not call" lists of those consumers who do not wish to be contacted by phone, to develop a written policy implementing this "Do not call" list-keeping requirement and to train its telemarketing personnel in these procedures.

Enforcement and Penalties

Calling a consumer who has requested not to be called is a Rule violation and could result in civil penalties of up to $10,000 per violation, nationwide injunctions prohibiting certain conduct or redress to injured consumers. If a written "Do not call" policy is in place and the call was the result of error, there may be no Rule violation, but the complaint could be subject to an enforcement investigation into the effectiveness of the "Do not call" policy, how it is implemented and if all personnel are properly trained in its procedures.

Ultimately, the seller is responsible for keeping a current "Do not call" list, whether it is through a telemarketing service it hires or through its own efforts. However, if the investigation reveals that the telemarketeer ignored the seller's written "Do not call" procedures, then the telemarketeer would be liable for the Rule violation. The Rule further states that, without an agreement to do otherwise, the seller must maintain advertising and promotional materials, information about prize recipients, sales records, employee records and all verifiable authorizations for demand drafts for a period of two years from the date that the record is produced.

The FTC, the states and private citizens may bring civil lawsuits in federal district courts to enforce the Rule. Actions by the states may be brought by the attorney general or any officer authorized to bring actions on behalf of its residents. Private persons may bring action if they have suffered $50,000 or more in actual damages. In both cases, written notice must be provided to the FTC prior to filing a complaint or immediately upon instituting the action.

ETHICAL MARKETING GUIDELINES
By American Teleservices Association

The American Teleservices Association is one of the key bodies laying down guidelines for the telemarketing industry I the US. The ATA promotes and supports courteous, ethical and relevant telephone communication between consumers and businesses. We promote adherence and compliance with all state and federal laws pertaining to telephone and marketing communications to our membership. We also strongly promote training and processes for our member employees to ensure that telephone marketing is professional and consumer friendly.

The ATA develops, promotes and supports ethical marketing guidelines created by best practices developed within the industry that support professional, accurate and courteous communication.

The ATA encourages its members and member clients to use on-going quality and feedback programs that allow consumers to provide feedback to the business and industry relating to personal teleservice experiences.

General: ATA requires (1) that members adhere to state and federal laws, (2) adopt professional communication standards and practices that minimize potential annoyance associated with telephone marketing offers; (3) develop marketing processes and targeting to ensure the call has relevance; (4) develop and use procedures to control the timing and frequency of communication.

Target Marketing & Frequency

ATA supports a targeted marketing approach, recognizing that untargeted calling is not in the best interest of consumers, businesses or the telemarketing industry. Calls should always be targeted to people or companies likely to have a use for the particular product or service being offered. With the exception of legitimate market research requiring random sampling, the ATA does not condone random or sequential dialing without regard to the potential usefulness of the product or service offered to the call recipient.

ATA recognizes that consumer interest may change over time and therefore an offer that was not relevant may become so in the future. Consumers receive multiple targeted offers throughout a year and the ATA supports a time span between marketing promotions from the prior contact (excepting follow-up service, customer satisfaction and new account introduction calls).

Attempted Contact Frequency

For any given marketing, political or charitable calling program, consumer contact should be limited to avoid excessive contacts. The ATA supports limiting the number of maximum attempts to reach an individual regardless of who answers the phone. Placing a limit on attempting to reach a specific individual will minimize the frustration experienced by any other individual answering the phone who is not the targeted recipient of the call. This limit is supported for those calls that are answered by an individual and not by an electronic device.

In addition to the contact limit, if the individual answering the phone requests that the telemarketeer not call again or requests a specific time for a call back, such a request should be honored whether or not the individual is the targeted recipient of the call.

Consumer Requests and Feedback

Consumer requests should be explicitly honored by industry. For example :

- Customers declining an offer should not be called again during that marketing campaign or for the recommended 'rest period' between marketing campaigns. Members are encouraged to educate their telephone representatives to recognize early refusals and only continue if the customer needs additional information to understand the offer.
- Requests to be placed on company/client specific do not call lists should be handled expeditiously, and such requests should be recognized and honored and not requiring the consumer to use specific language to distinguish a do not call request from a refusal request.
- The request to be placed on company/client do not call requests should be consumer friendly and not require the consumer to place additional calls.

In accordance with the TCPA, consumers should be provided with a method to contact marketeers to ask questions or provide feedback. ATA strongly recommends that every contact be provided a toll free number to call that is answered during business hours by an industry professional who can respond to the consumer's needs. Members are encouraged to use timely and efficient multi marketing media that makes it convenient and easy for customers to ask questions, follow-up on orders and provide other feedback to the respective business

"Do Not Call" Compliance

ATA strongly advocates and promotes the value of company/client specific do not call lists. Federal law mandates that companies maintain internal, company/client specific do not call lists to honor requests from consumers to not receive future solicitation calls. All such requests from consumers should be honored. Companies must adhere to this mandate whether using internal or contracted telephone representatives. Policies and procedures must exist to ensure that all Do Not Call requests are honored. Training should be frequently conducted with all representatives regarding how to correctly respond to the consumer and handle any such requests.

ATA requires all members comply with federal and state laws, including those relating to state and federal do not call lists. Marketeers should adhere to the various frequency guidelines relating to downloading the updated state/federal lists of those consumers who have requested not to receive solicitation calls for those marketing programs and industries that are bound by such laws.

Business Relation & Prospect Inquiry Definition

ATA supports the business relationship exemption present in federal and most state do not call laws. The definition of business relationship should be legislated to ensure a standard interpretation. ATA supports a business relationship definition to be defined for customers with current and recent relationships with marketeers, as well as a definition for prospective customers who inquire about a company's product or service.

Call Flow Adherence

Outbound solicitation communication should be brief and engaging to allow consumers to state interest and engage in conversation if they choose. ATA supports laws that require marketeers to engage consumers by restricting the initial solicitation pitch to include an introduction, purpose of call and gaining of the consumer's interest to proceed. Delivering efficient communication is beneficial to both consumers and business and allows interested consumers to assess their interest in the offer being presented.

Consumers who express no interest in the offer or call should be respected. Marketeers should not continue the call once they have offered a response to a consumer's objection unless the customer asks additional questions or clearly states interest in the offer. Continuing dialogue with a consumer who expresses no interest is not in the best interest of consumers, businesses or the telemarketing industry.

Call Abandon Rules

Federal law requires that those calls abandoned/not

answered by a live operator have a recorded message delivered to the consumer stating the marketeer's name, reason for calling and phone number that is answered during business hours. ATA supports this law and practice. The message allows consumers to receive information regarding who has attempted to reach them and services that may be of value. Requiring this message eliminates 'phantom' calls. In addition, the ATA requires its members to comply with all federal legislation which requires that no more than 3% of all callers attempted on a given day for a campaign would receive an automated voice recording due to the unavailability of a live representative.

Calling Hour Restrictions

The ATA requires members to adhere to the federally mandated calling hours for marketing offers and promotes member companies to use those same calling hours for non-marketing calls. Any state laws further restricting calling hours or days must be honored by all ATA members.

What the ATA and these Ethical Guidelines are all about

The American Teleservices Association (ATA), a not-for-profit trade association founded in 1983 to represent and serve the telemarketing profession for all industries that use the telephone as a means to communicate with customers and prospective customers. It is committed to meeting the needs of its members, as well as protecting the rights of consumers and businesses who have telephone contact with its members.

Through professional programs and activities, the ATA attempts to educate its members, the public and public officials concerning the ethical behavior for both inbound and outbound telemarketing. We have also developed these Ethical Marketing Guidelines to help any business, consumer or legal entity objectively measure telemarketing program integrity and professional performance.

- The ATA supports the Federal Trade Commission (FTC) Telemarketing Sales Rule and the Federal Communications Commission (FCC) Telephone Consumer Protection Act.

- The ATA strongly encourages its members to review all federal, state and local laws for compliance before initiating any telephone solicitation campaign.
- The ATA advocates the highest standards of professionalism and ethical behavior for all telemarketing operations. These guidelines, when conscientiously adhered to and practiced call-by-call; help assure the long-term satisfaction of ATA members, their employees and customers while preserving the future of the call Centre industry.

This Ethical Guidelines are an educational tool developed under the premise that professional, reputable programs have specific goals, achieved through closely supervised high-quality performance, with the public interest—business and consumer—in mind. It is anticipated that these Ethical Marketing Guidelines will be an evolving set of principles that should grow over time as changes in the industry and changes in the various laws governing the industry come about.

As direct marketeers ("sellers") move forward with telephone solicitations, several do not call compliance issues must be considered pursuant to the FTC's Telemarketing Sales Rule (the "TSR") and the FCC's rules under the Telephone Consumer Protection Act (the "TCPA Rules"). Generally, in order to ensure compliance, it is imperative that sellers: (a) develop, implement and follow a written Do Not Call Policy; (b) train personnel and third party telemarketeers ("telemarketeers") in procedures established as part of the Do Not Call Policy; (c) scrub calling lists against the Registry, as well as any remaining state lists; (d) understand the parameters of the existing business relationship exemption for themselves and their affiliates; (e) ensure compliance with company-specific internal do not call obligations; (f) keep accurate, detailed records of compliance; and (g) appoint a specific person to be a "Chief Telemarketing Officer".

Develop a Written Do Not Call Policy

Both the TSR and TCPA Rules offer a "safe harbor" pursuant to which sellers and telemarketeers will not be liable for calling a number on the Registry, if: a call is the result of an error and the seller or telemarketeer can demonstrate that its routine business practices include: (a) establishment and implementation of a written policy for compliance procedures; (b) training in the compliance procedures for its personnel and any other entities assisting in compliance; (c) main-tanence of a company-specific list of telephone numbers that must not be called; (d) a process to prevent calling numbers on the Registry; and (e) the monitoring and enforcement of its written compliance policy on an on-going basis.

Creating a written Do Not Call Policy is the first step to establish compliance and without it, sellers and telemarketeers will never be able to meet the remaining prongs of the safe harbor. The written policy must explain the seller's or telemarketeer's procedures forcomplying with the Registry. The policy should, at a minimum, address the following:

- Subscribing to and paying for the use of the Registry.
- Downloading telephone numbers on a timely and quarterly basis from the FTC's website at https://telemarketing.donotcall.gov/.
- Procedures for accepting and recording company-specific do not call requests, and maintaining a company-specific do not call list ("Company Specific List").
- Time frame for responding to requests to be placed on the Company Specific List.
- Scrubbing calling lists against the Registry and the Company Specific List.
- Procedures for dealing with a person who claims his or her number is on the Registry or the Company Specific List.
- Procedures for dealing with an inadvertent call to a person whose number is on the Registry or the Company Specific List.
- Training personnel and, in the case of sellers, third party telemarketeers, to comply with the requirements of the Registry and the Company Specific List.

- Use of the Registry list and the Company Specific List is prohibited for any purpose other than to honor such do not call requests.
- Ensuring that compliance with the Registry and the Company Specific List is monitored.

Once the written Do Not Call Policy has been completed, it can be used as a road map for working out the specific technical details of how to comply. The written Do Not Call Policy should be used as general guide for all internal and external operations that are implicated in telemarketing activities.

Train Personnel and Vendors

Sellers and telemarketeers must periodically train their own personnel, and, in the case of sellers, any telemarketing vendors acting on their behalf, with respect to the practices and procedures that are necessary to comply with the policy and ideally, the laws that impact telemarketing activities.

Scrub Calling Lists

While the Do Not Call safe harbor is helpful, it cannot be relied upon as a substitute for scrubbing calling lists against the numbers on the Registry and on any Company Specific List.

Don't Forget About State Specific Lists

There are two important issues to be aware of with respect to state-specific lists. First, the states have been given approximately eighteen months to download any existing state do not call registries into the Registry. Even though most states have folded their state specific lists into the Registry, there are a few hold-out states, including Alaska, Georgia, Idaho, Indiana, Louisiana, Missouri, Texas, Wisconsin and Wyoming. Therefore, marketeers must still scrub against these state lists in addition to the Registry. In November 2003, the State of Texas demonstrated its strong enforcement posture with respect to its state do not call list when the Texas Attorney General brought lawsuits against fifteen telemarketeers that allegedly violated the "Texas No-Call" law.

Second, even in those states which have merged their lists into the Registry, state regulators retain their ability to enforce do not call violations made to state residents under state specific statutes. This leaves open the possibility of both state and federal regulatory action, as well as private causes of action, for violation of both state and federal do not call provisions.

Be Wary of Affiliates' Existing Business Relationships

Sellers can take advantage of an exemption to the do not call provisions of both the TSR and TCPA Rules, if there is an "existing business relationship" ("EBR") between the seller and the person being called. An EBR exists where a purchase or transaction has occurred within eighteen months, or where an inquiry or application regarding offered products or services has been made within three months, immediately preceding the solicitation and the relationship has not been terminated by either party.

Whether an affiliate or company otherwise related to the company with which the EBR exists can also take advantage of the EBR is a much more complicated issue. The test here is the reasonable expectation of the consumer. The FTC has indicated that "[a]n established business relationship is between a seller and a customer; it is not necessarily between one of the seller's subsidiaries or affiliates and that customer. The test for whether a subsidiary or affiliate can claim an established business relationship with a sister company's customer is: would the customer expect to receive a call from such an entity or would the customer believe such a call is inconsistent with having placed his or her number on the National Do Not Call Registry".

In considering whether or not a consumer would reasonably expect to be called by an affiliate, one must ask are the affiliate's goods or services similar to the seller's and is the affiliate's name identical or similar to the seller's? The greater the similarity between (1) the nature and type of goods sold by the seller and any subsidiary or affiliate and (2) the identity between the seller and any subsidiary or affiliate, the more likely it is that the call would fall within the EBR exemption.

Both the FCC and the FTC make specific use of the words "affiliate" and "subsidiary" under their respective rules, and these terms generally have established meaning under corporate law. An "affiliate" is generally understood to mean a company, incorporated or not, in which a certain percentage or greater interest is owned, directly or indirectly, by another company. A "subsidiary", is generally understood to mean a company that is owned by another company and such other company has the ability to control the subsidiary. Entities such as franchisees or independent car dealerships, both of which are independently owned entities, would not typically be considered "affiliates" or "subsidiaries" of a marketeer under these definitions. Accordingly, a strict interpretation of the EBR exemption would suggest that these and similar types of entities could not take advantage of the EBR exemption with their franchisor or motor vehicle manufacturer, respectively, despite the fact that the goods and services offered and the names of the entities are likely to be virtually identical.

Don't Forget About Company Specific Do Not Call Obligations

One of the most important factors to remember in complying with the do not call provisions of the TSR and TCPA Rules is the need to maintain a Company Specific List. As a practical matter, scrubbing a calling list against the Registry is not enough, since a consumer's request to be placed on a company specific do not call list trumps any exemptions under the Registry between the seller and the consumer. Once a calling list has been scrubbed against the Registry, it must also be scrubbed against any Company Specific List.

Keep Records

Even if a written Do Not Call Policy has been developed, and all of the other procedures and practices necessary to meet the Do Not Call safe harbor have been implemented and followed, such efforts will be wasted if compliance cannot be proven. In general, the TSR requires records to be kept for a period of twenty-four months, and under the TCPA Rules, the retention period, for records of those consumers who have requested not to be called, is five years. Therefore, a document retention policy relating to telemarketing records must be implemented and followed. Detailed and accurate records may be the only defense against claims of a Do Not Call violation.

Put Someone in Charge

All of the foregoing is meaningless if someone is not appointed to oversee and ensure compliance with the TSR, TCPA Rules and state telemarketing laws. A responsible person must be appointed to monitor and ensure compliance with the Do Not Call Policy and applicable laws—a "Chief Telemarketing Officer". This person must be familiar with the company's telemarketing practices and related laws and act as a central point of contact for coordination and compliance questions. Without designating such a person, adherence to regulations and policies may lapse and the risk of regulatory action is likely to rise.

Chapter 265 of the Acts of 2002
AN ACT REGULATING TELEMARKETING SOLICITATION

Be it enacted by the Senate and House of Representatives in General Court assembled, and by the authority of the same, as follows:

SECTION 1. The General Laws are hereby amended by inserting after chapter 159B the following chapter:

CHAPTER 159C
TELEMARKETING SOLICITATION

Section 1. As used in this chapter, the following words

shall, unless the context clearly requires otherwise, have the following meanings:—

"Caller identification service or device", a telephone service or device which permits a consumer to see the telephone number of incoming calls.

"Consumer", an individual who is a resident of the commonwealth and a prospective recipient of consumer goods or services.

"Consumer goods or services", an article or service that is purchased, leased, exchanged or received primarily for personal, family or household purposes including, but not limited to, stocks, bonds, mutual funds, annuities and other financial products.

"Doing business in the commonwealth", conducting telephonic sales calls: (i) from a location in the commonwealth or (ii) from a location outside of the commonwealth to consumers in the commonwealth.

"Existing customer", a residential telephone subscriber with whom the person or entity making a telephonic sales call has maintained an account or had a business relationship within the previous 24 months.

"Marketing or sales solicitation", the initiation of a telephone call or message to encourage the purchase or rental of, or investment in, property, goods or services, that is transmitted to a consumer, but not including a telephone call or message: (i) to a consumer with that consumer's prior express written or verbal invitation or permission; (ii) by a tax-exempt nonprofit organization; (iii) by an individual or organization for a noncommercial purpose, such as a poll or survey; or (iv) to a consumer in response to a visit made by such consumer to an establishment selling, leasing or exchanging consumer goods or services at a fixed location.

"Office", the office of consumer affairs and business regulation.

"Telephonic sales call", a call made by a telephone solicitor to a consumer for the purpose of: (i) engaging in a marketing or sales solicitation; (ii) soliciting an extension of credit for consumer goods or services; or (iii) obtaining information that will or may be used for marketing or sales solicitation or exchange of or extension of credit for consumer goods or services.

"Telephone solicitor", an individual, association, corporation, partnership, limited partnership, limited liability company or other business entity, or a subsidiary or affiliate thereof, doing business in the commonwealth who makes or causes to be made a telephonic sales call.

"Unsolicited telephonic sales call", a telephonic sales call other than a call made: (i) in response to an express written or verbal request of the consumer called; (ii) primarily in connection with an existing debt or contract, payment or performance of which has not been completed at the time of the call; (iii) to an existing customer unless such customer has stated to the telephone solicitor that such customer no longer wishes to receive the telephonic sales calls of such telephone solicitor; or (iv) in which the sale of goods and services is not completed, and payment or authorization of payment is not required, until after a face-to-face sales presentation by the telephone solicitor or a meeting between the telephone solicitor and customer.

Section 2. The office shall establish and maintain a no sales solicitation calls listing of consumers who do not wish to receive unsolicited telephonic sales calls. The office may contract with a private vendor to establish and maintain such listing, provided that: (i) the private vendor has maintained national no sales solicitation calls listings for more than 2 years; and (ii) the contract requires the vendor to provide the no sales solicitation calls listing in a printed hard copy format and in any other format offered at a cost that does not exceed the production cost of the format offered. The office shall provide notice to consumers of the establishment of a no sales solicitation calls listing. A consumer who wishes to be included on the listing shall notify the office by calling toll-free number provided by the office, or in such other manner and at such times as the office may prescribe, which may include electronic notification. A consumer on such listing shall be deleted from such listing upon the consumer's written request or in such other manner and at such times as the division may prescribe, which may include electronic notification. The office shall update such listing not less than quarterly and shall make such listing available to telephone solicitors and other persons for a fee as the office shall prescribe.

Section 3. A telephone solicitor shall not make or cause to be made an unsolicited telephonic sales call to a consumer: (i) if the consumer's name and telephone number appear on the then current quarterly no sales solicitation calls listing made available by the office under section 2; (ii) to be received between the hours of 8:00 p.m. and 8:00 a.m., local time, at the consumer's location; (iii) in the form of electronically transmitted facsimiles; or (iv) by use of a recorded message device.

Section 4. No telephone solicitor shall intentionally cause to be installed or shall intentionally use a blocking device or service to circumvent a consumer's use of a call identification service or device.

Section 5. (a) A person who obtains the name, residential address or telephone number of a consumer from published telephone directories or from any other source and republishes or compiles such information, electronically or otherwise, and sells or offers to sell such publication or compilation to telephone solicitors for marketing or sales solicitation purposes shall, in accordance with this chapter, exclude from any such publication or compilation and from any database used exclusively for marketing or sales solicitation purposes, the name, address and telephone number of a consumer whose name and telephone number appears in the then current quarterly no sales solicitation calls listing made available by the office under section 2.

(b) This section shall not apply to: (i) a telephone company, subject to the authority of the department of telecommunications and energy, for the sole purpose of compiling, publishing or distributing telephone directories or causing the compilation, publication or distribution of telephone directories or providing directory assistance; and

(ii) a person, for the sole purpose of compiling, publishing or distributing telephone directories for such telephone company pursuant to an agreement or other arrangement with such telephone company.

Section 5A. (a) A telephone solicitor shall disclose all of the following information within the first minute of a telephonic sales call and before requesting, accepting or arranging for payment by a consumer: (i) that the purpose of the telephone call is to make a sale or solicit funds; (ii) the correct name of the telemarketing company that employs the individual telemarketeer who is making the call; (iii) the correct name of the ultimate seller whose goods or services are being offered by means of the telemarketing call; and (iv) a complete and accurate description of the goods or services being offered including, but not limited to, the retail market value of the goods or services.

(b) The telemarketeer shall provide all of the following information before requesting, accepting or arranging for payment by a consumer: (i) the cost to the consumer of the goods or services that are the subject of the telemarketing sales call including, but not limited to, any applicable tax, shipping and handling fees; (ii) any restrictions, limitations or conditions attached to purchasing the goods or services; (iii) the complete terms of any applicable refund, return, cancellation, exchange or repurchase policies; (iv) any material aspect of an investment opportunity being offered including, but not limited to, the price of the land or other investment, the location of the investment and the fact that an investor may lose some or all of their original investment.

Section 6. The office shall promulgate regulations to carry out this chapter which shall: (i) require each local exchange company to inform consumers of the opportunity to provide notification to the office or its contractor that such consumer objects to receiving unsolicited telephonic sales calls; (ii) specify the methods by which each such consumer shall give notice to the office or its contractor of the consumer's objection to receiving such sales calls or revocation of such notice; provided, however, that there shall be no cost to the consumer for joining the listing; (iii) specify the length of time for which a notice of objection shall be effective and the effect of a change of telephone number on such notice; (iv) specify the methods by which such objections and revocations shall be collected and added to the no sales solicitations calls listing; (v) specify the methods by which a person or entity desiring to make telephonic sales calls may obtain access to the no sales solicitation calls listing as required to avoid calling the telephone numbers of consumer included in such listing; and (vi) specify such other matters relating to the listing that the office deems desirable.

Section 7. If the Federal Communications Commission establishes a single national database of telephone numbers of consumers who do not wish to receive unsolicited telephonic sales calls pursuant to 47 U.S.C. section 227(c)(3), the office shall include that part of such single national database that relates to the commonwealth in the listing established pursuant to this chapter.

Section 8. (a) The attorney general may initiate proceedings relating to a knowing violation or threatened knowing violation of this chapter. Such proceedings may include, without limitation, an injunction, a civil penalty of not more than $5,000 for each knowing violation, but not less than $1,500 for a knowing violation involving a consumer who is 65 years of age or older, and additional relief in a court of competent jurisdiction. The attorney general may also issue investigative demands and subpoenas, administer oaths and conduct hearings in the course of investigating a violation of this chapter.

(b) A person who has received more than 1 unsolicited telephonic sales call within a 12-month period by or on behalf of the same person or entity in violation of this chapter may: (i) bring an action to enjoin the violation; (2) bring an action to recover for actual monetary loss from such knowing violation or to receive not more than $5,000 in damages for such knowing violation, whichever is greater; or (iii) bring both such actions.

(c) In a civil proceeding resulting from a transaction

involving a violation of this chapter, the prevailing party, after judgment in the trial court and exhaustion of all appeals, if any, shall be awarded reasonable attorney's fees and costs from the nonprevailing party.

Section 9. It shall be a defense in any action or proceeding brought pursuant to this chapter that the defendant has established and implemented, with due care, reasonable practices and procedures to effectively prevent unsolicited telephonic sales calls in violation of this chapter.

Section 10. No action or proceeding shall be brought pursuant to this chapter: (i) more than 3 years after the person bringing the action knew or should have known of the occurrence of the alleged violation; or (ii) more than 3 years after the termination of a proceeding or action arising out of the same violation by the commonwealth, whichever is later.

Section 11. Information contained in the no sales solicitation listing established pursuant to this chapter shall be used only for the purposes of compliance with this chapter or in a proceeding or action under section 8. Such information shall not be subject to public inspection or disclosure.

Section 12. A court of the commonwealth may exercise personal jurisdiction over a nonresident or his executor or administrator as to an action or proceeding authorized by this chapter.

Section 13. The remedies, duties, prohibitions and penalties provided in this chapter shall not be exclusive and shall be in addition to all other causes of action, remedies and penalties provided by law, including any applicable remedies pursuant to chapter 93A.

Section 14. The office shall establish an advisory group comprised of government entities, local telecommunications companies, businesses, senior citizens and other community advocates to compile and promote a list of educational literature to help consumers understand their options with regard to telephonic sales calls. The office shall work with local telecommunications companies to disseminate to their residential subscribers information about the availability of and instructions on how to request educational literature from the office. The office shall include on its internet website information that informs consumers of their rights to be placed on the no sales solicitation calls listing and the various methods, including notice to the office, of placing their names on the no sales solicitation calls listing.

SECTION 2. This act shall take effect on January 1, 2003.

Approved August 10, 2002.

Glossary

A

Abandonment. As in the phrase "call abandonment". This refers to people who, being placed on hold in an incoming call, elect to hang up ("abandon") the call. Call Centres monitor closely the "abandonment rate" as a measure of their inefficiency.

ACD. Automatic Call Distributor. A complex machine used in modern call Centres for incoming calls. It routes calls to available agents, holds overflow calls, gives and takes messages, provides reports. A must for modern database marketing.

Acquisition Cost. The cost of signing up a new customer. Lifetime Value is often used to compute the maximum allowable acquisition cost.

Ad Clicks. When a visitor uses an advertisement link to go to another web site.

Ad Copy. The text used for an advertising campaign.

Ad Inventory. The number of ads a website or publication can sell in a given period.

Ad Views. When a visitor pulls an advertisement's image from the server, it is assumed they saw it and have the opportunity to visit the advertiser's website by clicking on the link. One person looking at one ad.

Ad-hoc Report. A reporting method which permits you to ask questions like: How may women over 60 have bought more than $200 from us in the last 4 months?

Address. A computer term for the location on a disk or in memory of a piece of information. Addresses help the computer to find things rapidly, and to store them for later retrieval.

Affiliate Program. An advertising program offering a monetary incentive for webmasters to drive traffic to the advertiser's web site. This eliminates the necessity for the advertiser to find web sites with related content to list their banners. It also increases the response rate by giving the "affiliate" web sites a stake in the response rate. Affiliate programs are a great plan for the websites offering them, but the web sites that participate often become underpaid sales representatives.

Affinity. People who are similar in lifestyle.

Affinity Analysis. A process of finding relationships between customer purchases. People who buy skis buy snow tires.

Affinity Matrix. A cross tab showing cross buying patterns by customers who did or did not buy products A, B, C and D.

Affluents. Households with 30% or more than the cost of living plus taxes.

Agent. The word for a telephone operator in a modern inbound call Centre in a company that takes a lot of customer service and sales calls.

Analog. Regular telephone service comes over analog lines. Modern improved service (often used for data lines) comes over DIGITAL lines in which all the sounds are converted to 1's and 0's. For database marketing computer communications, digital is better.

Auto attendant. A computer system or program that is capable of independently responding to customer's needs and questions without human intervention. Auto attendants (see also Interactive Voice Response Systems/IVR's and Voice Response Units/VRU's), can be integrated with ACD's, other call handling systems and databases. Today's more sophisticated menus allow callers to interact using speaker independent speech recognition technology along with traditional touch-tone options.

Auto Available. An ACD feature whereby the ACD is programmed to automatically put agents into Available after they finish Talk Time and disconnect calls. If they need to go into After-Call Work, they have to manually put themselves there. See Auto Wrap-up.

Abandoned Calls. In outbound teleservices, a call initiated by a predictive dialer that is disconnected when no agent is available. In inbound teleservices, abandoned calls are ones that are terminated by the caller before a representative answers.

Activity Codes. See Wrap-Up Codes.

Automatic Call Distributor. An Automatic Call Distributor (ACD) is a call Centre systems resource that processes, distributes, tracks and reports incoming call activity. Depending on systems features and defined business rules, ACD systems can perform a wide variety of tasks in the contact Centre including queuing of calls, routing of calls, tracking and reporting of call statistics and other key management functions.

Automatic Call Distributor (ACD). The specialized telephone system used in incoming call Centres. It is a programmable device that automatically answers calls, queues calls, distributes calls to agents, plays delay announcements to callers and provides real-time and historical reports on these activities. May be a stand-alone system, or ACD capability built into a CO, network or PBX.

Automatic Call Sequencer (ACS). A simple system that

is less sophisticated than an ACD, but provides some ACD-like functionality.

Average Delay of Delayed Calls. The average delay of calls that are delayed. It is the total Delay for all calls divided by the number of calls that had to wait in queue. See Average Speed of Answer.

Adherence To Schedule. A general term that refers to how well agents adhere to their schedules. Can include both (a) how much time they were available to take calls during their shifts, including the time spent handling calls and the time spent waiting for calls to arrive (also called Availability), and (b) when they were available to take calls (also called Compliance or Adherence). See Real-Time Adherence Software and Occupancy.

After-Call Work (ACW). Also called Wrap-up and Post Call Processing (PCP). Work that is necessitated by and immediately follows an inbound transaction. Often includes entering data, filling out forms and making outbound calls necessary to complete the transaction. The agent is unavailable to receive another inbound call while in this mode.

Agent. The person who handles incoming or outgoing calls. Also referred to as customer service representative (CSR), telephone sales or service representative (TSR), rep, associate, consultant, engineer, operator, technician, account executive, team member, customer service professional, staff member, attendant and specialist. Did we miss any?

Agents. See Average Number of Agents.

Agent Group. Also called Split, Gate, Queue or Skills Group. A collection of agents that share a common set of skills, such as being able to handle customer complaints.

Agent Out Call. An outbound call placed by an agent.

Agent Status. The mode an agent is in (Talk Time, After-Call Work, Unavailable, etc.).

All Trunks Busy (ATB). When all trunks are busy in a specified trunk group. Generally, reports indicate how many times all trunks were busy, and how much total time all trunks were busy. What they don't reveal is how many callers got busy signals when all trunks were busy.

Analog. Telephone transmission or switching that is not digital. Signals are analogous to the original signal.

Announcement. A recorded verbal message played to callers.

Automatic Number Identification (ANI). A telephone network feature that passes the number of the phone the caller is using to the call Centre, real-time. ANI may arrive over the D channel of an ISDN PRI circuit (out of band signalling), or before the first ring on a single line (inband signalling). ANI is delivered from long distance companies. Caller ID is the local phone company version of ANI, and is delivered inband. ANI is a North American term and Calling Line Identification (CLI) is an alternative term used elsewhere.

Auxiliary Work State. An agent work state that is typically not associated with handling telephone calls. When agents are in an auxiliary mode, they will not receive inbound calls.

Availability. See Adherence to Schedule.

Available State. Agents who are signed on to the ACD and waiting for calls to arrive.

Available Time. The total time that an agent or agent group waited for calls to arrive, for a given time period.

Average Handle Time (AHT). The sum of Average Talk Time and Average After-Call Work for a specified time period.

Average Holding Time on Trunks (AHT). The average time inbound transactions occupy the trunks. It is: (Talk

Time + Delay Time)/Calls Received. AHT is also an acronym for Average Handling Time, which has a different meaning.

Average Number of Agents. The average number of agents logged into a group for a specified time period.

Average Speed of Answer (ASA). Also called Average Delay. The average delay of all calls. It is total Delay divided by total number of calls. See Average Delay of Delayed Calls.

Average Time to Abandonment. The average time that callers wait in queue before abandoning. The calculation considers only the calls that abandon.

Answer Supervision. The signal sent by the ACD or other device to the local or long distance carrier to accept a call. That's when billing for either the caller or the call Centre will begin, if long distance charges apply.

Answered Call. When referring to an agent group, a call counted as answered when it reaches an agent.

Application Service Provider (ASP). Also known as "apps-on-tap", an ASP is a company that offers access to software and/or network applications, typically via an Internet connection. ASP services provide an attractive option to companies wishing to minimize up front costs and reduce internal support requirements.

Application Based Routing and Reporting. The ACD capability to route and track transactions by type of call, or application (*e.g.*, sales, service, etc.), versus the traditional method of routing and tracking by trunk group and agent group.

Architecture. The basic design of a system. Determines how the components work together, system capacity, upgradeability and the ability to integrate with other systems.

Audiotex. A voice processing capability that enables callers to automatically access pre-recorded announcements. See Voice Processing.

Auto Greeting. Agent's pre-recorded greeting that plays automatically when a call arrives.

Auto Wrap-up. An ACD feature whereby the ACD is programmed to automatically put agents into After-Call Work after they finish Talk Time and disconnect calls. When they have completed any After-Call Work required, they put themselves back into Available. See Auto Available.

Automated dialer. A computer program or machine responsible for making phone calls for a telephone representative by using a list of phone numbers previously provided by a list broker.

Automatic Number Identification (ANI). The telephone network feature that allows the transmission of the ten-digit area code and telephone number of the originating telephone to the receiving telephone line. Telephone lines and handsets subscribing to "Caller I.D." are able to view the ANI of the calling party.

B

Base Staff. Also called Seated Agents. The minimum number of agents required to achieve service level and response time objectives for given period of time. Seated agent calculations assume that agents will be ñin their seatsî for the entire period of time. Therefore, schedules need to add in extra people to accommodate breaks, absenteeism and other factors that will keep agents from the phones. See Rostered Staff Factor.

Basic Rate Interface (BRI). One of two basic levels of ISDN service. A BRI line provides two bearer channels for voice and data and one channel for signalling (commonly expressed as 2B+D). See Primary Rate Interface (PRI) and Integrated Services Digital Network.

Beep Tone. An audible notification that a call has arrived (also called Zip Tone). Beep tone can also refer to the audible notification that a call is being monitored.

Benchmark. Historically, a term referred to as a standardized task to test the capabilities of devices against each other. In quality terms, benchmarking is comparing products, services and processes with those of other organizations, to identify new ideas and improvement opportunities.

Benchmarking. A benchmark is a standard that provides a measuring-stick for relative performance. Benchmarking is critical to formulating a knowledge-based plan of action to achieve objectives.

Best in Class. A benchmarking term to identify organizations that outperform all others in a specified category.

Blockage. Callers blocked from entering a queue. See Blocked Call.

Blocked Call. A call that cannot be connected immediately because (A) no circuit is available at the time the call arrives, or (B) the ACD is programmed to block calls from entering the queue when the queue backs up beyond a defined threshold.

Busy Hour. A telephone traffic engineering term, referring to the hour of time in which a trunk group carries the most traffic during the day. The average busy hour reflects the average over a period of days, such as two weeks. Busy Hour has little use for incoming call Centres, which require more specific resource calculation methodologies.

Blended Centre. A call Centre that conducts programs that process both inbound and outbound call activity at the same agent station/desktop.

Bonding requirements. Some states have enacted laws requiring that telemarketing firms post surety bonds in order to do business within the state boundaries. The bond provides the state with assets that can be claimed in the event of fraud.

C

Contact Centre/call Centre. A facility designed to support customers using the telephone as well as other contact channels. A contact Centre may receive inbound calls, make outbound calls, receive or send email, white mail, fax or support chat, VoIP or other communication mediums employed by customers or prospects.

Call. Also called Transaction and Customer Contact. A term referring to telephone calls, video calls, Web calls and other types of contacts.

Call Blending. Combining traditionally separate inbound and outbound agent groups into one group of agents responsible for handling both inbound and outbound contacts. A system that is capable of call blending automatically puts agents who are making outbound calls into the inbound mode and *vice versa*, as necessitated by the incoming call load.

Call By Call Routing. The process of routing each call to the optimum destination according to real-time conditions. See Percent Allocation and Network Interflow.

Call Centre. An umbrella term that generally refers to reservations Centres, help desks, information lines or customer service Centres, regardless of how they are organized or what types of transactions they handle. The term is being challenged by many, because calls are just one type of transaction and the word Centre doesn't accurately depict the many multi-site environments.

Call Control Variables. The set of criteria the ACD uses to process calls. Examples include routing criteria, overflow parameters, recorded announcements and timing thresholds.

Call Detail Recording. Data on each call, captured and stored by the ACD. Can include trunk used, time in queue, call duration, agent who handled the call, number dialed (for outgoing) and other information.

Call Forcing. An ACD feature that automatically delivers calls to agents who are available and ready to take calls. They hear a notification that the call has arrived (*e.g.* a beep tone), but do not have to press a button to answer the call.

Call Load. Also referred to as Work Load. Call Load is the product of (Average Talk Time + Average After-Call Work) × call volume, for a given period.

Caller ID. An electronic, telephone related device that allows individuals to identify callers before answering the telephone. When a telephone rings, an electronic display registers the caller's name and phone number. Individuals often use caller *id* to screen their calls.

Caller. Entered Digits (CED). Digits callers enter using their telephone keypads. The ACD, VRU, or network can prompt for CEDs.

Calling Line Identity (CLI). See Automatic Number Identification.

Calls In Queue. A real-time report that refers to the number of calls received by the ACD system but not yet connected to an agent.

Carrier. A company that provides telecommunications circuits. Carriers include both local telephone companies and long distance providers.

Cause-and-Effect Diagram. A tool to assist in root cause identification, developed by Dr. Kaoru Ishikawa.

CD-ROM. Compact Disc Read Only Memory. These discs hold as much as 660 megabytes of memory.

Central Office (CO). Can refer to either a telephone company switching Centre or the type of telephone switch used in a telephone company switching Centre. The local central office receives calls from within the local area and either routes them locally or passes them to an inter-exchange carrier (IXC). On the receiving end, the local central office receives calls that originated in other areas, from the IXC.

Centum Call Seconds (CCS). 100 call seconds, a unit of telephone traffic measurement. The first C is the Roman numeral for 100. 1 hour = 1 Erlang = 60 minutes = 36 CCS.

Chief Information Officer (CIO). A typical title for the highest ranking executive responsible for an organization's information systems.

Circuit. A transmission path between two points in a network.

Client/Server Architecture. A network of computers that share capabilities and devices.

Collateral Duties. Non-phone tasks (*e.g.*, data entry) that are flexible, and can be scheduled for periods when call load is slow.

Common Causes. Causes of variation that are inherent to a process over time. They cause the rhythmic, common variations in the system of causes, and they affect every outcome of the process and everyone working in the process. See Special Causes.

Compliance. See Adherence to Schedule.

Computer Simulation. A computer technique to predict the outcome of various events in the future, given many variables. When there are many variables, simulation is often the only way to reasonably predict the outcome.

Computer Telephony Integration (CTI). The software, hardware and programming necessary to integrate computers and telephones so they can work together seamlessly and intelligently. In General it is the software, interfaces, and processes used to integrate telephone and computer networks in order to provide a more efficient and seamless customer interaction and reporting mechanism.

Conditional Routing. The capability of the ACD to route calls based on current conditions. It is based on "if-then" programming statements. For example, "if the number of calls in agent group 1 exceeds 10 and there are at least 2 available agents in group two, then route the calls to group two".

Continuous Improvement. The ongoing improvement of processes.

Control Chart. A control chart sifts out (identifies) two types of variation in a process, common causes and special causes. See Common Causes and Special Causes.

Controlled Busies. The capability of the ACD to generate busy signals when the queue backs up beyond a programmable threshold.

Cost Centre. An accounting term that refers to a department or function in the organization that does not generate profit. See Profit Centre.

Cost of Delay. The money you pay to queue callers, assuming you have toll-free service.

Cost Per Call. Total costs (fixed and variable) divided by total calls for a given period of time.

Customer Contact. See Call.

Close. A statement that ends the sales-pitch and asks the customer to purchase the product

Closed sale rate. The number of sales finalized as a result of telemarketing efforts. A telemarketing company may report the rate on an individual or company level.

Closed-ended question. A closed-ended question is a question which allows only a yes, no, or another either/or option provided by the questioner.

Coaching. In teleservices, coaching is the process of providing instruction, direction, feedback and support to agents in order to improve performance and results.

Common carrier. A telephone service provider.

Company-specific do not call lists. Company-specific do not call lists contain the names of people who have asked not to be contacted by telephone by specific companies. Under the Telephone Consumer Protection Act of 1991, most companies doing business over the phone are required to keep such lists and honor the customer's request.

Confirmation. The confirmation is the point in a sales presentation when the representative completes the sale and confirms the payment type, length of the commitment, and the address of the customer.

Contact Conversion Rate. The ratio of successful calls (whether a completed sale, survey, or follow up call) to the total number of contacts expressed as a percentage. See also: List Conversion Rate.

CSR. Customer Service Representatives (CSR) answer consumer questions and resolve customer problems.

Customer Relationship Management (CRM). The strategies, processes, people and technologies used by companies to successfully attract and retain customers for maximum corporate growth and profit. CRM initiatives are designed with the goal of meeting customer expectations and needs in order to achieve maximum customer lifetime value and return to the enterprise. As a primary sales, service and retention touch point for many companies, the Contact Centre is a critical component of a successful CRM strategy.

D

Database Call Handling. A CTI application, whereby the ACD works in sync with the database computer to process calls, based on information in the database. For example, a caller inputs digits into a voice processing system, the database retrieves information on that customer and then issues instructions to the ACD on how to handle the call (*e.g.*, where to route the call, what priority the call should be given in queue, the announcements to play, etc.).

Data mining. Data mining entails analyzing information for previously undiscovered correlations between two markets. Data mining connections can be made through associations (baseball fans also watch football), sequences (buying wood and then buying paint), forecasting (based on patterns found) and clustering (grouping information in a new way).

Day of Week Routing. A network service that routes calls to alternate locations, based on the day of week. There are also options for day of year and time of day routing.

Delay Announcements. Recorded announcements that encourage callers to wait for an agent to become available, remind them to have their account number ready, and provide information on access alternatives. In some systems, delay announcements are provided through recorded announcement routes (RANs).

Delay. Also called Queue Time. The time a caller spends in queue, waiting for an agent to become available. Average Delay is the same thing as Average Speed of Answer. Also see Average Delay of Delayed Calls.

Delayed Call. A call which cannot be answered immediately and is placed in queue.

Dialed Number (DN). The number that the caller dialed to initiate the call.

Dialed Number Identification Service (DNIS). A string of digits that the telephone network passes to the ACD, VRU or other devise, to indicate which number the caller dialed. The ACD can then process and report on that type of call according to user-defined criteria. One trunk group can have many DNIS numbers.

Digital. The use of a binary code Ü 1s and 0s Ü to represent information.

Direct Call Processing. See Talk Time.

Dual-Tone Multifrequency (DTMF). A signalling system that sends pairs of audio frequencies to represent digits on a telephone keypad. It is often used interchangeably with the term Touchtone (an AT&T trademark).

Dynamic Answer. An ACD feature that automatically reconfigures the number of rings before the system answers calls, based on real-time queue information. Since costs don't begin until the ACD answers calls, this feature can save callers or the call Centre money when long distance charges apply. Electronic Mail (E-mail). Electronic text mail.

E

Email management services/software. A company or software that helps its clients sort, manage and respond to email communications.

Envelope Strategy. A strategy whereby enough agents are scheduled for the day or week to handle both the inbound call load and other types of work. Priorities are based on the inbound call load. When call load is heavy, all agents handle calls, but when it is light, some agents are reassigned to work that is not as time-sensitive.

Erlang B. A formula developed by A.K. Erlang, widely used to determine the number of trunks required to handle a known calling load during a one hour period. The formula assumes that if callers get busy signals, they go away forever, never to retry (ñlost calls clearedî). Since some callers retry, Erlang B can underestimate trunks required. However, Erlang B is generally accurate in situations with few busy signals.

Erlang C. Calculates predicted waiting times (delay) based on three things: the number of servers (reps); the number of people waiting to be served (callers); and the average amount of time it takes to serve each person. It can also predict the resources required to keep waiting times within targeted limits. Erlang C assumes no lost calls or busy signals, so it has a tendency to overestimate staff required.

Erlang, A.K. A Danish engineer who worked for the Copenhagen Telephone Company in the early 1900s and developed Erlang B, Erlang C and other telephone traffic engineering formulas.

Erlang. One hour of telephone traffic in an hour of time. For example, if circuits carry 120 minutes of traffic in an hour, that's two Erlangs.

Error Rate. Either the number of defective transactions or the number of defective steps in a transaction.

Escalation Plan. A plan that specifies actions to be taken when the queue begins to build beyond acceptable levels.

Exchange Line. See Trunk.

Executive Summary. A brief summary of the key points of a more detailed report or study.

F

Facsimile (FAX). Technology that scans a document, encodes it, transmits it over a telecommunications circuit, and reproduces it in original form at the receiving end.

Fast Clear Down. A caller who hangs up immediately when they hear a delay announcement.

Fax on Demand. A system that enables callers to request documents, using their telephone keypads. The selected documents are delivered to the fax numbers they specify.

Flowchart. A step by step diagram of a process.

Flushing Out the Queue. Changing system thresholds so that calls waiting for an agent group are redirected to another group with a shorter queue or available agents.

Full-Time Equivalent (FTE). A term used in scheduling and budgeting, whereby the number of scheduled hours is divided by the hours in a full work week. The hours of several part time agents may add up to one FTE.

Fulfillment services. A company that provides facilities, systems and personnel to process mail, package products, or perform other customer requests for a marketeer. Fulfillment services companies may be stand-alone providers or may provide integrated services including call Centre, database, list or other marketing support services.

G

Gate. See Agent Group.

Gateway. A server dedicated to providing access to a network.

Grade of Service. The probability that a call will not be connected to a system because all trunks are busy. Grade of service is often expressed as "p.01" meaning 1% of calls will be "blocked". Sometimes, grade of service is used interchangeably with service level, but the two terms have different meanings. See Service Level.

H

Handled Calls. The number of calls received and handled by agents or peripheral equipment. Handled calls does not include calls that abandon or receive busy signals.

Handling Time. The time an agent spends in Talk Time and After-Call Work, handling a transaction. Handling Time can also refer to the time it takes for a machine to process a transaction.

Handsets. Handsets are traditionally thought of as the telephone receivers one holds in their hand. While still hand-held, new models may possess full Internet access and video display, as well as traditional functions.

Headsets. Hardware for hands-free telephone use consisting of a set of earphones and a microphone suspended from one of the earpieces so that the microphone sits in front of the mouth. It serves the same purpose as a telephone receiver.

Help Desk. A term that generally refers to a call Centre set up to handle queries about product installation, usage or problems. The term is most often used in the context of computer software and hardware support Centres.

Historical Reports. Reports that track call Centre and agent performance over a period of time. Historical reports are generated by ACDs, third party ACD software packages, and peripherals such as VRUs and Call Detail Recording Systems. The amount of history that a system can store varies by system.

Holding Time. See Average Holding Time on Trunks.

Home Agent. See Telecommuting.

I

Imaging. A process whereby documents are scanned into a system and stored electronically.

Immutable Law. A law of nature that is fundamental, and not changeable (*e.g.*, the law of gravity). In an inbound call Centre, the fact that occupancy goes up when service level goes down, is an immutable law.

Inbound Centre. A contact Centre that receives and processes inbound transactions. Inbound Centres may handle traditional telephone activity as well as email, chat, white mail and other functions for sales, service, retention, research, data collection or other applications.

Incoming Call Centre Management. The art of having the right number of skilled people and supporting resources in place at the right times to handle an accurately forecasted workload, at service level and with quality.

Incremental Revenue (Value) Analysis. A methodology that estimates the value (cost and revenue) of adding or subtracting an agent.

Index Factor. In forecasting, a proportion used as a multiplier to adjust another number.

Integrated Services Digital Network (ISDN). A set of international standards for telephone transmission. ISDN provides an end-to-end digital network, out-of-band signalling, and greater bandwidth than older telephone services. The two standard levels of ISDN are Basic Rate Interface (BRI) and Primary Rate Interface (PRI). See Basic Rate Interface and Primary Rate Interface.

Interactive Voice Response (IVR). A software application, enables users enter data on a telephone keypad or input information by voice. The software can then process the input and route the caller to the appropriate extension. IVR can be used for specific information lookup, call forwarding, polls and simple order entry transactions.

Internet Service Provider (ISP). A company that provides other companies with the equipment and information they need to access the Web. ISPs may host websites and/or supply the necessary telecommunication lines.

Internet telephony. Internet telephony is the use of the Internet in place of the traditional telephone company infrastructure and rate structure to exchange telephone information.

Interactive Voice Response (IVR). See Voice Response Unit.

Interflow. See overflow.

Internal Help Desk. A group that supports other internal agent groups, *e.g.* for complex or escalated calls.

Internal Response Time. The time it takes an agent group that supports other internal groups (*e.g.*, for complex or escalated tasks) to respond to transactions that do not have to be handled when they arrive (*e.g.*, correspondence or e-mail). See Response Time and Service Level.

Internet "Call Me" Transaction. A transaction that allows a user to request a callback from the call Centre, while exploring a Web page. Requires interconnection of the ACD system and the Internet by means of an Internet Gateway.

Internet "Call Through" Transaction. The ability for callers to click a button on a Web site and be directly connected to an agent while viewing the site. Standards and technologies that provide this capability are in development.

Internet Phone. Technology that enables users of the Internet's World Wide Web to place voice telephone calls through the Internet, thus by-passing the long distance network.

Intraflow. See overflow.

Invisible Queue. When callers do not know how long the queue is or how fast it is moving. See Visible Queue.

IXC. Inter-exchange carriers (IXC) are telephone companies that provide connections from local exchanges in one geographic region to local exchanges in different areas.

J

Judgmental Forecasting. Goes beyond purely statistical techniques and encompasses what people believe is going to happen. It is in the realm of intuition, interdepartmental committees, market research and executive opinion.

L

LAN/WAN. A Local Area Network (LAN) is a group of computers and related devices that are connected to each other so that information can be easily accessed on all computers. Computers in a LAN generally share a single processor or server and are found in smaller, localized areas (such as one floor of an office building). A Wide Area Network (WAN) is very similar to a LAN except that it is dispersed over a much larger geographical area. Because it is spread over a larger area, it requires telecommunication technology to make the connection possible.

Law of Diminishing Returns. The declining marginal improvements in service level that can be attributed to each additional agent, as successive agents are added.

Lead generation. In either inbound or outbound teleservices, the process of gathering information from a prospect or customer in order to qualify and score the opportunity for future follow-up. Subsequent follow-ups may be conducted via face-to-face, telephone, e-mail, mail or other method.

List brokers. List brokers are companies and individuals that research and provide for the sale and/or rental of marketing lists.

List Conversion Rate. The ratio of total successful calls to the total number of records in a given list. See also: Contact Conversion Rate.

List managers. List managers are companies and individuals who compile, update, manage and rent information including names, addresses, phone numbers and other data for use by direct marketeers, teleservices marketeers and others wishing to prospect to those names or update databases. Lists are typically segmented by business and consumer listings and compiled through a variety of sources. Vertical lists are those compiled from a specific industry or source where the source is disclosed. Compiled lists are those assembled from a variety of sources (often public information) where the specific source is not known.

Telephone data append and other services are provided by list management companies and telephone data providers.

List seeding. List seeding is a way of checking delivery and detecting unauthorized list usage by adding false names to the mailing or calling list.

Live-chat. A method of responding to customer's questions and needs in-real time through the use of recent internet "chat" technology. Customer service representatives respond directly to customers through the use of online computer chat software.

Load Balancing. Balancing traffic between two or more destinations.

Local Exchange Carrier (LEC), ILEC and CLEC. A LEC is simply a telephone company that provides service to a local calling area. An ILEC (incumbent local exchange carrier) is a telephone company that provided local service prior to the Telecommunications Act of 1996. Competitive Local Exchange Carriers (CLECs) have come into existence since the Telecommunications Act of 1996. CLECs attempt to compete with pre-existing LECs by using their own switches and networks.

Long distance reseller. A company that purchases blocks of long-distance telephone service in bulk at a reduced price and then sells the long-distance to consumers at a rate below that which they would normally pay.

Logged On. A state in which agents have signed on to a system (made their presence known), but may or may not be ready to receive calls.

Long Call. For staffing calculations and traffic engineering purposes, calls that approach or exceed thirty minutes.

Longest Available Agent. A method of distributing calls to the agent who has been sitting idle the longest. With a queue, Longest Available Agent becomes ñNext Available Agent.î

Longest Delay (Oldest Call). The longest time a caller has waited in queue, before abandoning or reaching an agent.

Look Ahead Queuing. The ability for a system or network to examine a secondary queue and evaluate the conditions, before overflowing calls from the primary queue.

Look Back Queuing. The ability for a system or network to look back to the primary queue after the call has been overflowed to a secondary queue, and evaluate the conditions. If the congestion clears, the call can be sent back to the initial queue.

Lost Call. See Abandoned Call.

M

Monitoring. Monitoring is a quality function used within contact Centres to assure quality communications, coach and counsel telephone agents and identify opportunities for operating and marketing improvements. The process of listening to agents' telephone calls for the purpose of maintaining quality. Monitoring can be: (A) silent, where agents don't know when they are being monitored, (B) side by side, where the person monitoring sits next to the agent and observes calls or (C) record and review, where calls are recorded and then later played back and assessed.

Middleware. Software that mediates between different types of hardware and software on a network, so that they can function together.

Modem. A contraction of the terms Modulator/Demodulator. A Modem converts analog signals to digital and *vice versa.*

Multilingual Agents. Agents that are fluent in more than one language.

Multimedia. Combining multiple forms of media in the

communication of information. (*e.g*, a traditional phone call is "monomedia" and a video call is "multimedia").

Murphy's Law. If anything can go wrong, it will. Not a good perspective to live by, but worth considering when designing agent groups, routing configurations and disaster recovery plans.

Multilingual teleservices. Multilingual teleservices describe a teleservices company that offers services in various languages. Such services enable companies to serve a broader market or target a specific ethnic group that might otherwise be beyond reach.

N

Network Control Centre. Also called Traffic Control Centre. In a networked call Centre environment, where people and equipment monitor real-time conditions across sites, change routing thresholds as necessary, and coordinate events that will impact base staffing levels.

Network Inter-flow. A technology used in multi-site call Centre environments to create a more efficient distribution of calls between sites. Through integration of sites using network circuits (such as T1 circuits) and ACD software, calls routed to one site may be queued simultaneously for agent groups in remote sites. See Call by Call Routing and Percent Allocation.

Next Available Agent. A call distribution method that sends calls to the next agent who becomes available. The method seeks to maintain an equal load across skill groups or services. When there is no queue, Next Available Agent reverts to Longest Available Agent.

Noise Cancelling Headset. Headsets equipped with technology that reduces background noise.

Non ACD In Calls. Inbound calls which are directed to an agent's extension, rather than to a general group. These may be personal calls or calls from customers who dial the agents' extension numbers

No rebuttal laws. If a consumer states that they are not interested in the product or service as offered, the seller must discontinue the call in Arkansas, Idaho, Illinois, Kansas, Kentucky, Mississippi, Oregon, Pennsylvania, South Carolina, South Dakota, Utah and Washington without further sales attempts (as of 10/2001).

O

Occupancy. Also referred to as agent utilization. The percentage of time agents handle calls versus wait for calls to arrive. For a half-hour, the calculation is: (call volume × average handling time in seconds) / (number of agents × 1800 seconds). See Adherence to Schedule.

Off The Shelf. Hardware or software programs that are commercially available and ready for use "as is".

Offered Calls. All of the attempts callers make to reach the call Centre. There are three possibilities for offered calls: (1) they can get busy signals, (2) they can be answered by the system, but hang up before reaching a rep, (3) they can be answered by a rep. Offered call reports in ACDs usually refer only to the calls that the system receives.

Off-Peak. Periods of time other than the call Centre's busiest periods. Also a term to describe periods of time when long distance carriers provide lower rates.

Off shore call Centres. A call Centre that uses personnel and/or a location found outside of the United States.

Open Ticket. A customer contact (transaction) that has not yet been completed or resolved (closed).

On hold service. Music and announcements provided for the enjoyment and/or information of customers who are waiting to be attended to by the next available telephone representative. "On hold service" can be purchased by a company wishing to provide that service to its customers.

Open-ended question. An open-ended question allows for more than just a one or two word response.

Outsourcing. Contracting some or all call Centre services to an outside company.

Overflow. Calls that flow from one group or site to another. More specifically, Intraflow happens when calls flow between agent groups and Interflow is when calls flow out of the ACD to another site.

Overlay. See Rostered Staff Factor.

Outbound Centre. An outbound Centre conducts outgoing telephone calls and may be engaged in a variety of functions including sales, research, fundraising, appointment setting, collections or informational messaging.

P

PBX/ IP-PBX. A Private Branch Exchange (PBX) is an internal telephone system within a company that switches calls between internal lines while allowing all users to share a certain number of external phone lines. The primary role of the PBX is to save the cost of requiring a separate telephone line for each user.

Permission to continue laws. This law states that a sales representative may only continue a sales presentation if the prospect gives permission, or otherwise shows strong interest in what is being sold. Illinois, Kentucky, North Carolina, Oregon and South Dakota are currently the only states with permission to continue laws (as of 10/2001).

Predictive dialer. A predictive dialer is an outbound call processing system designed to maintain a high level of utilization and cost efficiency in the contact Centre. The dialer automatically calls a list of telephone numbers, screens the unnecessary calls such as answering machines and busy signals and then connects a waiting representative with the customer.

Q

Qualifiers. Qualifiers are questions used in a sales presentation, which are designed to capture information from a prospect to assist the sales agent in presenting appropriate information and closing a sale.

Quality assurance/ control representative. In the teleservice industry, an individual engaged in the process of listening, scoring and reporting on call interactions. The quality process is designed to assure that the manner in which calls are conducted is in compliance with the established guidelines of the program and other established legal and ethical requirements.

R

Registration requirements. States have a variety of laws, which may require telemarketing companies to formally register with the state before conducting business in that state. Different states maintain different regulations and requirements with some requiring the posting of a bond and/or paying a registration fee.

Remote agents. A remote agent is someone who works outside of the actual office or call Centre while maintaining real time telephone and computer access to information required to process contacts (*i.e.* phone calls, email, etc.).

Retention rate. In teleservices human resource management terms; the percentage of a company's employees that remain with the company during the course of a year. Conversely, the churn or turnover rate is the percentage of employees who will leave within the course of a year.

S

Sales channel. A sales channel is the avenue through which a company or representative completes transactions with consumers. Channels include the telephone, the Internet (web sites, e-mail, web-chat), mail response and face-to-face interaction.

Sales per hour. Sales per hour is the average number of sales a caller makes in an hour. To find sales per hour, divide total sales by calling hours. The Sales per hour number is one of the key metrics used in the measurement of an agent's success as well as the overall success of a sales campaign.

Script/Call Guide. In either inbound or outbound teleservices, a script or call guide refers to the written presentation or outline of the verbiage a representative uses in conversation with a customer or prospect. Call Guides may be designed in such a way as to be delivered verbatim, semi-verbatim, bulleted or free form depending on a company's business philosophy or program requirements.

Simultaneous voice and data. A telecommunication line that allows spoken information and electronic data to be transmitted through the same line at the same time. A Digital Subscriber Line (DSL) is a simultaneous voice and data line.

Site selection. Site selection is the process by which a company analyzes the merits of prospective locations in which the company potentially intends to locate a branch or headquarters. Relevant factors include an area's average education level, availability of labor, market wage prices, proximity to large cities and access to high-speed technological equipment, among others.

Speech recognition. A machine or software capable of recognizing spoken language. The machine or software may take the spoken language and translate it into written text, or follow the spoken instructions to perform other functions.

State-based do not call lists. A practice in which states maintain a blanket list of those wishing to avoid unsolicited calls. Telemarketeers are prohibited by law from calling individual who's names are on the do not call list (DNC). States currently with do not call lists include Alabama, Alaska, Arkansas, California, Colorado, Connecticut, Florida, Georgia, Idaho, Illinois, Indiana, Kentucky, Louisiana, Maine, Missouri, New York, Oregon, Tennessee, Texas, Wisconsin and Wyoming (as of 1/2002).

T

Talk time. In either inbound or outbound, talk time represents the average amount of time the representative spends on the phone either handling a customer inquiry or making a presentation.

Telco. Short for "telephone company". The term Telco may include a local phone company or a long distance phone provider.

Telecommuting. Telecommuting uses telecommunication technology such as the Internet to work outside of the traditional workplace. An individual may be on a company's payroll, but perform his or her duties from the home.

Telephone Data Provider. A company that provides a variety of telephone data services such as telephone append, real time telephone append, demographic append and other services for inbound and outbound teleservices companies wishing to better target or qualify customers.

Telephony. Transmitting voice or digital information between two parties by using the telephone or telephone-related technology.

Teleservices Provider. Teleservices providers are companies that provide teleservices, whether those services include telemarketing (inbound or outbound) or customer service. Many provide custom teleservices—that is, they operate call Centres on behalf of other companies.

Third party verification. After a representative completes certain transactions the caller is transferred to a separate entity (normally outside the company) to verify the transaction.

TSR (Telesales Representative). A TSR uses the telephone or telephone related technology to contact potential customers and make sales.

Turnover rate. Turnover (or churn) rate is the rate at which employees enter and leave a company. The more loyal employees are to a firm, the lower the turnover rate. A 100 percent turnover rate from year to year means that as many people left the company as were hired.

U

Unified messaging. Unified messaging, also known as unified messaging systems and UMS, enables a user to access voice, fax and text messages via one single email or telephone account.

Unified queues. Lines, or queues, are created to funnel calls into the call Centre and distribute them based on given criteria (such as chronological order or customer priority). Unified queuing means to queue all calls, regardless of the line through which they came, in one manner.

V

Virtual call Centres. A virtual call Centre is made possible by telecommunication and Internet technology. Virtual call Centre employees use the Internet to work from their own homes or de-centralized locations.

Voice over Internet Protocol (VoIP). VoIP is a term used for a set of facilities designed to manage the delivery of voice information using Internet Protocol. In general, this means sending voice information in inconspicuous digital form rather than in the traditional circuit-committed protocols of the public switched telephone network (PSTN). A major advantage of VoIP and Internet telephony is that it eliminates ordinary toll charges.

W

Web callback. Web callback is a feature that enables a consumer visiting a company's website to schedule a time at which a company sales or service representative can call back. The consumer also leaves a phone number and, sometimes, the reason for the appointment. The representative then calls at the allotted time, when both parties are prepared.

Web-collaboration/ Cooperative Browsing. An Internet-related technology that enables a sales or service representative to assist a customer in using a website. While a customer is chatting with an online representative, the representative can temporarily manipulate the customer's web browser to display requested items or information.

Web-Enabled Centre. A call Centre is web-enabled if it can conduct business, be it customer service or sales, through various Internet features. Such features include correspondence via e-mail, cooperative browsing and live web chat wherein call Centre representatives answer various questions for consumers online in real time.

Workforce scheduling/Management software. In order to best serve their companies, their clients and their agents, contact Centre managers must effectively balance several factors, some of which include optimal staff levels, anticipated workloads, campaign timetables, resource availability and technological capability, all while considering elements such as agent preferences and unexpected absences. Due to the challenges involved with tracking these factors, managers rely upon management software programs designed to track resources and respond to changes.

Written sales contract requirements. Some states require a written contract to enforce and/or collect upon certain telemarketing transactions. The following states have specific contract guidelines pertaining to phone transactions: Alabama, Alaska, Arizona, Arkansas, California, Connecticut, Delaware, Florida, Idaho, Illinois, Kansas, Kentucky, Louisiana, Maryland, Massachusetts, Michigan, Minnesota, Mississippi, Montana, Nevada, New Mexico, North Carolina, North Dakota, Ohio, Pennsylvania, Rhode Island, South Dakota, Utah, Vermont, Virginia and Wisconsin (as of 5/2001).

Case Studies

- **The Problem**

This case study is presented by Nortel Networks

In the highly competitive luxury vacation destination business, Kerzner International has built a reputation for creating not just a hotel and casino, but an entire vacation experience. Enchanting new visitors and keeping delighted guests coming back to their two resort properties in The Bahamas—the largest island resort destination in the world—is not easy. Telephone communications—from the very first reservation inquiry to the on—site guest experience—must be gracious, efficient and accommodating in every way. To attain this goal, Kerzner International needed a sophisticated contact Centre solution that would support two separate resort properties and improve customer service. Poor call handling was becoming an increasing complaint—dropped calls, disconnects, long waits, inaccurate call routing—the problem was put on the critical priority list. The challenge was in defining the source of the guest service problem.

About Kerzner International

Kerzner International Limited is a resort and gaming company incorporated in The Bahamas which develops and manages premier resort and casino properties. The company, through its subsidiaries, currently operates resort hotels and/or casinos in The Bahamas, the Indian Ocean and Dubai. In addition, the company earns income based on the gross revenues of the Mohegan Sun Casino Resort in Connecticut.

On Paradise Island, Bahamas, Ocean Club- once a private estate—is now an exclusive resort treasured by discerning travellers. Luxury bedrooms, suites and poolside cottages rest between miles of pristine beach and exquisite gardens, inspired by the romantic grandeur of Versailles. Fragrant blossoms of hibiscus and bougainvillea, along with hand-laid rock ledges and stone steps, ascend the terraced garden decorated with bronze and marble statues from Europe. At its apex stand the dramatic arches of a 12th century Augustinian cloister that boasts a spectacular view of the sunset over Nassau Harbour. Ocean Club Spa is undeniably one of the finest and most luxurious spas in The Bahamas and the Caribbean.

Sharing Paradise Island—the sister resort to Ocean Club and the company's largest property—is Atlantis, Paradise Island resort and casino, a 2,317-room resort and casino. Larger than life, as dramatically fanciful as it is magnificent in scope and concept, the $850-million Atlantis is a glorious and wonderfully playful celebration of the legends of the lost continent of Atlantis, as seen in original artwork and in the design and decor throughout the resort. Unique entertainment attractions include The Dig-a fanciful journey into the world of the ancient Atlanteans, water rides, and three towers which provide the foundation for a 2,300-room resort that is as much fun for every kind and age of traveller as it is breathtaking and bold. In addition to a wide variety of accommodations, Atlantis offers a unique entertainment Centre with the Caribbean's largest casino, 38 restaurants and lounges, and extensive meeting facilities, including the largest ballroom in the Caribbean/Bahamas. More than 11 million gallons of water activities and attractions—including water slides and rides, swimming pools, waterfalls, fountains, snorkeling and swimming lagoons—plus one of the world's most beautiful beaches delight the guests. The focal point of the 34-acre Atlantis is the largest tropical marine habitat in the world, second only to Mother Nature herself, and home to 50,000 fish and sea animals from around the world.

- **Solution**

Supporting the world's largest island luxury resort destination with efficient and personalized communications service may seem like a dream job for many people, but was no easy task for Desmond Parker, VP of Information Technology for Kerzner International. "We have separate contact Centres for the Casino, VIPs, Spa, Restaurant Reservations, Room Service, and Ocean Club and Atlantis Guest Services. Our contact Centre also manages calls for general administrative functions such as Human Resources and the IT Help Desk. We were getting increasing complaints from guests about abandoned calls, misrouted calls, and long waits. We needed to address this fast. The problem was we did not know where to fix it. We needed a better contact Centre solution that would give us realtime visibility into call activity across all of our Centres so we could make informed decisions for change. I also felt we needed to look further into call routing and prioritization, peak call flow trends, staffing balance and individual performance of the agents answering the calls".

Prior to installing Symposium Call Centre Server and Symposium Call Centre Web Client, they did not have the flexibility to allow contact Centre supervisors and executive management to easily monitor each agent's personal performance. "Reporting was cumbersome", said Parker. "We used eight computers to manage 20 contact Centres, each with a separate proprietary client application to manage a defined group. We were unable to obtain an integrated report across all contact Centres, and management could only access reports and performance displays from the computers where a proprietary client application was installed. This management implementation required that we be in a specific location to pull reports, not to mention the significant time and expense to maintain current software functionality for over 100 agent and supervisor stations".

Kerzner International chose the Nortel Networks Symposium* Call Centre Server to help improve customer relationships and enhance contact Centre capabilities. This solution would enable them to fully leverage skill-based routing and support separate branding for their two properties from one centralized system located at the Atlantis resort on Paradise Island. Kerzner International also deployed Symposium Call Centre Web Client-a browser-based thin client—to provide an easier way of making immediate call flow changes and to monitor real-time performance and trends of the entire contact Centre operation.

Result

Atlantis deployed the Nortel Networks Symposium Call Centre Server and Symposium Call Centre Web Client to fulfill the Kerzner mission of delivering outstanding guest communications services. Positive change was immediate. Approximately 100 agents on-site now use the Agent Desktop Displays, which allow the agents to monitor the performance for the skill sets they are answering and make adjustments to improve their performance, if necessary. In addition, contact Centre supervisors can see up-to-the-second real-time statistics for each of the skill sets that agents are answering using Symposium Call Centre Web Client. Real-time displays are shown on 42 inch plasma monitors—so when they see that a specific skill set is getting an overflow of calls, they can respond immediately, so guests are not kept waiting. Supervisors are able to monitor the performance of each agent on their team—including breaks, time-outs, abandoned calls, length of calls and wait period. They also have the flexibility to quickly reassign supervisors and agents for breaks, sick leave, or vacation. "Individual agent service is an area that has shown immediate improvement with the Symposium solution", exclaimed Parker enthusiastically. "Our agents now know we can track every activity of their shift and monitor their calls, and that has really motivated them to perform at a significantly higher level. And with the new ability to respond immediately to changing conditions and make adjustments, we can provide the highest level of service to our guests and reduce wait times".

Executive management are also using the Symposium Call Centre Web Client historical reports-total volume of calls, abandoned calls, and calls presented are generated from a single desktop source and sent to supervisors and management on a weekly basis to keep everyone informed. They can then choose to delve deeper into specific areas by pulling their own reports in more detail. The reporting and the scripting changes can be done from anywhere via the Web interface. "I frequently travel between Fort Lauderdale, Florida, and Paradise Island, Bahamas. This new solution, which enables me to connect to historical reports and real-time displays through a standard Internet Explorer browser, makes it easier to get integrated data and work with it, and has made my job so much more productive and flexible", Parker explains.

"The new call Centre technology has really saved us money in time and productivity as well. Instead of having to install proprietary software and updates on 100 agent PCs separately, we now send out one electronic update with simple instructions for each agent to update their own desktop display.

The separation of property branding was a success as well. Although Atlantis and Ocean Club are sister properties on Paradise Island, they each have distinctive personalities. With Symposium Call Centre Server's flexible routing and scripting, we are able to treat each property separately, even at the detail of the on-hold music and announcements.

The installation of Symposium Call Centre Server and Symposium Call Centre Web Client has helped us to improve our methodology in doing business overall, and enabled immediate improvement in service levels, as evidenced by the greatly reduced number of guest complaints. We continue to evolve and find new ways to improve our contact Centre operations and are pleased to know that Symposium Call Centre Server has the scalability to change with our business."

Conduit PLC.

• The Problem

This case study is presented by Performix Technologies Conduit, a European based directory service provider, is one of the fastest growing information services companies in Europe. Founded in 1997, the company quickly and firmly established itself in the most competitive and difficult sector of the international contact Centre business. Conduit provides services in four countries through six outsource contracts and three own-branded access codes. These services are provided through the Group's contact Centre facilities in Dublin, Ireland and Vienna, Austria and more recently from the Group's new facilities in Cardiff, UK and Biel, Switzer-land.

The company's contact Centres operate 7 days a week, 24 hours a day and handle over 200,000 incoming calls daily. One of the keys to their success is the intelligent use Conduit has made of the Emvolve Performance Manager solution from Performix Technologies.

Critical To Success

As a relatively new entrant to the market place Conduit faced significant competitive challenges to achieving their business goals of market penetration, growth and market share. Four factors were identified as critical to success.

Firstly, the achievement of a consistently high level of customer service that eliminates the need for callers to hold while waiting to have their enquiry dealt with.

Secondly, rigorous cost management based on having agents handle a high number of calls, within a 45 second average, while decreasing the number of searches on the database to find the correct information.

Thirdly, increased revenue arising from up selling of direct customer call connections.

Fourthly, control and effective management of employee attrition and absenteeism levels. The clever use of Emvolve Performance Manager™ has made it possible for Conduit to address these challenges and achieve their business goals.

"The clarity of this system focuses agent's attention on what they need to do to consistently deliver a high level of service to customers, reduce costs and increase revenue while at the same time boosting their take home pay", states Katherine Whidden, Call Centre Director, Conduit plc.

• Solution

Emvolve Performance Manager takes data from Conduit's eight monitoring systems including the ACD, the scheduling system and the call monitoring database. The solution links this data to their performance standards and key indicators and streams it into a coherent picture of performance. The information is displayed in a visually simple format and available at the click of a button on everyone's desktops. Everyone in the organization can see the numbers that relate to their own performance.

Delivering Success

"The success of our contact Centre business is highly dependant upon individual performance", says Katherine Whidden, Call Centre Director with Conduit. "To get the right numbers at the top you have to get the right numbers at an individual level. That's where Emvolve helps us".

Through intelligent use of the Emvolve solution Conduit has successfully increased agents adherence. This underpins the delivery of consistently high service levels to their customers. Conduit measures service level by the number of incoming calls received combined with the number of calls handled within 15 seconds. This requires agents to be logged on and receiving calls 93% of the time.

The Emvolve solution brings visibility to such key targets and links individual's rewards to achievement of the same. "It's totally transparent. This transparency is the key to its success", says Katherine Whidden, Call Centre Director, Conduit plc.

Conduit has successfully reduced the average number of searches on their database per call, which represents over a 60% cost saving that is crucial to the success of the business. This has been achieved by agents using the feedback from the Emvolve solution to focus on more effectively understanding the customer query and resolving it quickly and simply. Likewise, they have used Emvolve to increase the number of interconnections their agents make. This increased level in revenue is a result of the up selling of direct customer call connections and directly improves profit margins.

This has been achieved by using Emvolve to empower the agents to manage their own performance. Emvolve has played a key role in helping Conduit reduce attrition and absenteeism. The combined improvements delivered by the Emvolve solution enabled Conduit to achieve a return on their investment in less than 3 months.

Implementation

With a clear understanding of Conduit's business, Performix firstly mapped their organizational structure within the Emvolve solution and secondly developed comprehensive matrices of individual goals for all employees across the organization. Performix implementation experts used the Emvolve solution to automate the extraction of appropriate activity data from Conduit's diverse measurement systems and linked this to the matrices of goals. Having consolidated the data on activity and linked it to the correct individual goals, each employee was provided with security access to performance information live from their desktops.

Result

"The success of our call Centre business is highly measurable thanks to the Emvolve solution", concludes Katherine Whidden, Call Centre Director, Conduit plc. "We use it to measure the success of our business firstly in terms of service levels, secondly in terms of quality and thirdly in terms of direct cost of each call".

The transparency of the system, the easy access to

feedback on performance and the direct link to the reward system means that agents are able to watch their numbers unfold, learn from them and do things to improve their performance.

"I couldn't imagine us operating without Emvolve as all our daily performance reports are available on it. Our incentive performance scheme is on it as well so agents can see what they are earning. The information is critical to running our business", states John Connolly, Resource Manager, Conduit plc.

Medical Transcription

Introduction

Medical transcription programs prepare people to type verbatim reports from tapes recorded by doctors. Students learn medical terms and how to translate complex information. They also learn to use computers.

Medical Transcription is conversion of voice to electronic text form. Medical Transcription is an IT enabled service that requires specialized skills in utilizing Information technology in converting the voice data of the doctors who are in the US or in other countries, consisting of patient history and medical advises into electronic documents.

A medical Transcriptionist is thus a medical language specialist who interprets and transcribes dictation by medical professionals especially by professional doctors. This dictation covers pretty much everything that takes place between the health care provider and the patient. Usually, the information is recorded either into tape or onto digital voice processing systems.

Overview

Everybody knows that doctors write prescriptions that are hard to read. Doctors don't have much time to write, so after they see a patient, they often dictate a recording that summarizes what they just saw and did. Just as pharmacists can read the prescriptions that don't make sense to us, likewise, medical transcriptionists can make sense of these often-rushed recordings.

Doctors use a lot of specialized terms to describe their work. So in this program you study medical terminology. You study the structures and functions of the human body. You learn the names of various diseases and disorders. You become familiar with procedures that doctors perform and the drugs they prescribe. Your goal is to understand medicine so well that you can spot when the doctor says something inconsistent with the case or forgets to mention something. In your training, you learn how to check with the doctor to make sure the record is correct.

The purpose of your work is to produce a document. So you improve your keyboard skills and learn how to word-process according to formats that are commonly used in medical records. You learn how to keep a computer in good running condition. And you learn how to work the device, often controlled by a foot pedal, that allows you to start and stop the recording as you transcribe the information.

Because you will work in a medical office, you learn about its various business functions. You study the computer software packages that are used in office management. You study the laws that apply to healthcare. Especially important are those that specify how patient records are to be kept confidential.

A knowledge of these thing required for working in this :

study courses such as :
Computer Fundamentals
College English
Medical Terminology
Human Anatomy and Physiology
Keyboarding and Formatting
Office Management and Procedures
Medical Transcription Procedures
Pharmacology
Medical Ethics and Law
Spreadsheet Applications
Medical Transcription Internship
And Supervised training

In India, Medical Transcription business is some 3-4 years old. The Medical Transcription has its origin in USA where it is a well-established industry and it is of 25 years old. A study done by NASSCOMM predicts that this industry is here to stay in India for atleast 10 years. More and more Transcription services are outsourced to India because of the cheap and highly efficient work force thus making it an attractive market for transcription not only in Medical transcription but also in other transcription services also.

In U.S and other western countries Maintenance patients' record has been made mandatory and doctors dictate for transcribers to make the document and save their valuable time.

India provides affordable and superior medical transcription service with our specialized workforce. India has successful integrated advancements in Information technology to its transcription services. We offer our service, as a one-stop-shop for all Medical Transcription needs.

India offers genuine expertise and an excellent track record in Medical transcription and Media and business or Legal transcription services.

Medical transcriptionists translate and edit recorded dictation by physicians and other healthcare providers regarding patient assessment and treatment. Using a transcribing machine with headset and foot pedal, medical transcriptionists listen to recordings by physicians and other healthcare professionals dictating a variety of medical reports such as emergency room visits, diagnostic imaging studies, operations, chart reviews and final summaries. To understand and accurately transcribe dictated reports into a format that is clear and comprehensible for the reader, the medical transcriptionist must understand the language of medicine, anatomy and physiology, diagnostic procedures, and treatment, and must be able to translate medical jargon and abbreviations into their expanded forms. Editing as necessary for grammar and clarity, the medical transcriptionist transcribes the dictated reports and returns them in either printed or electronic form to the dictator for review and signature, or correction. These reports eventually become a part of the patient's permanent file. Credential/Licensure/ Registration/Certification.

Employers prefer to hire transcriptionists who have completed postsecondary training in medical transcription, offered by many vocational schools and community colleges. Completion of a 2- year associate's degree program—including coursework in anatomy, medical terminology, medical legal issues, and English grammar and punctuation—is highly recommended.

Services in Medical Transcription
General Correspondence,
History and Physicals
Patient Progress Reports
Consultations and discharge Summaries
Chart Notes and Narratives
Radiology Reports
Hospital Progress Notes and Procedure Notes
ER Reports and Surgical Procedures
Operative Reports

Independent Medical Evaluations and Peer Reviews

India's mission is to provide our clients with acceptable medical transcription services, healthcare management services at an affordable price.

India offers a number of significant factors that makes us our customer's choice for their next medical transcription service. We give international quality within an affordable budget, and our prompt deliverability has made us a top medical Transcription service provider in India.

We believe in accuracy and specialized attention is given to every detail. We have Excellent English speaking work force who can deliver their best in the field and assure you their best service.

Medical Transcription Process

Medical Transcription service from India gives the valuable customers a complete transcription service to medical coding and Medical Billing service.

The process of medical transcription is transferring this information using word processing.

Total Dictation & Transcription Solutions
Record Conversion & Migration
Electronic Medical Recording
We Maintain & Customize EMR For Your Practice
Maintaining Patients Record
Maintaining Patients progress
We maintain complete secrecy of the patient's records
Workforce:

Our work force consists of Graduates in science with good command over English. Our work force is dedicated to welfare of our customers and offers their best service in Medical Transcription. Our Medical transcription service uses state-of-the-art technology, infrastructure and highly qualified and skilled manpower to provide end-to-end solutions for our customers.

Working Conditions

The majority of these workers are employed in comfortable settings, such as hospitals, physicians' offices, clinics, laboratories, medical libraries, government medical facilities, or at home. An increasing number of medical transcriptionists telecommute from home-based offices as employees or subcontractors for hospitals and transcription services or as self-employed independent contractors.

Work in this occupation presents few hazards, although sitting in the same position for long periods can be tiring, and workers can suffer wrist, back, neck, or eye problems due to strain and risk repetitive motion injuries such as carpal tunnel syndrome. The pressure to be accurate and fast also can be stressful.

Many medical transcriptionists work a standard 40-hour week. Self-employed medical transcriptionists are more likely to work irregular hours—including part time, evenings, weekends, or on an on-call basis.

Employment

Medical transcriptionists held about 102,000 jobs in 2000. As of February, 2002, a Medical Records Transcriptionist earned annually, on average, a low of 26,751.00 USD to a high of 31,541.00 USD. About 2 out of 5 worked in hospitals and about another 2 out of 5 in physicians' offices and clinics. Others worked for laboratories, colleges and universities, transcription services and temporary help agencies.

Related Industries

Digital Dictation, Transcription And working

If you are a Medical Transcriptionist, you no longer can afford to ignore the slow but sure move away from tapes as a medium used for recording dictation. Although many, many physicians are still using tapes to record their dictation, it becomes more obvious daily that there also are more physicians using digital voice recorders to hold their dictation. There are obvious benefits to using the digital format for recording such as: being able to use a small handheld voice recorder; larger capacity recording time due to the various, but similar, types of storage methods used; better features on voice recorders such as separate directories, so, for instance, urgent dictation, chart dictation, personal dictation, medicolegal dictation, etc., may be separated for ease of access. The audio quality is usually superior to tapes. (This is especially important in light of the fact that most physicians think recording tapes last forever and rarely toss them out without a fight, as many veteran MTs will attest.)

How does digital dictation work?

The process begins when your client dictates into a digital voice recorder, much the same way s/he would dictate into any handheld voice recorder. When finished, s/he simply uploads the files from their digital voice recorder into their computer. To upload the files from the recorder, the recorder is connected to the computer with a USB cable, usually included with the digital voice recorder at time of purchase. At this point, software either included with the digital voice recorder or other software, recognizes there has been a connection made and a window will pop up asking the user where the files should be saved. Your client saves the files to the directory of their choice. Once the files are uploaded to the computer, the process is finished and the connection can be removed. The client then opens their e-mail program and prepares a message to send to his/her Transcriptionist and, using the "attach a file" feature available in most e-mail programs, attaches the digital files that were just uploaded and saved from their handheld recorder to a directory on their computer. The e-mail is then sent to the transcriptionist with the file attached.

It is very important to note that each and every e-mail, especially those containing a digital file whose contents are personal and confidential health information on individuals, should only ever be sent by encrypted e-mail. If you do not encrypt e-mail that includes private patient health files, it makes the e-mail a possible target for hackers who may intercept and open the e-mail. Once intercepted, the hacker may use the contents somehow to their advantage, *i.e.,* to embarrass the physician and/or transcriptionist, citing their lack of concern about privacy, or use the private patient information for personal, financial, or other gain. If you do not want to risk your reputation or that of your client, and want to ensure that a patient's health records are always protected in transit, you have to use e-mail encryption.

When the medical transcriptionist receives an encrypted e-mail, the file is opened and then brought into your PC transcription system using software like that included with the WAVpedal system. The MT may convert the digital file to any number of many formats, but the most popular one that most MTs use or convert to is the "wav" format, as in "filename.wav". In conjunction with the software the MT can then manipulate the digital voice file with the WAVpedal foot pedal. From there, everything works just as it does on a regular tape transcriber. The foot pedal controls movements through the voice file just like moving through a conventional tape. The software includes features not found on a tape transcriber machine, including being able to move immediately to certain points in the dictation with no time delay and usually far greater control over the speed of the playback. After finishing transcribing the files, the MT simply e-mails the finished reports, as an attachment (digitally signed and encrypted, of course), back to the physician's office for filing or printing there.

That is the process generally, and some things may differ according to the type of system, recorder, software, being used. The point we want to make is that it is not a difficult process. It is efficient, secure and easy to get started. It will allow MTs to receive work from larger companies who are always looking for MTs to do work from home. These MTs will need to be familiar with the digital process.

What do I need to transcribe digital dictation files?

You will need a special foot pedal required to manipulate digital files, such as the WAVpedal software and foot pedal. Your physician client will need a digital voice recorder. If you use the WAVpedal system, the brand of digital voice recorder does not really matter. To use the special foot pedal required to manipulate digital files, you will need to have a computer with an available USB port or serial port connection. Most new computers come with at least one serial port connection and at least one USB connection—some come with two or more USB connections.

Almost every computer comes with a serial port connection at the very least, even very old computers. (You should know that there are converter cables that will convert a serial connection to a USB connection, and ones that convert a USB connection to a serial connection, if that will help in your situation. Visit your local computer store for help.) You also need an Internet connection, telephone or cable and an e-mail account. Lastly, you need to have a software program to open and manipulate the digital files. Please realize that to manipulate the digital files, you need a foot pedal that connects to your computer. (A foot pedal that comes with a tape transcriber will not work.) The WAVpedal foot pedal and software package that fulfill these two last, but very important, requirements. You also have a choice of ordering the WAVpedal with a serial connection or USB connection. There are other foot pedals available on the market that do much the same thing as the WAVpedal system. The reason for recommend the WAVpedal system is that the WAVpedal is the original pedal system designed for manipulating digital files. The WAVpedal has features that other systems do not, including the ability to convert files recorded on almost every type of digital handheld recorder. This allows the MT to perform transcription for many client physicians, regardless of the type of digital voice recorder they use.

What does my client (physician) need?

All your client needs is a digital voice recorder and, ideally, a computer with Internet connection and e-mail account.

If your client does not have a computer or cannot or will not e-mail her/his digitally recorded dictation for some reason, there is still a way for you to transcribe it. Your client will need to send you the "memory stick" or "smart card" or whatever storage medium is used in their particular recorder, from their recorder with the completed dictation on it. (Some basic recorders do not have removable media, so if your client does not have a computer or does not want to e-mail the files, be sure s/he buys a digital voice recorder with removable media.) If the client sends the dictation to you this way, they will need one or more additional memory sticks or cards for their digital voice recorder to use while you are working on the files on the one you were sent. Also, if your client sends you a memory stick or smart card, you will need a special adaptor to plug into a USB port on your computer, so you can access the memory card or memory stick. The kind of adaptor you need depends upon the type of digital media their recorder uses. You can find Sony memory sticks. You can find Sony memory stick adaptors. You can find other types of memory cards. You can find other types of memory card adaptors. A few top quality digital recorders, which you may read about. Unfortunately, using the digital voice recorder files this way is really just substituting digital media for tape media. You will still have to deal with pick-up and delivery of the media, as you did with tapes. Unfortunately, one of the best features of digital dictation is the ability to e-mail it instead of physically send it, but at least you will have the benefit of other features of digital files during transcription.

This is the future of MT and if you are not actively looking into this type of system you may miss out on opportunities to engage new clients or perform transcription on a contract basis for others. It doesn't cost much, it's easy to install, and a lot of physicians/dictators really like it. If you are an independent contractor (IC), a good method of introduction to this system of dictating is to provide your client with a digital voice recorder (just on-loan while they are your client, of course) and you should find their acceptance of the new technology and procedures to be more positive.

Service provide by call Centre

Convert various audios and video formats into digitally remastered or encoding.

Guarantee best service because of our wide network and professional touch.

Every medium received from clients is verified for its quality and amount of time to be spent for the work for converting them to digitally remastered one. The cost is estimated depending on the time required and effort needed and they are conveyed to our clients before we start our work on them.

Medias that are of broadcast quality requires less time

to transcription while medias of lesser quality takes longer time.

All types of media from poorer quality into a high quality digital media.

Services are listed below:—

Video Captioning

Audio Transcription

Text Conversion

Regular Transcription and Manuscript Typing

Proofreading

Copy Editing and Publication Design

Medical, Legal and Technical Transcription

Transcription Summaries

Digital Audio Editing

Audio or Video Encoding

Materials having lot of technical, business, financial or computer terms usually take between 7 or 8 hours of work per hour of audio. Focus groups with multiple participants and overlapping conversations may take 10 hours per hour of audio to transcribe and proofread.

The work efficiency depends upon the quality of material received from our client while a Broadcast-quality material usually results in 100% accurate transcripts. Lesser quality audio results in a decline of accuracy, but with our professional service we can generally achieve 98% accuracy or better on most material.

Our professional expertise comes into fore with our job giving a better result even in hard to transcribe material.

Our rates include proofreading and fast turnaround times. The philosophy of is to provide a manuscript-quality finished product rather than an industry-standard -rough draft.

Media transcription

- DIGITAL REMASTERING AND ENCODING
- AUDIO RESTORATION AND FORENSIC TRANSCRIPTION
- DATA CONVERSION AND CONTENT REPURPOSING
- HIGH SPEED TAPE DUPLICATION

DIGITAL REMASTERING AND ENCODING

Transcripts can digitize and encode any format of audio or video into any number of formats to streamline from Web sites, broadcast over intranets, or play back from CDs, VCDs and CD-ROMs.

- Conversion of Audio and video into the three major formats, Real Media, Windows Media and MPEG (MP3 for audio, MPEG-1 for video).
- Audio typing and tape transcription of mini, micro, standard and mini disc tapes, plus digital DSS and WAV sound files.
- The material we encode includes conferences, speeches, investor calls, training tapes, radio shows and more for such clients.

In addition, we can burn your audio to a music CD, which will play on any CD video transcription, and we can burn your video to a Video CD, which will play on any computer with a CD drive and most DVD video transcriptions being sold today. Feel free to ask us for prices for your particular needs.

AUDIO RESTORATION AND FORENSIC TRANSCRIPTION

A growing area for us is restoring poorly recorded and hard-to-hear audio, on which we became expert at as part of our forensic transcription work. We can digitally boost low volume recordings, eliminate electrical hums, reduce hiss, equalize voices and reduce echoes and background noises.

We can deliver the restored audio on a cassette, on an audio CDs, or on a CD-ROM as WAVs, MP3s, Real Audio or Windows Media files.

Please keep in mind that while not every tape can be saved, we might be able to turn a flawed recording into something that is audible and usable, or be able to extract a transcription from it.

Call or e-mail us for details. There is no charge for a tape we cannot improve.

DATA CONVERSION AND CONTENT REPURPOSING

Data conversion service for converting audio files into text or text to media or other types like digital to analog or *vice versa*. Some of the conversions we've done recently include repurposing interactive CD-ROMs into Websites, transcribing interviews directly into databases, and archiving teleconference calls onto audio CDs. We have also done captioning work for the deaf and have worked to redesign Websites to comply with the American with Disabilities Act

HIGH SPEED TAPE DUPLICATION

High speed Tape duplication service is available. If you need cassette copies of your tape, we can duplicate them with our high-speed tape duplicator. A copy of a tape can be made within six minutes. Copies are slightly softer than their originals, so we recommend only good quality tapes be duplicated in this fashion.

Legal transcription

Legal transcriptions of video and audiotapes for attorneys from United States. Legal transcriptions services are quality-controlled service. This service will free your highly skilled, trained and paid staff giving them other important responsibilities that they can concentrate their efforts on more important and cost-effective responsibilities of your company. In addition to these we also provide the following services:

General Correspondence—letters to clients, other attorneys, judges, court clerks, agencies-Legal pleadings-Interrogatories-Bankruptcies-Realestate-Subpoenas-briefs-CourtProceedings-Trials-Wire Taps.

- Same Day Turnaround is available for emergency documents.
- Customized Internet Servers
- Deposition Summaries and Police Reports By

Security-Rated Employees

- Transcription Of Meetings, Interviews, Internal Affairs and Investigations

Legal Transcription services online

Transcription services using your video and audiotapes and legal digital transcription services using your digital voice recordings. Every data's can be transferred to us via Internet your transcribed data's will be delivered right in your desktop via Internet. Your legal files are totally protected and secure as they are sent to and from us on our secure server. We give you a personal code and password, which enables you to access and retrieve your files at any time.

For security, all your transcribed files on our system for an entire year, so that you can easily look up files that may have accidentally been misplaced in your office.

Digital legal transcription gives you faster turn-around time as well, eliminating the time and expense of transport and mailing of tapes. Transport files in any format that you need, *i.e.* DSS, WAV files or MP3. You can also send your recorded voice or data's from your computer, and upload the voice file to us via the Internet using FTP or email service.

Record your proceedings; transcribe them in more than 100 languages including English and with our certified translators. Transcribers and translators are professionally chosen such that for their linguistic skills and their expertise in specialized subject areas.

Legal Transcription service Infrastructure

The company must have complete infrastructure facilities like high performance PC and a broadband connection supported by our network and hardware engineers who take care of it round the clock. The company's work force consists of graduates who are fluent in English and professional's trainers from Law Colleges train them. The "Transcriptionist" the job only provided if they fullfill the minimum requirement stipulated by us during our training.

The offshore outsourcing keeps rolling on inexorably to India. This despite severe protests arising over shifting of hundreds of call centre jobs from the United Kingdom and the United States to low-cost countries like India, China and the Philippines, more and more firms and professionals are coming to realize the benefits of outsourcing.

The latest to join the BPO wagon are British and Welsh lawyers, planning to move legal transcription production overseas, particularly to India, says BBC News.

The movement of more legal transcription work to India shows the confidence of them in Indian Companies. The advances in technology mean that solicitors can drastically reduce the number of legal secretaries they employ and at less than half the cost then it costs in UK.

In general the legal secretaries produce legal documents dictated by solicitors, prepare legal files and liaise with clients. A number of law firms are cutting jobs and moving legal document production to India, where transcription Centres give quality service at an affordable rate.

UK's Law Society—wants the offshore companies to do the transcribing work in strict confidentiality and security and that liability remains with the UK firm.

Some solicitors believe clients might be unhappy about their legal work not being done directly by the firm they employ. But those who are promoting the idea say the cost savings will prove increasingly attractive.

Legal Transcription Outsourcing

Legal Transcription is virtually transcribing everything that takes place in the civil and criminal court systems into hard copy documentation. The information that are either dictated or recorded in the courtroom or at deposition hearings, as well as in law offices in less official settings. This data may include testimonies, pleadings, interrogatories like questions and answers, reviews of administrative hearings and the like. The process used for operations in these legal transcription service in India uses similar process like legal and medical transcription industry in U.S.

The legal transcription services in India will hugely benefit both the attorney and consumers at large as specifically delegated and supervised legally substantive work is performed and distributed. The attorneys also realise that their own productivity and cost efficiency is maximised through utilising paralegal services and legal transcription services, demand will increase and new opportunities will arise for those offering these services. The demand for paralegals and legal transcriptionists has been increasing rapidly and it is estimated that by 2005, there will be a need for between 150,000 and 176,000 paralegals requirement in the US this has led to positive átmosphere in India.

Legal Transcription Service Users

The main users of these services are attorneys and law firms, courts, public defenders' and prosecutors' offices, public utility companies, publicly funded legal service projects and community legal service programmes. The other users would be corporate legal departments, insurance companies, financial institutions, real estate and title agencies, state and federal government agencies. These users would be largely benefited because of lower cost rate available for the Legal Transcription service in India.

The Legal Transcription work may include drafting and filing legal documents, calendaring and tracking important deadlines, assisting attorneys to prepare for trials, documenting relevant facts and information pertaining to a lawsuit, using computers and related software and other reference material to research and document law and to prepare the documents used. Legal transcriptionists can become so proficient that they can actually undertake paralegal duties as well.

To be a legal transcriptionists, one needs to be proficient in the knowledge of American law, law in general and its origin, various court systems, cases, both legal application and reasoning and many other details. Companies in Legal transcription services in India commonly beyond this, one can specialise in various types of law like real estate, criminal, family, personal injury, business and so on.

Legal Transcription from Home

Legal Transcription services can be done from home. Legal Transcriptions service from Home is for those interested in working on contract basis in their home. The jobs are available only through the agency which offers job on a contract basis and let them know you are available for independent contract work in the future. The legal transcription from home service requires agreements to be signed with the company offering you the contract. After establishing a relationship with the firm you might be able to land contract work. Most firms would never use an untested independent contractor.

Each week there are many job listings in Internet and local newspapers and other resources for the best jobs at home and telecommuting jobs. Also, many companies that may require legal transcriptionists actually post their requirement at many websites that lists online job opportunities. These companies are screened by theses web sites to make sure the jobs are legitimate and offer their service free for thousands of home based transcriptionists, do not charge a fee.

Legal Transcription services can be done from home. Legal Transcriptions service from home is for those interested in working on contract basis in their home. The jobs are available only through the agency which offers job on a contract basis and let them know you are available for independent contract work in the future. The legal transcription from home service requires agreements to be signed with the company offering you the contract. After establishing a relationship with the firm you might be able to land contract work. Most firms would never use an untested independent contractor.

Each week there are many job listings in Internet and local newspapers and other resources for the best jobs at home and telecommuting jobs. Also, many companies that may require legal transcriptionists actually post their requirement at many websites that lists online job opportunities. These companies are screened by theses web sites to make sure the jobs are legitimate and offer their service free for thousands of home based transcriptionists, do not charge a fee. Then these jobs are then posted on our job board! You can immediately view and apply for these jobs! New Companies are signing up all the time looking for people just like you to fill their work at home jobs!

It would literally take you hundreds of hours of your valuable time trying to track down these legitimate, work at home jobs. That is why we have been providing this valuable service for over four years to people just like you!

Are you tired of searching through all the work at home jobs only to find out they are scams, charge a fee or are a home biz opportunity? Wouldn't you like to have access to jobs that have been screened and do not charge a fee and are not MLM's, home biz opps or assembly jobs?

Legal/medical transcription is one of the better known work-from-home opportunities. For people without on-the-job transcription training, companies and community colleges will offer transcription courses --and sometimes promise large profits.

It's true that you can make money transcribing. Before you sign up for your courses, ask yourself the following questions:

1. Is this something you *want* to do, or are you doing this because you think it's a "hot" business? Do you have a passion for transcribing notes? Fantastic! Not sure? Consider starting another business. The *worst* thing you can do is create an at-home business that you won't or can't enjoy.
2. What research have you done? Does your local market need more legal/medial Transcriptionist? Have you talked with doctors, attorneys, etc. to determine if they may be interested in your services? Have you chatted with someone that is already in this line of work?
3. What is your background? If you have a medical/legal background, great! You're halfway there. If you don't have an applicable background, consider how you are going to market your services. Many doctors or attor-

neys prefer someone with some related on-the-job transcription experience.

4. What do you know about the company offering the course? Unless you're taking classes through a community college, check up on the company. A couple of calls to the Better Business Bureau and the Attorney General's office can put your mind at ease--and keep you safe from scams.

India offers best outsource talents in the legal transcription field. The company based in India with world-class infrastructures like advanced communication setup and high end PC's and servers. The company has a broadband Internet connection for dealing transcription service online for our clients.

Our legal transcription service involves following procedures:

General Correspondence—letters to clients, other attorneys, judges, court clerks, agencies-Legal pleadings-Interrogatories-Bankruptcies-Real estate-Subpoenas-briefs-Court Proceedings- Trials-Wire Taps.

- Same Day Turnaround is also available for emergency documents.
- Customized Internet Servers
- Deposition Summaries and Police Reports By

Security-Rated Employees

Employment In legal Transcription: The outlook for work in the legal Transcription profession is expected to be in a high growth through 2006, driven by a steady increase in demand by the legal profession for various legal assistance. The outsourcing is becoming necessary for American companies for cutting costs.

There are many state-of-the-art on-line home training program consists of two sections plus 5 hours of dictation for transcription practice.

The courses are streamlined, comprehensive and completely interactive. You will learn to enter the legal field and do a variety of things. It is designed to teach the functions and processes of institutions in the U.S. legal system, roles and issues in the field and selected specialties of law.

These programs discusses employment opportunities and provides dozens of websites for research purposes to enhance your educational skills on-line, in addition to opportunities to network for working possibilities and resources after you're working.

They cover's issues relevant to the profession, an overview of American Law, court systems, litigation and an overview of all the different law specialties. It includes dozens of samples of dictation types and formats, terminology used in the law, complete with an abridged Latin dictionary. It reviews English grammar and provides all the typing rules, complete with the captions for different types of courts and actions.

A legal Transcriptionist does word-processing and document preparation in a legal office. These program emphasizes keyboarding skill, computer software, grammar and punctuation skills, legal transcription and document preparation. This program is ideal for someone who is currently doing office work but would like to move to a legal setting.

Privacy Risk in Outsourcing

Healthcare providers can outsource transcription, but they can't outsource their obligation to safeguard privacy.

Method to minimize risk

Healthcare providers are faced with multiple pressures, many of them financial. The need for management to meet financial constraints often translates into a desire to contract with vendors at the lowest possible immediate cost, sometimes without thought as to the non price issues in a contract.

It is important to linger over the legal issues that may be associated with vendor contracts, especially with vendors that may subcontract portions of their tasks. The October

2003 incident in which a Pakistani subcontractor, in a dispute with a medical transcription company, threatened to release patient information on the Web provided a dramatic reminder of this. Provider and vendor liability has become even more important in light of HIPAA privacy and security regulations, which place an obligation on covered healthcare providers to ensure that their vendors safeguard confidentiality.

This article discusses specifically the considerations that should be given by healthcare providers when choosing a medical transcription vendor, and it offers tips to protect providers when entering into a medical transcription contract.

Transcription Outsourcing

Medical transcription is a vital part of healthcare operations. Accurate, timely transcription of daily notes such as operating room reports, discharge summaries and radiology reports is essential for communication among healthcare providers. Transcription further factors into accurate coding and billing of services, satisfaction of regulatory requirements, and defense of medical malpractice suits. In recent years it has become important in the development of electronic health records.

Transcription is also a frequent candidate for outsourcing. Healthcare providers often contract out their transcription as a cost-saving measure (though cost savings may not be possible in all circumstances). Providers also choose outsourcing to meet staffing challenges posed by local labor markets, the need for specialized training and their own staffing limitations.

Whatever the motivation for outsourcing, transmission of confidential medical information outside of facility walls places an obligation on the provider to ensure that the vendor protects the confidentiality of the information. HIPAA requirements make this issue more critical than ever before.

The case in which the Pakistani subcontractor threatened to release patient information illustrates how important it is for providers to choose vendors carefully to complete due diligence with regard to chains of subcontracting and to protect themselves contractually from liability for acts of the vendor or the vendor's subcontractors.

The above story started in fall 2003 when the University of California at San Francisco Medical Centre (UCSF) forwarded a portion of its transcription work to Transcription Stat, a company it had used for two decades. Transcription Stat employs 15 subcontractors throughout the US to handle the large volume of files it receives daily from UCSF. One of those subcontractors, a woman in Florida, further subcontracted the work to a man in Texas named Tom Spires.

HIPAA Requires

The privacy regulations of the federal HIPAA law, effective April 14, 2003, were intended to ensure the privacy and confidentiality of personal health information. HIPAA's privacy rules apply only to healthcare providers, payers and clearing houses that are covered entities. Because the law does not directly apply to other parties that may handle medical information (*e.g.*, transcription companies and other vendors), HIPAA attempts to stretch its coverage by requiring healthcare providers to take certain actions when entrusting medical information to vendors.

HIPAA requires that if a provider releases medical information to another person or entity to perform a function on the provider's behalf (the provider's "business associate"), the provider must enter into an agreement obliging the business associate to maintain the confidentiality of the medical information.

HIPAA's privacy regulations require that business associate contracts contain several specific provisions. The contract must specify the permitted uses and disclosures of information by the business associate. The contract also must require the business associate not to use or further disclose the information except as permitted by the contract and to use appropriate safeguards to prevent use or disclosure of the information other than as allowed by the contract. The contract must "ensure that any agents, including a subcontractor", to whom the business associate provides medical information agree to the "same restrictions and conditions that apply to the business associate with respect to such information". The contract must authorize termination if the business associate violates a material term of the contract.

When the HIPAA security rule goes into effect, medical transcription vendors will be covered as business associates under this rule also, because the security rule applies to electronic medical information, both in storage and in transmission. The rule requires that when providers contract with business associates who "create, receive, maintain or transmit electronic protected health information", the contract specify appropriate use of the information.

Additional security provisions may need to be added to business associate contracts with transcription vendors and other business associates that receive or transmit electronic information. For example, the security regulations require that any business associate shall—

(i) implement administrative, physical, and technical safeguards that reasonably and appropriately protect the confidentiality, integrity and availability of electronic protected health information that it creates, receives, maintains or transmits on behalf of the covered entity, as required by the security standards,

(ii) ensure that any agent, including subcontractors to whom the business associate provides such information, agrees to implement reasonable and appropriate safeguards to protect it.

(iii) Rreport to the covered entity any security incident relating to the electronic information that the vendor maintains for the provider.

Providers Should Determine

Providers should therefore determine how a medical transcription vendor maintains the privacy of medical information and how the vendor safeguards the security of electronic information. Providers should get answers to the following questions:

- Does the vendor have security safeguards for information that is maintained at the vendor's data headquarters (*e.g.*, is each employee required to have a secure password)? Are voice files and data files maintained in a secure data safe?
- Is there an audit trail that shows who has accessed data in the vendor's archive system?
- How long are data files maintained, and are they destroyed after that period? Are voice files automatically deleted within a reasonable time after being transcribed? The provider may wish to specify that data is maintained only until the provider ensures that the transcribed report is in the medical record (*e.g.*, no more than one year).
- Is electronic medical information transmitted from the vendor to the provider in a secure fashion-for example, through encryption?
- How does the vendor regulate provider access to the provider's directory on the vendor server? For example, is it safest to allow only one person authorized by the provider (*e.g.*, the director of medical records) to draw data down from the transcription vendor's computer system?
- If the vendor employs home-based transcriptionists, does the vendor have policies to safeguard workstations? Are home-based transcriptionists allowed to store provider files on their home computers?

Minimizing Risk

Providers can consider a number of options when entering into a contract for medical transcription services. These options can clarify the mutual understanding of the contractual relationship, minimize the chance of a HIPAA or confidentiality violation, and ensure that the provider will be able to take appropriate action should a vendor fail to meet required standards.

1. Ensure that the contract with the medical transcription company obligates the vendor to not only maintain

confidentiality itself, but to require any person or entity to whom the vendor sends information to maintain confidentiality and security of information. The vendor should require that the person or entity comply with all of the obligations of the vendor under the vendor's business associate agreement with the provider.

In the UCSF case, the transcription vendor, the first subcontractor, and second subcontractor were simply intermediaries. That realization makes a provider wonder how many transcription vendors operate by simply contracting with another party whose cost is low enough to allow the first vendor to skim off a profit, and so on down the line until the only person left to do the work is someone whose wages are below those livable in the US. It is difficult to ascertain how HIPAA's privacy or security requirements can be satisfied if a transcription company is simply a pass-through: can anyone identify who has the data, how it is stored, or where it is? Nevertheless, the HIPAA rule assists providers by making clear that vendors are responsible for the privacy and security of the data given to them.

The obligations of both provider and business associate become further complicated if some of the parties receiving information are not located inside the United States. Entities not domiciled in the US may not be subject to, or even aware of, US laws.

2. Require indemnification from the vendor for any breach of the contract (including confidentiality), not only by the vendor but by any of the vendor's subcontractors or entities to which the subcontractor may send information.
3. Consider placing restrictions on the subcontractors that a vendor may use; for instance, explicitly requiring that any subcontractor receiving medical information from the vendor be physically located in the United States and that, in addition, the vendor's subcontractors be explicitly prohibited from sending any of the provider's information outside the US. Although this will not obviate the problems that can occur if a subcontractor isn't paid and threatens release of information, for

example, it will ensure that any such subcontractor is subject to US law and may be less likely to make such threats. Also, providers can consider asking vendors outright for a full disclosure of subcontracts.

4. Consider using a medical transcription company that does not subcontract any work at all. Some vendors are staffed with full-time employees who receive benefits, and some offer incentives to staff for meeting high performance standards. Some vendors assign transcriptionists responsibility for a single client, fostering familiarity with the client's transcription needs. Such vendors may charge a premium for that level of service, but providers may want to balance that cost with the potential benefits of a stable, dedicated staff.
5. Consider whether the transcription company is making investments to obtain and retain the provider as a customer. Is it purchasing computers and equipment for use on the account, or is it simply subcontracting all work and keeping a percentage of the fee ? The answer gives the provider a clue as to how much the vendor values the relationship and how carefully other contract terms should be reviewed.
6. Ensure protection by including specific performance standards in the contract. These should include turnaround time, error rate and template consistency (so that the documents follow a standard format). Not only are written performance standards important to give the provider the ability to terminate the contract if standards are not met, they also can help identify hidden costs. Although one vendor may appear to be less costly than another, does a high error rate require the provider to allocate time from other employees to review, edit and correct the vendor's work?
7. Weigh the cost of training staff regarding confidentiality. HIPAA requires that all persons with access to personal health information receive training on the confidentiality requirements of the law. In addition, laws in some states require additional staff training for specific situations, such as New York's AIDS confidentiality law. It can be easier for the provider to place the burden of training

on the transcription company.

8. Ensure that the contract contains the protection terms standard in any contract: (1) the ability (of both parties) to terminate the contract for cause (*e.g.*, failure to comply with the terms of the contract) and not for cause (if the vendor has made a substantial capital investment in the provider's account, this clause may only be agreed upon if the provider takes some responsibility for the investment); (2) an appropriate length of time for the contract; (3) inability of the vendor to assign the contract without the provider's permission; and (4) a requirement that any claim be brought in the state in which the provider is located.

In the wake of the UCSF case, a California state senator discussed introducing legislation that would prohibit provider and payer organizations in California from sending confidential medical information outside of the United States for transcription or other outsourced data processing activities.

Such a law would ensure that all vendors and their subcontractors are subject to US laws, but it would not alter a provider's core responsibilities when transmitting confidential records to a vendor. Meeting responsibilities and minimizing risk will still require asking the right questions, weighing the options and establishing an appropriate business associate agreement.

Advancement in technology is rapidly changing the global economy and work place. The field of medical transcription has undergone tremendous progress because of constant advances in communication and Internet technology. Outsourcing medical transcription has proved to be an extremely popular and profitable option for the medical industry.

Outsourcing medical transcription profitable?

The concept and benefits of outsourcing medical transcription is well known to the medical industry.

The direct and immediate advantage of outsourcing medical transcription is cost reduction, reliability in turn around time and total security.

Why outsource medical transcription to India?

In the last few years India has shown amazing success in this field. The large pool of IT professionals, the internet revolution and the encouraging policy changes have catapulted India to a top position as a quality source of medical transcription services.

Advantages

Advantages of outsourcing medical transcription to India—

There are several advantages in outsourcing medical transcription to India:

- **Language**—India has a vast pool of English speaking resources. Medical transcriptionists are graduates and most of them are science majors. Their qualifications teamed with fluency in the language makes training easier and the quality of results delivered is high.
- **Cost Savings**—The wage levels of medical transcriptionists in India are considerably lower than those in the US or other developed countries. Indian companies can offer highly competitive rates for comparable services. This translates into big savings for hospitals. Global medical transcription companies can bolster their bottom-lines by sub-contracting to Indian medical transcription companies.
- **Turn-Around-Time**—Turn around time is critical in this industry. Since India is several hours ahead of America and Europe, Indian medical transcription industries can offer the natural advantage of quicker turn around time.

Cost savings of 10%—50%

The degree of saving depends on your current medical transcription service method. Regardless of what method that is currently being used, Celtic Transcripts Ltd. can guarantee substantial savings.

Freelance transcription

- High Volume medical transcription service
- Internationally based transcription company
- In-house employees Large and Responsible Workforce
- Responsible staff ready and waiting to assist you with your transcription needs.
- Firm plans are in place to grow this to 200+ employees. Staff Trained to High
- Standards
- Each member of staff has been certified to national standards for medical transcription.
- A licensed RN and qualified staff of assistants carry out all in house training.
- High Speed Connection to the Internet
- Satellite connections and an oncoming broadband connection, will give bandwidth to handle a planned workload of up to 1000 doctors per day.
- Return Policy
- A 24-36 hour turnaround time will be provided
- Expedited and rush jobs can be accommodated at a small premium.

Security and confidentiality

- All data will be transferred using secure file transfer protocol.
- A 128-bit SSH encrypted file transfer system will be used to ensure data integrity.

Costing Methods

Costing can be made available to clients in their preferred method:

- Per line costing
- Per page costing
- Per hour costing
- Per minute

Discounts of up to 20% on our already guaranteed lowest costs are available on high volume workloads.

MT Course description

- **Instruction Module 1**
  - Learning Strategies
    Identifying and implementing a successful study method; planning when, where and how you'll study; creating effective and efficient study tools; using study tools to improve chances for success.
  - Introduction to Medical Transcription
    What a medical transcriptionist does; skills and personal qualities required; work settings; the origin and history of medical transcription; role of the AAMT; the CMT designation.

- **Instruction Module 2**
  - Time and Stress Management
    The art of relaxation; stress reduction techniques that should be avoided; coping strategies; common stressors and symptoms of stress; dealing with emotional and social stress; the basic philosophy of mental health; lifestyle and lifetime goals; increasing your energy; establishing effective daily routines.
  - Interpersonal Communication
    The components of communication; interpersonal relations in the medical office; effective oral communication; interacting with patients; scheduling; patient reception; patients with special needs; health factors that contribute to wellness.

At this point in the program, you will need to have access to an compatible PC with the following minimum system requirements

Intel Pentium® 233 MHz or higher processor, Pentium III recommended; Memory, 128 of RAM or above recommended; 400MB of available hard disk space; 190MB of hard disk space for Microsoft® Office Outlook® 203 with

Business Contact Manager; Optional installation files cache (recommended) requires an additional 290MB of available hard disk space with a sound card; Microsoft® Windows® 2000 with Service Pack 3 (SP3) or later; Windows XP or later; Display, Super VGA (800x 600) or higher-resolution monitor; USB port connector. You will also need Internet access.

- **Instruction Module 3**
  - o Law, Ethics and Medicine
    The difference between laws and ethics; patient rights; physician's and medical office professional's responsibilities; professional liability; malpractice and determining negligence; health care issues.
  - o Keyboarding and Word Processing
    Keyboarding techniques; developing speed and accuracy; creating, editing, formatting, saving and printing documents; formatting business correspondence, simple reports and tables.

- **Instruction Module 4**
  - o Practices in Medical Law and Ethics
    Consent; access to medical charts; defamation and the difference between libel and slander; protection against malpractice claims; legislation on reporting abuse of children.
  - o Introduction to Medical Terminology
    Root words, prefixes and suffixes and their use in medical terms; determining a medical term's meaning by analyzing its parts; basic structures of the human body; anatomical position and directional terms; the six major body cavities.

- **Instruction Module 5**
  - o Body Systems Terminology 1
    The organs of the digestive, urinary and reproductive systems; the function and structure of these three systems; common pathology, symptoms of disease and treatments for each system; tests and procedures for these three systems.

- o Body Systems Terminology 2
  The major structures of the musculoskeletal, nervous and special sense systems; terms related to diseases, diagnosis and treatment of diseases of these three systems; using combining forms to build and analyze terms related to each of these systems.

- **Instruction Module 6**
  - o Body Systems Terminology 3
    The parts of the endocrine and circulatory systems; the function and structures of these two body systems; the pathology, symptoms of disease, and treatments for each system; common tests and procedures for each system; abbreviations relating to these systems.
  - o Body Systems Terminology 4
    The organs and appendages of the integumentary and respiratory systems; the function of each organ and appendage; possible diseases and disorders of each of these body systems; laboratory and radiology tests of each body system; clinical and surgical procedures of each body system.
  - o Advanced Medical Terminology and Pharmacology
    How cancer develops; benign and malignant tumors; types, grades and stages of cancer; four major methods of cancer treatment; the types and uses of x-ray, ultrasound, MRI and nuclear medicine tests; drug names and references; agencies of drug regulation; drug action and effect; surgical positions and supplies.

- **Instruction Module 7**
  - o Written Communication 1
    The parts of speech; determining sentence patterns; types of sentences; common errors in sentences; the purpose of punctuation; the usage of various punctuation marks; the basic rules for capitalizing words.
  - o Written Communication 2
    The principles of unity, coherence and emphasis; editing and proofreading; processing information requests and correspondence; writing original letters; formatting business letters; formatting formal and informal reports.

- o Written Communication 3
  Expanding reading recognition, writing and speaking vocabularies; figuring out the meaning of unfamiliar words with context clues, prefixes and suffixes; using a thesaurus; using synonyms, antonyms and homonyms; denotation and connotation; forming plurals and possessives of nouns.

- **Instruction Module 8**
  - o Medical Filing
    A practical approach to filing; "hands-on" exercises in checking and applying your knowledge.
  - o Creating and Maintaining Medical Records
    The purpose of medical records; creating accurate and complete medical records; different formats; maintenance; the difference between medical records and business records; equipment and procedures of medical transcription; full-block, modifed-block, indented and run-on report formats; preparing physicians manuscripts for submission to medical journals.

- **Instruction Module 9**
  - o Technologies in the Office
    The impact of telecommunications technologies in the office; network systems; transmitting information using telephone systems; present and emerging telephone communications technologies and services; the use of computers in today's offices.
  - o Learning Lab 1
    "Hands-on" practical exercise in medical transcription. You will transcribe the following medical reports: History and Physical, Request for Consultation, Operative Report, Radiology Report, Pathology Report and Discharge Summary.
  - o Learning Lab 2
    "Hands-on" practical exercise in medical transcription with emphasis on spelling, word usage, punctuation, sentence structure, format and appearance.

BPO [Business Process Outsourcing]

BPO [Business Process Outsourcing] has been the latest mantra in India today. As the current sources of revenue face slower growth, software companies are trying new ways to increase their revenues. BPO is top on their list today. IT services companies are making a quick entry into the BPO space on the strength of their existing set of clients.

BPO is the delivery of business functions to a customer through a multi-year contract. The term covers a wide range of white-collar processes, from 'horizontals' such as :

HR

Finance and procurement to a growing number of vertical-specific processes across sectors including financial services utilities and local government.

Actually, setting up a call Centre is capital intensive. An ordinary BPO Centre that takes care of pure back office operation [*e.g.* payroll, data entry] will not be as expensive as a call Centre.

The philosophy behind BPO is specific, do what you do best and leave everything else to business process outsourcers. Companies are moving their non-core business processes to outsource providers. BPO saves precious management time and resources and allows focus while building upon core competencies. The list of functions being outsourced is getting longer by the day. Call centres apart, functions outsourced span purchasing and disbursement, order entry, billing and collection, human resources administration, cash and investment management, tax compliance, internal audit, pay roll...the list gets longer everyday. In view of the accounting scandals in 2002 [Enron, WorldCom, Xerox etc], more and more companies are keen on keeping their investors happy. Hence, it is important for them to increase their profits. BPO is one way of increasing their profits. If done well, BPO results in increasing shareholder value.

Typically, a customer calls the call Centre [usually a toll-free number]. After pressing numerous numbers [1 for

English, 2 for Spanish, 3 for bank balance!] the operator will answer your query by accesing the database. Call centres address sales support, airline/hotel reservations, technical queries, bank accounts, client services, receivables, tele marketing, market research.

If a bank shifts work of a 1000 people from US to India it can save about $18 million a year due to lower costs in India. According to Mckinsey, giant US pharma firms can reduce the cost of developing a new drug, currently estimated at between $600 million and $900 million by as much as $200 million if development work is outsourced to India.

Benefits derived from BPO can be summarized as follows:

1. Productivity Improvements
2. Access to expertise
3. Operational cost control
4. Cost savings
5. Improved accountability
6. Improved HR
7. Opportunity to focus on core business

Outsourcing is not new—it has been a popular management tool for decade. One can safely say outsourcing has evolved:—

- 1960's—time-sharing
- 1970's—parts of IT operations
- 1980's—entire IT operations
- 1990's—alliances/tie-ups
- 2000's—IT-enabled services

India has one of the largest pool of low-cost English speaking scientific and technical talent. This makes India one of the obvious choice to outsource to. Dell, Sun Microsystems, LG, Ford, GE, Oracle all have announced plans to scale up their operations in India. Others like American Express, IBM and British Airways are leveraging the cost advantage India has to offer while setting up call centres. Several foreign airline and banks have too set up business process operations in India. Indian revenues from BPO are estimated to have grown 107 per cent to $ 583 million and this particular area employs 35,000 people in the year ending March 31, 2002.

Many European and US companies have realized that they should focus on their main business and outsource their Human Resource Department, accounting department etc. Bingo! it is here exactly India fits in! Today US corporations have embraced BPO wholeheartedly.

Managed Care Companies, which is more popularly known as Healthcare payers, are increasingly outsourcing business processes due to changing and challenging business environment and technological and legislative changes. There is a good opportunity for Indian BPO vendors in this space. BPO vendors will need to have good domain knowledge, process know-how and competence with technological solutions to cater to these Manage Care Companies.

Need for Outsource

Flexibility

Outsourcing smoothens out the ups and downs of business cycles. When an IT company outsources most of its business processes, there are fewer assets to carry when the going gets tough.

Helps keep pace with technology

Outsourcing ensures access to the right resource mix without overloading your own overheads. If a new technology affects your business, you do not have to invest heavily in retraining and commit time and resources in course correction.

Greater focus on core competence

The demands of support and maintenance can distract you from your core competence. Once you outsource your secondary functions, you can afford to focus on what you do best with just enough resources to do it well.

Converts fixed costs to variable

If you forego the outsourcing option, you may need to

invest more in fixed assets and people and ensure optimum utilization to stay profitable. Outsourcing, on the other hand, is a variable cost and frees you from inflexible, long-term burdens.

Out sourcing

For most business organizations across the globe, offshore outsourcing is an interesting option, but they are reluctant to explore this option. The major reasons being most are not aware of the benefits of offshore outsourcing & the possibilities in outsourcing. Occasional failures of outsourced software projects have been discouraging people to entertain the various options that the fast changing globally competitive markets have to offer. Whether it is a service or a product to sustain an organization's competitiveness, one has to relentlessly pursue cost reduction goals without compromising the quality of the solutions. The biggest boon outsourcing has given to the global business community is the strength to upgrade their core business while being at the cutting edge of technology.

There are a few logical and important guidelines that any organization has to follow to be successful in outsourcing software to offshore businesses. India has established itself as one of the most competitive destinations for software outsourcing development services.

Unlike in house development or on site development, the offshore software development has certain peculiarities associated with its process. Most of the steps that are involved in onsite development are present in offshore development. Critical steps have been included in the process to ensure successful completion of the project.

Software outsourcing though in huge demand & profitable proposition, if not handled properly can become a pain also. But professional organizations outsourcing software or hardware functions are very cautious these days & do they due diligence before selecting the right software outsourcing partner. Given below are 5 modes of avoiding the common pitfalls in outsourcing.

Even as the scope, speed and scale of outsourcing increase, companies fail to take full advantage of the benefits outsourcing has to offer. Instead, they're falling into the booby traps along the way. To take one well-publicized example, Dell's enterprise customers barraged the computer maker with negative feedback after their experiences with Dell's offshore customer support. That led to some managerial backpedaling and questions about whether off shoring had gone too far.

Areas in Outsourcing

Outsourcing is undergoing a radical transformation. Transparent geography is one of the many emerging trends. Dramatic benefits such as cost savings and time to market reductions have been reported by its pioneers. New trends in outsourcing are defying speculators' predictions about a slowdown. Here are some of the new areas in outsourcing:

E-governance

- E-governance or electronic governance may be defined as delivery of government services and information to the public using electronic means.
- The private partner brings in specialized IT skills and other resources. Outsourcing helps the government, generally lacking in the knowledge of current and emerging IT technologies, to make the right choice of technology.
- Project management skills in government are also quite poor and by outsourcing, services can be digitized with least penalty in time, cost and other resources. The private vendors would generally work more efficiently and effectively for faster development of projects at a lower cost. Day-to-day hassles of running, maintaining and managing the system can be left to the more specialized private partner.

  Outsourcing also allows mountains of inherent legacies of the government systems to be by-passed. Legacies reside in the organization, the hierarchy, the processes, decision-making and in the people involved. Dozens of approvals required in the sanction of projects result in huge delays in implementation of projects and, finally, poor quality of service delivery. The choice of outsourcing makes it possible to jump over these legacy systems in one go, bringing relief to the government IT-administrators, who need not then be afraid of the auditors and their guillotines.

- The most important advantage of outsourcing lies in the fact that the government can concentrate on their core competencies. Productivity can thus be enhanced.

Retail Services Outsourcing

- Geographic borders and time zones mean little for retail and manufacturing enterprises competing for mind share and market share in the global economy.
- With supply chains that span the globe, businesses are pushing to get their products to market and into the hands of their customers more quickly and more efficiently than ever before, little or no margin for error, they need experienced partners who can help them get the job done right, the first time.
- Major chains are expanding their presence across geographic regions and, in many cases, across national boundaries. Additionally, they are expanding into new markets that extend their brand to new product categories.
- Meanwhile, with the Internet has raised expectations for customer services. Customers are expecting retailers to deliver a consistent experience, regardless of whether they are inside the store, phoning a call Centre, or at their computer. Outsourcing these services proves both cost effective and leads to increased productivity.

Pharmaceutical research

- From drug discovery to selling, the pharmaceutical industry needs new solutions. Utilizing information technology efficiently is a critical component for business success and gaining the competitive edge.

- Outsourcing provides the small pharmaceutical company the ability to take new drugs through clinical trials by avoid the investment in infrastructure which would normally be necessary.
- After InfoTech firms, it's the turn of biotech and pharma companies to look at outsourcing from India. According to Proximare Inc, a consultant for pharma and related companies, over $200-million worth work is likely to be outsourced from India over the next 12 months in the field of biotechnology and pharmaceuticals.
- These companies are mostly looking at collaborative research outsourcing work to be done out of India. Collaborative research outsourcing (CRO) is likely to become the next big wave after contract research outsourcing

Financial Services

- The role of outsourcing in financial services is undergoing fundamental, industry-wide changes. Financial services providers and vendors of IT products and services to the financial sector have long used outsourcing to meet their limited tactical goals.
- Enterprises are relying on outsourcing as part of their broader strategic sourcing plans. Their goal is to improve competitiveness while reducing costs.
- A recent study conducted by The Economist Intelligence Unit shows that approximately 30 percent of the companies (in the study) outsource finance and accounting functions, with two-thirds of those (65 percent) characterizing the arrangement as successful (57 percent) or very successful (8 percent).
- While cost savings and increased productivity are key motivators for outsourcing, the study determined that finance and accounting outsourcing is increasingly being used as a catalyst for business transformation.

Healthcare

- IT will provide healthcare organizations opportunities in 2004 to improve quality and reduce costs, while presenting challenges to the security and privacy of patient data.

- Healthcare's provider sector is opening its minds to the possibilities of business transformation through BPO. Rather than just focusing on the bottom line, they're realizing that savings from reduced operating costs can be redirected to investments in improving patient care quality, medical facilities or equipment and salaries.

Importance of outsourcing

Call Centre Outsourcing is becoming an increasingly popular trend among businesses. By focusing energy and resources towards the goods and services unique to one's company, call Centre outsourcing can allow for more effective specialization and a stronger bottom line.

There are two classes of outsourcing:

On-shore call Centre outsourcing, (using a call Centre within a given country) can still provide significant cost benefits with the added security of a stronger language base and potentially more secure systems.

Off-shore call Centre outsourcing, (using a call Centre outside of a given country), is often cheaper and just as effective.

Benefits of Call Centre Outsourcing

- No need for overhead investment: By outsourcing calls to specialized Centres, you can avoid the overhead costs associated with call Centre management, hardware and software.
- Lesser Personnel costs: On-shore providers (such as Canada and Mexico for America) and off-shore providers (such as India and the Philippines) can provide a tremendous cost benefit.
- Stability and Consistency of 24x7 coverage: The sun never sets for customers of many different companies. Providing affordable and reliable 24×7 support through call Centre outsourcing can strengthen customer loyalty and satisfaction.
- Specialization Advantage: Call Centre Outsourcing Centres have the training and skills that come with years of experience. Many problems and learning curves associ-

ated with call Centre management and utilization can be eliminated by the experience and understanding of these professionals. This specialization can mean greater service customers and less time, money and stress for your company.

Risks of Call Centre Outsourcing

A Call Centre's Past performance is their best indicator of future performance. Always be sure to get references from Call Centre Outsourcing companies. Call previous clients and evaluate their responses.

- **Security:** Although most call Centre outsourcing companies have powerful information security and encoding, preventing information theft during data transfer is never completely fool proof. If your company is working with very sensitive information, shop around for a call Centre outsourcing company that has security you understand and feel comfortable with. For extremely sensitive information, it may be wisest to do data collection and gathering in-house.
- **Complex/Sensitive Material**: For material that requires special care because of complicated or sensitive steps, call Centre outsourcing may not be the best option. Asking outsourcing agents to demonstrate their ability to successfully fulfill a task may be necessary before signing a contract.
- **Legalities:** Laws and regulations regarding call Centre outsourcing vary from region to region and country to country. Payment, job content and more may be subject to policy and regulations that you are unaware of. Be sure to become familiar with the laws and customs unique to your line of work and location.

Stage of outsourcing success

There are 5 stage to ensure your outsourcing success. Regardless of where you are in the program lifecycle we can cater to your requirements. Depending on your needs we can manage a part of your program or the entire program life cycle.

Stage 1—Situation Analysis

Situation analysis is not just understanding your stated needs, but carrying our analysis beyond that to provide solutions to enhance your business. It is our experience that customers tend to underestimate the extent and nature of work that can be outsourced.

Conducting a comprehensive study of the processes involved and give our input on the "outsourceable" components of your business. An outsourcing strategy is devised that will fulfill immediate requirements, or if you choose can be carried even further to provide solutions to expand and increase your business.

Stage 2—Pilot Project

Proof of concept even before you enter a formal arrangement by conducting a pilot project. This will clearly define parameters of quality, productivity, turn around time and cost efficiency.

Strive to exceed expectations right from this stage. This is a point where customers realize the enormous potential of outsourcing when they see the value that is created.

Typically, a pilot program is carried out over a 30 day period, but this could vary depending on the service you are seeking.

Stage 3—Transition Management

This process in place to ensure flawless performance during the critical phase of migrating customer processes to offshore locations. The challenges in this stage are different from actual execution. This is why a specialized team who would work with you and the execution team to make sure that standards and efficiency do not drop. Defining of Service Level Agreements (SLAs), which commit to mutually agreed upon levels of quality and productivity and schedules, the finalization of the contract, and the facilitation of customer visits, if required, are carried out during this stage.

Stage 4—Program Management

Program management is carried out at two levels. At the executional level we supervise the program to ensure the smooth functioning of operations and that agreed upon parameters of quality, productivity and turn around time are met. Primarily the objective of this stage is to consistently meet expectations. In case there is a failure to meet your expectations we have a process in place to address the problem and not only improve the situation, but also exceed your expectations.

At a higher level we can, if you choose, go beyond mere execution to provide value added inputs to ensure that your unstated goals are met. This is done through a thorough understanding of the program as well as your business.

In our experience customers outsource in order to cut costs while either maintaining current standards of or compromising slightly on quality. Our aim is to establish that these two are not mutually exclusive. For example, in a program we are managing for a large trucking company we have consistently improved quality over the level at which it existed.

Stage 5—Customer Relationship Management

Customer Relationship Management is as important to us as Program Management and would continue for the entire lifecyle of the program. With weekly telephone reviews, daily reports, a single point of contact, and a program management tool which allows tracking of a program on a daily basis, we ensure that you not only have a comfortable outsourcing experience, but never lose control over the entire process.

Initially, when a customer enters into a outsourcing relationship with us, they are unaware of the potential of the interaction that follows. We strive to go beyond what is expected by adding value to your business and enhancing your outsourcing experience.

Through this 5-stage process we strive to build long-term partnerships with our customers by delivering year on year productivity benefits, maximizing customer profitability, increasing and expanding their business.

This will relate real value which will impact not only your business and generate tangible benefits, but extend beyond that to create value in the society you live in.

FAQ

1. **What does BPO stand for? What does it mean?**
   BPO stands for Business Process Outsourcing. Major corporations in the US and Europe are outsourcing their back office operations to India to save costs. e.g. employee payroll is maintained in India for their employees worldwide. Although these jobs usually are not directly IT-related, their data-based orientation often means that they require IT departmental support to be successfully outsourced.
2. **What does ITES stand for? What does it mean?**
   ITES stands for IT-enabled services. IT-enabled outsourcing can be defined as,
   - o Those outsourcing services that use information technology in the processing and delivery of the service.
   - o Services are typically delivered through a telecommunications or data network, or other electronic media
3. **What is near shoring?**
   The practice of sending outsourced functions of any sort, whether IT-based or business process positions, to a nearby country rather than choosing markets such as India or Malaysia that are thousands of miles away. For *e.g.* US nearshores the work to Canada and Mexico. The physical proximity of these "nearshore" countries is a big threat to India.
4. **What are the reasons for outsourcing?**
   Cost reduction
   Focus
   Access to special enterprise
   Resource related reasons {relieve resource constraints, reduce IT staff and augment IT staff}

5. **What exactly does the BPO market comprise of?**
   There is a disagreement as to what exactly constitutes BPO. With the rapid expansion of the BPO industry and the extent of its reach, it is becoming increasingly difficult to define what a BPO exactly means. It encompasses a wide variety of activities such as human resource, accounting, financial research, marketing, sales, legal work, logistics and so on. Software services are also regarded as a part of the BPO market by many firms.
6. **What is BPM?**
   BPM stands for Business Process Management, basically this is about outsourcing the business processes.
7. **Now what is BTO!! ?**

o BTO stands for Business Transformation Outsourcing. Accenture defines BTO as a strategic partnership between the customer and the outsourcer with the advantage of sophisticated financing mechanisms. It would involve the firm acquiring strategic stakes in the BPO operations that companies have outsourced. BTO involves sharing risks and gains with an outsource business partner, measuring the performance improvement in dramatic gains in the share price, market position and return on capital.

o BTO also stands for Business Technology Transformation. It is a fast growing nice in BPO and is expected to become a $7 billion industry by 2007 from the current $2.5 million [2004]. BTO can reduce the overhead cost of enterprises by 20%. BTO is about governing the priorities, people and processes of organizations. It aligns IT and business strategy of a company while optimising quality, performance and business availability. According to Yankee Group, BTO enables companies measure and maximise business value across its IT investments.

8. **What is BPO2?**
   BPO2 stands for Business Process Optimization and Outsourcing.
9. **What is MBPO?**
   MBPO stands for Medical Business Process Outsourcing.

Apollo Hospitals is the first major hospital to be getting into this.

10. Can medical transcriptions be considered as BPO?

Yes.

11. What is RPO?

RPO stands for Research Process Outsourcing. This is popular in the biotech industry. Clients outsource their R&D work. This was termed reportedly by India's biotech queen Kiran Mazumdar-Shaw.

RPO also stands for Recruitment Process Outsourcing. RPO is a key component of Human Resource Outsourcing. The RPO team basically handles all the recruitment work for their clients.

12. What is defect density?

It is defined as the number of errors per 1000 lines of code. Accroding to Meta Group it has grown from 0.53 (2002) to 0.6 (2003) and is expected to further rise to 0.87 (2005).

13. What are the 4Es?

Engagement, education, enactment and enforcement framework is expected to ease the concerns of security and data privacy issue.

14. What is Procurement BPO?

Procurement BPO is transfer of management and execution of one of more procurement activities, transfer of the entire procurement sub-segments or transfer of the entire procurement business functions to an external provider. It offers increased productivity, cost reduction and business transformation to the client. It has a market potential of $10 billion by 2006.

15. What does BOT mean?

BOT stands for build, operate and transfer. BOT is not applicable only to BPO. Generally clients who wish to have their captive centre partner with a local company which builds and operates the centre for 2-3 years and then transfers it completely to the client.

16. What is HIPAA?

HIPAA stands for Health Insurance Portability and Accountability Act. The US healthcare industry has been interested in simplifying administrative processes and improving efficiency for several decades. The industry leaders concluded that greater standardization of data and transactions was necessary to improve efficiencies. This conclusion was subsequently memorialized by specific administrative simplification language included in the healthcare legislation called the HIPAA.

17. What is DNC [Do Not Call] list?

US Federal Trade Commission (FTC) Telemarketing Sales Rule bars companies from calling individuals who have registered themselves on DNC list. This hurts call centres that make outbound calls [cold calling]. This rule comes into effect from October 1, 2003. As of Sept 1, 2003 about 48 million individuals have registered on the DNC registry. If a company calls an individual on the DNC list, the fine can be approximately $11,000. Call centres have bought insurance to protect themselves from being fined.

18. What is Call Blasting?

Call Centre's sell by first playing a recorded message in American English. Then the real CSR speaks in neutral/American accent.

19. What does BFSI stand for?

Banking, Financial Services and Insurance.

20. Is there any restriction about women working in call Centres at night?

In Karnataka, the Legislative Assembly passed a bill in August 2002 which provides for the use of services of women employees during night. Section 25 of the Act was modified to accommodate this change. It is likely that all other states have a similar law. But the story seems to be a bit differcnt in Delhi.

21. What is BOSS?

BOSS stands for Burn-Out Stress Syndrome. BOSS syndrome is seen very commonly among young people working in call centres. The symptoms of this syndrome include chronic fatigue, insomnia and complete alteration of 24-hour biological rhythm of the body. Gastrointestinal problems are inevitable for those working at nights as the body is put under chronic stress. A potentially fatal increase in heart rhythm can result in severe chronic gynaecological problems in women and sleep disorders in both men and women. Guidance about physical and mental coordination to meet the demands of a call centre job is necessary.

22. Is it true that one needs very low skilled labor for a BPO operation?

Not true. It really depends upon what is the kind of job you are doing for your client. There are companies in India who are doing the R&D work for their clients. Is that low skilled labor?

23. What does captive operation mean?

The multinational company sets up its own BPO operation instead of outsourcing to a third party. e.g. GE Capital has its operations in Hyderabad and Gurgaon, Dell has an operation in Bangalore.

24. What is OTTS?

OTTS stands for Outsourcing Through Six Sigma

25. Are there any capability models for the ITeS industry?

Information Technology Services Qualification Centre (ITsqc) in Carnegie Mellon University has developed the eSourcing Capability Model (eSCMSM) for Service Providers to enable IT-enabled sourcing service providers to appraise and improve their capability to provide consistently high quality sourcing services. The eSCM framework also will enable service providers to establish and manage continually improving relationships with clients.

26. What do I need to enter the BPO arena?

The following list is no different than for any other business.

- o Domain or process knowledge—basically you need to know the customer's business. Yup, this is in short supply.
- o Customer access
- o Market reputation
- o Capital base

27. Do any associations cater to the BPO segment?

NASSCOM is the best organization that caters to the

BPO segment. They have done a wonderful job in addressing the issues with the government. They have a special group called SIGITES—Special Interest Group for IT Enabled Services.

28. What does "follow the sun" model mean?

India is situated 5 hours ahead of UK, 10 hours ahead of New York and 13 hours ahead of Los Angeles. US and UK companies can claim overnight response capability because during their night time, it is day time in India and agents in India can respond to emails during Indian business hours. This is known as follow the sun model.

29. Are there any setup guidelines from the govt. of India?

See guidelines. This is basically to get the DoT [Department of Telecom] clearance to operate a call centre. There is no prescribed application form, but you need to submit a set of documents. From what we have heard this office is very helpful and they don't harass you.

30. Can ITES companies share bandwidth?

As of Oct 22, 2002 the Govt. of India has decided that ITES can use the bandwidth on a time-sharing mode. It would not be treated as resale of bandwidth, which was banned in India. The move will allow firms to use the same facility and bandwidth to service Indian and international clients, which is not permitted under the present norms. BPOIndia.org would like to thank Confederation of Indian Industry (CII), which mooted the idea.

31. Why is it important to have the call centre in multi-locations?

- o BPO clients would not like their work to be disrupted. To ensure continuity it is essential to be multi-locational, at times this could mean in different countries also.
- o BPO companies need to constantly evaluate where they can get the best value for their money. Low-skill jobs like data entry could be outsourced to countries where labor is cheaper than in India.

- Few countries have data access legislation that prevents databases and information from crossing geographical boundaries. The best way to solve this problem is to have a BPO centre in that country itself. At times BPO client can take permission from the appropriate authorities and move the database outside the country. For *e.g.* in the case of EDS [Enhanced Directory Service] the operator needs to access a database which has the information of the residents/ businesses of the client country. Usually you are not allowed to ship this database outside that country, however clients have taken special permission to ship this database to countries like Philippines.

32. What is IVR?

IVR stands for Integrated Voice Response. IVR systems are automated systems installed in customer contact/ service Centres that help automate routine tasks such as account information, product information, schedule etc. IVR systems help automate many transactions that free employees tedious repetitive tasks. Customers can input their query using touch tone phones and these days advanced IVRs support speech recognition.

33. What is the bandwidth advantage talk about at Kochi (Kerala)?

Kochi has some of the cheapest available bandwidth in the country. It has the advantage of being located at the landing points of both satellite and submarine cable links. Both Sea-Me-We 3 and SAFE international submarine cables land at Kochi. Not only is bandwidth abundant, it is cheaper than at other locations. VSNL offers a 2 Mbps Internet leased line for Rs 12.5 lakh at Kochi. A 2 Mbps IPLC link costs Rs 40 lakh here. Nasscom has rated Kochi as one of the top two destinations in India for bandwidth intensive IT-enabled services. VSNL's International Gateway Exchange with 15 Gbps capacity is located next to the Cochin Special Economic Zone. Recently VSNL unveiled the SAT-3/WASC/SAFE submarine cable station in Kochi. With this, Kochi is one of the 16 landing points across the world for the submarine cable. The cable system has an ultimate capacity of 120 Gbps that enables it to convey a total of 5.8 million simultaneous telephone channels. VSNL operates a facility in the zone under the co-location scheme, offering global connectivity support to zone units at low-entry costs.

34. What is the talk about BPO companies being taxed?

The Indian government wants to examine whether a non-resident company, which has outsourcing deals with a BPO outfit in India, is subject to tax in India. Tax implications for the BPO sector (source Express Computer)

- o Taxing BPO clients will increase the cost of transacting in India. This will make India less cost-effective.
- o Companies will be discouraged from outsourcing their processes to India, this will slow down the growth rate of the Indian BPO sector.
- o Indian BPO sector will lose out *vis-à-vis* its competitors like Philippines, China, Ireland, Hong Kong, etc, if government adopts tough tax regimes.
- o The employment generated by the BPO sector might take a beating and the country will lose out significantly on the income tax charged on individual employees.
- o Overseas clients might perceive India as a country where taxation policies are not stable. India needs to project itself as a stable destination.

35. What is repetitive voice injury (call centre-itis)?

Call centre workers are suffering from a new industrial disease: repetitive voice injury, also dubbed as call centre-itis. Long hours and little opportunity for even a drink of water are behind the 'disease'.

36. What is glocalization?

Glocalization is basically globalization plus localization, your ability to take the best from the world's systems, best practices, best ideas, best brands and meld them with your own culture in a balanced way so that you don't feel overwhelmed by them.

Call Centres in India

Having a call Centre in India is the norm for several global companies today. In order to meet the growing international demand for cost-effective, customer-oriented call Centres, many organizations worldwide are outsourcing these services by setting up call Centres in India. But what makes call Centres in India such an attractive option? The country has intrinsic strengths which make it a major success as an outsource destination for call Centre work:

- A booming IT industry, with IT strengths recognized all over the world
- The largest English-speaking population after the USA
- A vast workforce of educated, English-speaking, tech-savvy personnel: A boon in a high-growth industry faced with a shortage of skilled workers
- Cost-effective manpower: In a call Centre operation, manpower typically accounts for 55 to 60 percent of the total cost. In India, manpower is available at a fraction of the cost overseas. However, some people get deterred by the fact that cost savings are not seen immediately. Initial investment in infrastructure and training can be expensive and make one believe that the promise of cost reduction is false. However, there will be savings and the fact that several global giants continue to set up call Centres in India is proof of this.
- The Government of India has recognized the potential of IT-enabled services and has taken positive steps by providing numerous incentives.
- The presence of most international technology vendors and solutions would enable creation of most advanced set-ups in this technology—intensive segment.

Call Centre industry in India

India's call Centre industry accounts for a quarter of all software and services exports from the country, according to industry association Nasscom, and Indian call Centres employ 160,000 professionals. Daimler-Chrysler, British Telecom, Barclays Bank, HSBC, Honeywell, Aventis and several others have come to India while the old timers of GE, British Airways, Citigroup, Amex and others have been around for a decade.

GE in India: an outsourcing success story par excellence

A large part of GE's business in India is in remote processing Centres. Success stories like GE's provide tremendous encouragement to both the Indian entrepreneur as well as potential business partners from overseas.

GE positions its call Centres as "productivity enhancers". According to GE, companies could be spending two-thirds or more of their time on things that have to get done but have little to do with what makes their business successful.

GE Business Productivity Solutions offer companies services and software that help them grow revenue faster than expenditures by reducing resources and time devoted to "back office" processes.

GE Capital International is employing over 1,000 people in its Centre of Excellence at Gurgaon near New Delhi in India. The Call Centre facility at Hyderabad is expected to be ready for use by March. These Centres provide IT-enabled business process outsourcing services to GE and non-GE customers around the world. GE's business objective is to consolidate back office processing into India for client organizations and to deliver quality services at competitive cost.

IT-Enabled Services Include

- Helpdesk Services and remote troubleshooting of IT-related queries from clients in the US
- Transaction Processing
- Accounting Services
- Call Centres
- Remote Network Management
- Service Bureau and Entrepreneur Systems
- End-to-end Processing Services with linkage to the parent company. The entire processing would be carried out in the facility in India, with a cost quality and service advantage to the parent organization

Product Specific Solutions Include

- Risk Modelling
- Data Mining
- Actuarial Services
- Underwriting Variation Analysis Analytic

Business Solutions

GE Capital India Business Solutions focuses on three areas:

1. Global business platforms
2. IT-enabled services
3. Product-specific solutions

GE's state-of-the art Decision Science Centre in Bangalore will develop predictive tools and models for all aspects of customer management.

India and Outsourcing

There are several factor under mentioned which make India a big hub as outsourcing

India Outsourcing History

The outsourcing history of India is one of phenomenal growth in a very short span of time.

India Outsourcing

The Indian outsourcing industry is expanding beyond Bangalore to smaller cities and towns in order to retain its competitive edge.

High Quality

Outsourcing to India is now more about high quality rather than cost. Indian companies are fast scaling up to match or surpass international quality standards and are ensuring that they stay ahead through stable quality systems and continuous quality improvement.

Outsourcing Engineering

Outsourcing engineering services to India holds

enormous potential. With a large number of labor driven and repetitive tasks, it fits the outsourcing bill to perfection. The labor-intensive engineering processes that can be outsourced are structural drafting and detailing, conversion services, cost estimations and a lot more

Data Privacy and Security

Indian companies are establishing India's reputation as a trustworthy outsourcing destination by proactively addressing data privacy and security concerns

Offshore Software Development

Offshore software development in India has evolved as software developers move up the value chain to offer custom software development. India emerged as a software service exporter in the late 1980s and early 1990s with the country's transition from centralized planning to a market-oriented economy. Today Indian companies have the lion's share in the global outsourcing market and compete with leading multinational suppliers across the IT solutions spectrum.

Network Outsourcing Services

Outsourcing network services to India is a relatively new practice, but there are a growing number of companies providing quality network management services. Several North American and European firms are realizing the potential of network outsourcing services in offshore locations like India. Several well established Indian IT companies have extended their gamut of services to include running networks operations Centres for global clients. These help to not only improve productivity and cut costs on the infrastructure side, but establish that cost efficiency and quality are not mutually exclusive.

Bangalore—Investment Hub

Bangalore possesses much of the attraction of other cities in India for the BPO sector; talented resources, good educational institutions, a large English speaking population, and technological prowess. However, it is a proactive state government that makes constant efforts to facilitate new investments, which gives Bangalore an edge over other Indian cities.

Outsourcing Writing

Outsourcing writing to India may seem unusual, but a high number of proficient writers and editors combined with a rich literary and film history makes this an area with huge potential. Whether it is writing of a technical nature, website content writing, journalistic writing, proofreading or manuscript editing, there is a vast range of services that can be outsourced to India.

HIPAA Compliance

Outsourcing healthcare services to India is extremely popular today. However, there are several concerns being voiced about data security and adhering to standard quality norms. The Health Insurance Portability and Accountability Act is widely acknowledged as the norm for healthcare services and Indian companies are well versed with the Act and other regulatory bodies.

New Areas

BPO is no longer restricted to back office work, and outsourcing processes as varied as e-governance to health care are rapidly gaining popularity.

Need for Outsource to India

If Software Engineering Institute's 'Capability Maturity Model Level 5' is the highest quality certification in the software industry, then India's the place to be. With 65% of the world's CMM Level 5 companies and one of the world's largest pool of scientific and technical talent, India is a logical choice for outsourcing.

Call Centres

In a highly competitive world, companies are looking

to outsource much of the work that needs to be done, but have little to do with it's success. As global companies such as GE and British Airways have found out, India, with its inherent strengths, has an advantage while setting up call Centres.

Global Giants

Looking at India as a possible outsource destination? Welcome to the gang. Sun Microsystems, LG, Cisco, Ford, GE, Oracle all have announced plans to scale up their operations in India. This article compiles recent announcements by some of the top global companies on their strategy regarding outsourcing work to India.

IT-Enabled Services Revolution

India's largest software house Tata Consultancy Services has tied up with finance company HDFC to provide IT enabled services to overseas clients. This is just one of the many such deals as more clients look seriously at India's low cost high quality talent. Call Centres and back office processing Centres are just two of the many avenues open for outsourcing IT enabled services.

Business Opportunities (Tax and Legal Issues)

Are you looking at reducing your software development costs? One attractive way would be to relocate some of the development work to countries like India. While there are tremendous opportunities in these countries, a clearer understanding of the tax and legal formalities could mean the difference between smooth outsourcing of work and a confusing tangle of delays and cost overruns. Here's an article that discusses these issues in depth, without the confusing legalese.

Chapter-Data Management Services

Information is vital in any scenario. Over time this information accumulates and it needs to be stored in a format that is easily accessible and understandable. How do you manage this labor intensive task, especially if you have huge volumes of data? Whether it is organizing years of official records or a library of books, data management is essential. Outsourcing data management is not a new practice. India is the one of the most popular outsourcing locations and there is international recognition of the technological knowledge and expertise here. Whether your requirements involve entry of data into an excel sheet or electronic document management, Indian companies provide high quality work and offer a range of data management services to suit your requirements:

Method with brief description are as

- Audio Tape Transcription

  The Internet has made it possible to send audio files to India and have them transcribed and returned within 24 hours. This is exactly what is happening when hospitals send their medical transcription to India. And because India is working when America is sleeping the text file is ready the next morning.

Potential

- Audio transcription started first with medical transcription but it will not be long before many other industries will be doing the same. For example here are a few other areas where audio can be transcribed in India.
- American TV shows for transcription for the hearing impared
- Film editors need to see text of the audio during editing.
- Seminar speeches are transcribed for publishing

Possible Problems

- Keep in mind that many Indians speak English as either a first or second language. There will, however, be minor problems in understanding accents or slang. However, transcriptionists are professionally trained to master the nuances of different accents.

Data Conversion

Data conversion is a necessity in this age of information as information is vital in any organization. In our modern day competitive world technology is constantly changing in order to improve and facilitate our lives. For an organization to function effectively data needs to be easily accessible. Most data is stored in the form of paper files or reports and accumulate over the years, resulting in data loss. It is a tedious process to find the necessary data when you need it and even to maintain the ever increasing flow. Data conversion is a necessity in a world where technology is constantly striving to make life easier.

The need for data conversion is at a peak now as there are several processes and challenges present in any enterprise: mergers, acquisitions and new technology developments. The accessibility, quality and diversity of information that a firm has at its disposal is becoming increasingly important to customers. Converting data to a readily available and easily accessible format is a must.

Some of the reasons why data conversion is important are:

- Sheer volume or bulk of information makes it difficult to manage
- Multiple input formats
- Multiple destinations
- Inconsistent styles
- Complexity of data

Use data conversion to transform your data

- From paper to computer
- From audio tape to CD
- From film to digital media
- From blueprints, maps and diagrams to editable, retrievable, shareable data
- From invoices and applications to intelligent systems
- From guarantee cards and contest forms to customer relationship management.

Data conversion services

The following are a list of data conversion services that can be outsourced to India :

- Data Capture, which involves defining forms to the system, scanning the forms, and executing Forms Processing (FP) which recognizes forms and text on forms.
- Data Validation, which provides for verification and correction of the data recognized by Forms Processing or for data entry when a form cannot be recognized.
- Data Output, which produces files based on the input from the forms and writes these files in a format suitable for processing by other applications or legacy systems.
- System Services, such as monitoring, indexing, printing and security; and other service functions, such as document querying
- Batch, sort and code records.

Data Entry or Processing

- Document preparation Handwritten, Machine Print, Reader Response
- Word Processing
- Image Keying
- Image Capturing
- Catalog Conversion (to digital format)
- COLD (Computer Output to Laser Disk / CD-ROM
- Document Management / Imaging
- Document Warehousing
- Document Retrieval
- Document Workflow
- Mail Processing Services
- Web Server

Other services

- Scanning
- Electronic Recognition: OCR (Optical Character Recognition) & ICR (Intelligent Character Recognition)
- Bar Code
- Marc Sense

Data Entry

The world of business is dynamic, fast paced and in constant flux. In such an environment the accessibility of accurate, detailed information is a necessity. It is irrelevant whether you are a small business or a sprawling global empire, as information is an asset in any scenario. The more you know about the market, your customers or clients, and other factors that influence an organization, the better you can understand your own business. There is usually an overwhelming amount of data entry required in order to progress.

In some companies the need for data entry is constant while for others there may be just a temporary requirement. Whatever the need may be, accurate and easily accessible data is a necessity. However, not many companies have the resources or finances to conduct data entry work in-house. Exploring alternative solutions like outsourcing your data entry work is a good idea.

Data Processing

Definition

Data Processing is a category of IT Enabled Services pertaining to capture, digitization and processing of data emanating from various sources. Traditional data processing services comprise of punching data from manually filled forms, images or publications; preparing databases and integrating them. However, with the advent of multimedia and internet, the scope and range of data processing has grown. Sources have widened to include manually printed documents, images, sounds and video. Equally diverse are the new output media which include databases on servers, hard copy publications, CD-ROM authoring and managing records emanating from internet based queries.

Organizations with extensive data turnover and customer interface can use high speed datacom links for their back office and data processing operations. This enables them to save costs and valuable resources.

Data Processing—The Process

Data Processing services cater to companies/organizations, which receive or generate large quantities of information that is handwritten/typed and time sensitive. These forms can be sent either physically or can be scanned and transmitted to the vendor's facility. The data processing may be done using high speed, automated systems reading hand print, check-boxes, mark sense, reader response, bar codes and most data slots that are on a form. Information can be processed from hard copy, fax or scanned version.

Many companies enter data manually (from image or paper) or through computer assisted data capture, using

- OCR (optical character recognition),
- ICR (intelligent character recognition),
- mark sense,
- MICR, and
- Bar code.

Information is checked by validation routines including table look-ups, data/range checks, and relationship validation. Processed documents are then sent to verification stations where experienced operators verify the accuracy of processed information. This product is then turned into Data, and properly formatted Data (record layout) is quickly transmitted to the client's computer.

Data Processing to India

Data processing is an essential process, which any organization requires. However, not many companies have either the expertise or resources to carry out this work in house. In such a scenario, outsourcing your data processing work is a wise option.

India is one of the most popular outsourcing locations. With it's vast pool of educated and professional resources, wealth of knowledge in several domains especially its growing prowess in the information technology field, and cost effective solutions, it is no surprise that several global companies have chosen India for their outsourcing needs. Indian Service Providers in the data processing and other

Information Technology enabled service fields are highly qualified and can cater to a vast array of data processing requirements.

Data Processing India—Services offered

There are several information technology enabled services related to data processing that are offered by Indian Service Providers.

Data Digitization

Digitization is the process by which physical or manual records such as text, images, video and audio are converted into digital forms. This is of paramount importance when projects need directions based on already established facilities and the implementing agency needs to find the scope for expansion.

Digitized data offers the following benefits: Long term preservation of documents, orderly archiving of documents, easy & customized access to information, easy information dissemination through images & text, CD-ROMs, internet, intranets and extranets.

The digitization process includes

- Identification of customer needs and the intended use of the digitized records.
- Translating customer needs to digitizing objectives by means of requirement specifications, system analysis and designing the system for the planned product.
- A pilot application of technology for approval and testing is then developed. On its approval by the customer, a data source chart for the source material is developed. The source material may include printed forms, images, sounds and video. The printed format requires maximum processing, as other formats can be easily converted into digital form.
- The documents are now printed so that their accuracy can be checked manually. These are scanned using special Optical Character Recognition (OCR) software and the historical documents are keyed in. The output is

checked manually by proofreaders before being converted to the desired format (ASCII, HTML, PDF, MS-Word).

- The images are scanned; old and faded images are recovered using advanced digital correction software. The sound and video data are captured through a data capturing software and hardware and converted into digital form; the quality of the digital version may be enhanced by filtering through an editing software.
- The digitized data are integrated into an easily accessible form by incorporating indexes and tables of contents. These are now authored on CD-ROMs or other suitable media depending on the intended use of the data.

Accuracy is achieved through a double keying system where every coding entry is made twice and automatically compared with proprietary software. Any discrepancy is rejected and the coding is done afresh for the rejected set of files.

E-Cataloging

E-Cataloging is a technology of processing paper catalogs to digitized data for the web. As virtual shopping is gaining ground throughout the world paper catalogs are no more a good approach to selling your products. E-Cataloging is a new technology that manufacturers and distributors throughout the globe are adopting to sell their products.

The process involves

- Paper Catalog from the manufacturer/distributor is collected.
- Duplicating(Documenting) the catalog for Analysis.
- Database Analysis to prepare the catalog database structure.
- Approval for the database structure from the client.
- Production of the catalog.
- Quality Assurance.
- Deliver.

There are several other related information technology services that India Service Providers offer :

- Web content development
- Animation
- Payroll processing services
- Write up services
- General Ledger services
- Financial Statement Preparation
- Tax Preparation
- Desk Top Publishing

Data Processing in India—The Advantages

India offers many advantages as an IT Enabled Services destination for major global companies. These include:

- 12-hour times zone difference with USA and other major markets for IT Enabled Services.
- A huge pool of English speaking and computer literate manpower who can continue to cater to the growing demand for professionals in IT Enabled Services. These professionals are skilled as well as quality conscious.
- Labour costs are significantly lower than in most other countries.
- Stable legislative and economic framework.
- Support of Government of India for all IT led industries—Many State
- Governments in India offer special incentives and infrastructure for setting up IT Enabled Services.
- India enjoys strong brand equity in major markets, thanks to its growing and globally competitive software industry.

Indian Service Providers are professional, quality conscious and offer cost effective solutions. They have:

- expertise
- a dedicated 24 × 7 × 365 support and a single point of contact
- a very reliable Quality Assurance System and a time bound project completion record.

- a full life cycle solution, which ensures your systems keep pace with your business, while providing saving in total cost of ownership.
- Flexibility whether it involves making necessary changes when situations for change arise or handling each project based on the requirements of the client.
- Personalized service as a team is assigned to each project. Apart from possessing an accurate knowledge of information technology services they offer valuable ideas, distinct service and complete solutions.
- Strict adherence to deadlines.

Outsourcing EDM

Why outsource document management?

Document management services help organizations better utilize and manage both old-fashioned paper documents and the modern computer printout reports. Each format comes with it's own unique set of problems with managing them. A well-planned document management system can offer a multitude of benefits. A centralized document archive that can manage paper-based information can handle documents stored in electronic format (TIFF) that are easily retrievable through a web browser. Compared to old-fashioned file cabinet solutions, this is definitely a lot easier.

Making the process cheaper and faster?

There are a number of things one can do to facilitate the document conversion process:

- Spend extensive time thinking through all the details. Write down all the rules you want to use during the conversions. For example, "How are post-it notes handled?"
- If you use a consultant, have him or her talk to your scanning service bureau as early as possible in the process.
- Thoroughly understand the indexing scheme you want to use, and whether you'll need OCR, formatted OCR or ICR.

- Work with your staff and consultants on all the "what if" scenarios.
- Get rid of "junk" documents you don't really need.
- Prepare your documents in-house before shipping them to your scanning service bureau. For example:
  - o Remove all staples.
  - o Mark each carton with a simple, effective serial number.
  - o If you'll need some of your documents while they are being converted, make copies for yourself.
  - o If you are giving your scanning service bureau documents in pieces (separate boxes), develop your own indexing scheme for the boxes so you'll have an audit trail of where the boxes are (service bureau will maintain a "mirror" trail with you).
  - o Preparation time is usually 15% of the total conversion—Preparation takes one to two hours per thousand pages.
  - o Do a trial run with your scanning service bureau to validate sample scans, file structures and indexing schemes. Provide samples of all sizes shapes of documents to be scanned.

Legal Considerations for document conversion

Copyrights In general, if you can scan someone else's copy righted material without their permission, you are breaking the law. Copying by the "extract means" of photographs, drawings, paintings and other documents by photography, scanning, or photocopying can be infringement of copyright laws. The persons doing the unauthorized copying could be potentially subject to a number of remedies, including actual and statutory damages, impoundment of materials and other penalties. GET PERMISSIONS FROM THE SOURCES FIRST! An exception to this is the concept of fair use—When the amount of work being copied is not substantial, or is for a different use than the original (Example: not for profit).

Legal documents

Scanned and electronically stored documents, especially on CD-ROM disks are often admissible as court evidence. The law varies from country to country. SEC, the IRS and many other U.S. Govt. agencies accept electronic documents. Be aware that there is a substantial rapidly changing body of U.S. law, which is still coming to grips with the implications of electronic data, scanned documents and Intellectual property in general.

Document Management application areas

1. Supporting organizational processes
2. Improving publication processes
3. Enhancing communication between teams
4. Improved access to external information
5. Maintaining corporate records
6. Promoting training and education
7. Creating knowledge management repositories

Challenges and opportunities in outsourcing document management

A challenge would be to use the right kind of technology. Technologies are evolving rapidly, but sometimes, when these emerging technologies are adapted in specific applications without any plan what you will have are "islands of automation". A document management system that uses the right technology appropriately, but also makes sure that a well thought out strategy is involved is what you should look out for. The objective is to manage data and not just the documents. The bottom line is that organizations need enhanced productivity and performance. Electronic Document management promises to leverage new technologies and generate improvements in productivity and performance.

Managers will need to educate the different departments within their organization about the benefits of Electronic Document Management. Complete coordination is essential to evolve the infrastructure and applications that are .eeded to support Electronic Document Management.

India is one of the most popular outsourcing locations with some of the finest information technology companies, products and services available. Technology companies possess the requisite knowledge, skills, and expertise to carry out even the most complex projects.

Data Entry Outsourcing

India is growing as a steady source of IT expertise. With it's increasing popularity as an offshore outsourcing location and it's strong domain knowledge it is a wise and profitable option to outsource data entry to India.

With a number of business processes being outsourced to the country, Indian service providers possess the necessary expertise and knowledge to handle even the most complex projects. India has some of the finest and most advanced technology companies. Here are just some of the possible data entry procedures that companies here can carry out:

- Data entry operators can input any type of data. They can develop and update databases and handle a high volume of data accurately at high speeds.
- Data entry Centres are equipped with facilities like a 64 KBPS Internet link, dedicated infrastructure and machines.
- The results obtained can be in the form of text annotations, images, or a mix of both.
- Paper documents can be converted to electronic media such as multimedia CD-ROMs, databases with tables of content and indices, PDF (Adobe Acrobat Format) files, HTML with full text search functionality or any specific Electronic Document Management System.

Data entry operators working in well-established systems are equipped to handle high volume image and paper-based data entry in any format, database design and management, SGML/HTML coding for the Internet and a host of other related services.

□□□